Suzy Gershman's

BORN TO SHOP

LONDON

The Ultimate Guide for
Travelers Who Love to Shop

11th Edition

Wiley Publishing, Inc.

For Ruth, the general manager of the Notting Hill Hilton Residence, with love and thanks for taking such good care of me.

Published by:

Wiley Publishing, Inc.
111 River St.
Hoboken, NJ 07030-5744

ISBN 0-7645-4218-4

Editor: David Allan
Production Editor: Suzanna R. Thompson
Photo Editor: Richard Fox
Cartographer: Elizabeth Puhl
Production by Wiley Indianapolis Composition Services

For information on our other products and services or to obtain technical support, please contact our Customer Care Department within the U.S. at 800/762-2974, outside the U.S. at 317/572-3993 or fax 317/572-4002.

Wiley also publishes its books in a variety of electronic formats. Some content that appears in print may not be available in electronic formats.

Manufactured in the United States of America

5   4   3   2   1

CONTENTS

MAP LIST

ABOUT THE AUTHORS

Suzy Gershman is a journalist, author, and global-shopping goddess who has worked in the fashion and fiber industry for more than 25 years. The Born to Shop series, which is now 20 years old, is translated into eight languages, making Gershman an international expert on retail and trade. Her essays on retailing have been used by the Harvard School of Business; her reportage on travel and retail has appeared in *Travel & Leisure, Travel Holiday, Travel Weekly,* and most of the major women's magazines. She is translated into French for Condé Nast's *Air France Madame* magazine.

Gershman is the author of *C'est La Vie* (published by Viking), the story of her first year as a widow living in Paris. She divides her time between an apartment in Montmartre, a small house in Provence, and the airport.

Ethan Sunshine is a 24-year-old male model, rap star, and television journalist who specializes in trends. He joins the Born to Shop team with jersey number 3.

Jenny McCormick, 22, is a graduate student and part-time Born to Shop editorial assistant who reports on young women's interests, fashions, and trends. She carries an expensive handbag.

TO START WITH

As this series moves into its 20th year, it seems that all things come round. When we started this series, the dollar was very strong, and people were shopping for shipping. Now it's the other way around. London is painfully expensive. The dollar is the weakest it has been in ages—which, of course, can change by the time you are reading this.

On the whole, London is a costly city—all the more reason to study these pages. There are good buys out there, as well as many consumer tricks to help you save time and money. And let's face it—there is no place like London. Even though I now live in France and go to London frequently (I even have my hair color done in London), I am struck dumb by the differences between the U.K. and France, from London to Paris. There are things to find and see and buy in London that simply can't be found elsewhere.

You even get to the point where the prices don't bother you too much—you just figure this is a one-off opportunity, and you'll cut back elsewhere. Tomorrow is another day . . . and all that.

To help you cope with tomorrow—when the bills arrive—I have changed the focus of much of this book. While I still have information on palace hotels, I have made the palace part a comparative feature, then concentrated on less expensive hotels and the kinds of places you want to stay but may not know about.

I have also added opinions from my young staff members—two under-25s—who have also worked on this edition. I thank them for including stores I didn't know or that didn't interest me and hope they provide another layer of context to you and yours.

I also send thanks from the wrong side of the road and hugs galore to (in alphabetical order) Anita Cotter, Martine de Geus, Paula Fitzherbert, Ruth Jacobs, Maria Kahn, John Prothero at Michaeljohn, and Anne Sweeney.

Chapter One

....

THE BEST OF LONDON AT A GLANCE

BULLETINS FROM BRITAIN

I may just as well have called this "Bullets from Britain": When you see the prices in the United Kingdom, you may feel like someone shot you . . . not in the heart, but in the pocketbook!

But wait, there are some buys and even some bargains, and there *is* value for money—things that are pricey but worth it, or expensive but still less in the United Kingdom than in the United States.

And there are plenty of price breaks to be found on airfare and hotels as well. You'll find all that stuff in the chapters that follow. *These* pages are meant to bring you the best of London's diverse shopping scene, including a few suggestions for gifts or personal trophies and indulgences to take home with you, faster than you can say "Trafalgar Square, please."

I hope that even those in a mad tear will find a moment to read the rest of the book because it lists many more stores, as well as tips for finding good values and other shopping strategies. Bargains in Britain are often hidden, and those on a flash dash don't always get the best buy. Thankfully, London has fabulous airport shopping, so you never have to go home empty-handed.

Okay, 'nuff said—let's go shopping, mates!

You Have Only 1 Hour to Shop in Mayfair

If I have a heavy day, I try to get people to come to me at my hotel or to keep my meetings in the **Mayfair area,** so that I can at least get outside. Though a walk along Regent Street or Oxford Street gives me more than a breath of fresh air . . . it gives me credit card debt!

If you do find yourself in Mayfair with 1 hour to shop and you want to go into just one place, your best bet is **Liberty of London,** if only to look around. But once you're there, you'll want to shop till you drop. Note that Liberty has reinvented itself; even if you knew the store before, you must see the new parts.

On the other hand, if you are more like me, with a little bit of funky in your heart, you may want something less uptown to do in your precious hour. I'll tell you what I generally do with my hour (and what I suggest for any die-hard shopper), and this is of course assuming I can easily get to the corner of Regent and Oxford streets:

- Head for **TopShop**—and be sure to go downstairs to find more women's things and browse the cheap copies of hot fashions.
- Dash into **SuperDrug** (across the street from TopShop, on Oxford toward Tottenham Court Rd.) for everything I need and don't need, and for loading up on stuff from Original Source, maker of my favorite bath products.
- Run into **Thornton's**—it's a candy store, and I'm addicted to their original toffee.
- Saunter along Regent Street, smelling the air and taking it all in; pop into Liberty; then turn left at the sign for Carnaby Street. Race for the **Lush** shop (no. 40) and buy all the gifts I've ever wanted or needed—and a few goodies for me, too.

You Have Only 1 Hour to Shop in Knightsbridge

If you are in Knightsbridge and want to spend your hour there, I suggest a trip to **Harvey Nicks** and then a quick whiz through the food halls at **Harrods** for souvenirs and a Stilton to go. Or just exit Harvey Nicks—if you can drag yourself away from one of the best department stores in London—by way of Sloane Street. Be dazzled at **Shanghai Tang,** where clothes, gifts, and fabrics from China offer a dizzying array of colors and energy. Then, make your way toward Sloane Square, popping into **Jo Malone** (no. 150) for scents and bath or beauty treatments that cost half their U.S. prices. When you get to the department store Peter Jones, turn right (you are now on Symons St.) and head into the new **General Trading Company,** which is a small department store with high style and gift items for the home; don't miss **The White Company,** next door.

You Have a Few Minutes to Shop (But Everything's Closed)

Assuming it's not Sunday night, there are a few places you can still have a little fun. (Remember, most shops in London close early by New York or Hong Kong standards—usually 7pm.) **Boots the Chemist** at Piccadilly is open until 10pm most nights. **Tesco Metro,** the grocery store, is open until 8pm most nights and 9pm on Thursday. On Sunday, hours are from noon to 6pm. During the week, it opens at 7:30am, when no other store is open! *Note:* The checkout lines are enormous at 9am.

Quick Spree That's Very London

- Head for **Covent Garden.** (Yes, there are branch stores of **Lush** here.)
- Explore Covent Garden's entire marketplace, but don't forget that if you need a few gifts, there's a tiny branch of **Hamley's** (great gifts for kids) and a **Culpeper the Herbalist** (wonderful bed and bath products, including aromatherapy gifts) here as well.
- Walk away from **Covent Garden** out the front end and go to **Neal Street** for an eyeful of cutting-edge British street fashion and shoes you just can't believe, as well as branches of stores such as **Mango,** a Spanish chain that makes inexpensive

copies of the latest fashions. There are also a lot of sneaker stores on Neal Street.

- Check out the mini-mall **Thomas Neals** by popping into tenant **SpaceNK,** which is a makeup and beauty store specializing in cult brands of makeup. Don't buy American brands, as they are very expensive. If you enjoy vintage clothes, there's a small shop in the mall that has some nice things.

- At the end of Neal, turn left and segue onto **Monmouth Street** for more vintage and fun finds.

THE BEST OF LONDON

....

Best New Shopping Area

This is tricky because you will read a lot of hype about the East End and even about Hoxton. I am not going to tell you that Hoxton is the best new neighborhood (no lemming me), but I am going to send you to **Borough Market,** which is way off near London Bridge and only open on Fridays and Saturdays. This is a food market, so it may not be to your taste—if you don't care about food—but I found it charming and, well, delish. Next door is Southwark Cathedral and nearby are the Globe Theatre—recently re-opened—and the Tate Modern.

The Best Department Store

SELFRIDGES
400 Oxford St., W1 (Tube: Bond St. or Marble Arch).

Selfridges has totally recreated itself so that if you remember a dowdy old British department store targeted to little old ladies, you can think again. This department store is now the talk of the town for all the young, hip designers' clothes; the grocery store; the designer boutiques; the clothes made especially for the store; and the largest makeup and beauty department in Europe.

The Best Specialty Store

HARVEY NICHOLS
Knightsbridge Rd. (corner of Sloane St.), SW1 (Tube: Knightsbridge).

Harvey Nicks sells style by the yard and is the specialty store of choice for Sloane Rangers; it was Diana, Princess of Wales's favorite department store—known for its blend of designers, home style, gourmet market, and good eats. *Note:* many of the fashion brands are American, which you do not want to buy in the U.K. as they are expensive.

The Best Chemist (Drugstore)

I do adore **Boots** and especially love the **Boots Well-Being Centre** (listed below in "The 10 Best Shops in London"), but for price and fun, I go with:

SUPERDRUG
Multiple branches around town. I'm usually at either Marble Arch (Tube: Marble Arch) or Oxford Circus toward Tottenham Court Rd. (Tube: Oxford Circus).

The Best Multiple (Chain) in Britain

LUSH
London addresses: Covent Garden, Units 11 and 7, The Piazza, WC2 (Tube: Covent Garden); 123 Kings Rd., SW3 (Tube: Sloane Sq.); 40 Carnaby St., W1 (Tube: Oxford Circus); 80–82 Regent St., W1 (Tube: Piccadilly Circus).

Several stores in London and branches all over the United Kingdom; now reaching into Canada, Australia, and, slowly, Europe. The first U.S. store has opened in San Francisco. Someday I'll yawn, but not yet; I'm still crazy for these bath-and-body stores after all these years.

The Best Places for Dishes

- Affordable: **Harrods,** Brompton Road, Knightsbridge, SW1 (Tube: Knightsbridge).
- Dream on: **Thomas Goode,** 19 S. Audley St., W1 (Tube: Hyde Park or Marble Arch, but really, no one takes the Tube to a store such as this).
- Discount, but with a limited selection: **Portobello China & Woollens,** 89 Portobello Rd., NW8 (Tube: Notting Hill Gate).

The Best American Moment

HARRODS
87–135 Brompton Rd., Knightsbridge, SW1 (Tube: Knightsbridge).

Newly arrived: Krispy Kreme doughnuts in Harrods, in case you're feeling a bit homesick.

The Best Designer Resale Shop

PANDORA
16–22 Cheval Place, SW7 (Tube: Knightsbridge).

The Best Flea Markets

- On Wednesdays: **Camden Passage,** Islington (Tube: Angel).
- On Fridays: **Bermondsey** (Tube: Bermondsey).
- On Saturdays: **Portobello Road** (Tube: Notting Hill Gate).
- On Sundays: **Brick Lane/Cheshire** (Tube: Liverpool St. Station).

Best New Market Experience

COLUMBIA ROAD FLOWER MARKET
Nearest Tube: Old St. Take a bus; it's easier.

Don't fret, it's not just flowers. Although the streets are filled with cut flowers, plants, herbs in pots, and small trees, there are shops selling antiques and fun home furnishings, and tiny outdoor markets with heaps of olives and so on. Several shops and bistros sell coffee, bagels, and other goodies. By 8:30am it's crowded; most of the stores open at 9am. They are only open on Sundays, so don't think you can come back during the week for a less-crowded stroll.

The Best Vintage Clothing (Upmarket)

STEINBERG & TOLKIEN
193 Kings Rd., SW3 (Tube: Sloane Sq.).

The Best Vintage Clothing (Downmarket)

PORTOBELLO ROAD MARKET
Pembridge Rd. & Portobello Rd., NW11 (Tube: Notting Hill Gate or Ladbroke Grove).

The Best Sunday in Town

Start at **Columbia Flower Market** (sorry, no really easy Tube . . . but there are buses).

Head to **Brick Lane** (it's not far, splurge for a taxi); then shop your way over to the street market on Cheshire Street. *Note:* the Brick Lane Market is nothing to write home about; the fun is on Cheshire Road, where things seem to have fallen off trucks.

Leave the area via the Liverpool Street Tube stop.

Head for **Camden Town** before a late lunch, Tube of the same name.

You want the **Stables Market** if you are over 25; the rest if you are under. This is a wide-flung series of markets, open until 5pm, and you may want to stay here the rest of the day. For me, it's the **Stables Market** and then I am outta there.

Fun lunch (your choice, but use the same Tube line to go from Camden Town to Tottenham Court Rd., then walk to Oxford Circus) . . . then shop department stores on **Oxford Street,** ending up at Marble Arch in time for a movie . . . or cut back toward the theatre district for a play. The play's the thing, as Shakespeare said.

The Best Place for Royal Souvenirs

BUCKINGHAM PALACE GIFT SHOP
Sorry, open only Aug–Sept. At the end of The Mall (on the road running from Trafalgar Sq.; Tube: St. James's).

ROYAL ENGLISH PALACES (INCLUDES TOWER OF LONDON)
Palaces have banded together to form a marketing confederation (how American!) and have redone their gift shops, offering replicas of the crown jewels at the Tower of London gift shop.

The Best Museum Store

VICTORIA & ALBERT MUSEUM
Cromwell Rd., SW7 (Tube: S. Kensington).

One-stop shopping for everything from postcards and posters to crafts (Crafts Council booths in the rear) to repro items (reproductions, to you newbies) and fun decorative touches including jewelry, tin dinner plates, Spode coffee cups, and so on. You may enter the store without paying the museum admission; tell them at the front desk. A specialty gift shop is usually set up to serve particular exhibits; this shop will be adjacent to the exhibit itself and sells merchandise that is not seen in the main gift shop.

The Best Bookstore

HATCHARDS
Piccadilly, W1 (Tube: Piccadilly Circus).

Some bookstores are larger, but none are more fun.

The Best Toy Store

HAMLEY'S
200 Regent St., W1 (Tube: Oxford Circus).

The Best Teenage Hangout

TopShop
214 Oxford St., W1 (Tube: Oxford Circus).

Great Gifts for Not Many £

- Anything from **Lush**—my faves are individual bath bombs or the Ballistic Barrel (three bombs in a container) and Red Rooster soap. I bought some baby bath bombs in pale blue for a novelty baby gift. Not every product they make is brilliant, so you'll need to experiment; their good ones are so good that you'll go back to buy more the next day—and rue the day you didn't bring home more.
- **Cashmere liquid washing soap from N. Peal.** OK, this is a novelty gift, but it goes a long way for the person who has everything.
- **Duchy Originals,** organic biscuits (cookies) from Prince Charles, available at all fancy food shops and food halls in department stores. *Note:* They have almost no sodium, making them a great gift for anyone on a salt-free diet.
- **Aromatherapy fan from Culpeper the Herbalist,** £15 ($25); with the scent of your choice, an additional £2 to £5 ($3.30–$8.25).
- **Feng shui products from Tesco,** about £3 ($4.95).
- **Silk-knot cuff links,** £5 ($8.25), from Thomas Pink.
- **Filofax or Filofax inserts.** Prices range with selection but are basically half the U.S. retail price.
- Bottle of **whisky.**

The Best Gifts Under £5

- **Designer-style plates printed on tin,** £4 ($6.60) each, at the Victoria & Albert gift shop.
- **Bath bomb from Lush** for £2 ($3.30) or bar of Red Rooster soap. (Prices depend on size, but £3/$4.95 will usually do it.)
- A **tabloid newspaper,** with at least one tacky headline and news of yet another royal scandal, 20p (33¢).

- **Original Source** shower gel, shaving cream, or moisture mousse. I'm nuts for Orange & Grapefruit as well as Tea Tree & Mint, which I use for shaving my legs because it smells great and leaves a tingle after I've shaved. The mousse is a lightweight foam that serves as a body oil after the shower. Available at all drug stores, less than £3 ($4.95) per product.

Unusual Gifts for the Person Who Has Everything

- **Desk gadgets and accessories from Smythson of Bond Street.** I buy the tiny magnifying glass as a 50th birthday gift for loved ones, £25 ($41); with an engraved case, £35 ($58), but there are all sorts of doodads and gadgets.
- **Columbia Flower Market original gray plastic tote,** only at Columbia Flower Market, £3 ($4.95).
- **Scent from Jo Malone,** £9 to £20 ($15–$33).
- The **Dorchester Hotel** has gift certificates for afternoon tea! They come wrapped in an elegant box that is perfect for presentation. Full tea is about £16 ($26) and champagne tea is about £22 ($35). If you would like the vouchers sent to you or sent directly to your gift recipient, call © 020/ 7629-8888 and ask for The Promenade. Credit card orders can be taken over the phone; however, there is an additional charge for international mail.
- A **dog portrait from Stephanie Poppen** on Walton Street.
- **Aroma Cushion,** available at many department stores—I found mine at Fenwick on Bond Street. These small pillows come with a variety of treatments—there's everything from Deep Sleep to Animal Spirit. Oh yes, don't forget Monthly Moon. Prices range from £15 ($25) to £20 ($33).
- Anything from **Basia Zarzycka** (52 Sloane Sq., SW1), where whimsy floats in the air and gift items range from decorated lampshades to fashion accessories, and prices soar on the wings of doves.

The 10 Best Shops in London

I hate lists like this because they don't really evaluate a store by taking on the city as a whole. On the whole, however, I like this list, which includes shops that happen to be close together so you can walk from one to the next. With the exception of two of the stores on this list, they are all on either King's Road (or nearby Sloane Sq.) or in Mayfair.

Also note that I have left out experiences, alternative retail, and entire events, such as Covent Garden or Greenwich on a Sunday or walking from Ledbury Street to Portobello Road along Westbourne Grove, and so on. My choices are based on thrills or chills.

BOOTS WELL-BEING CENTRE
127 Kensington High St., W8 (Tube: Kensington High St.).

I never met a Boots I didn't like, although I do like the superstores better than the average ones because they have a greater selection. The Well-Being Centre is nothing short of astonishing—perhaps the most exciting new store in London.

The store looks so average from the front that you will wonder if I am daft, so give me a break here. The space is very deep, gets wider in the rear, and has an upstairs with spa, herbal meds, and more.

Many brands of makeup and health, beauty, bath, hair, and sun products are sold on the ground floor. You can call ahead (© 0845/121-9001) to book spa appointments, which is a good idea since they do book up. Spa hours: Monday through Saturday, from 9am to 7pm; Sunday from 11am to 5pm.

GENERAL TRADING COMPANY
2–4 Symons St., Sloane Sq., SW3 (Tube: Sloane Sq.).

This is a totally new cup of tea for those of you who haven't stumbled onto the changeover on your own—the General Trading Company as Princess Di knew it ain't no more. That building is being converted into a housing block, so the icon store moved around the corner and fancies itself as GTC with a modern logo and a cool, Calvin Klein kind of environment. This is a mini-department store that has a lot of good gift and novelty items, but the new version reminds me of Gump's in San Francisco . . . very spare and minimalist, if that is possible, while still displaying heaps of merchandise.

GEORGINA VON ETZDORF
Burlington Arcade, W1 (Tube: Piccadilly Circus).

Etzdorf is a painter who scribbles and scrawls on fabric, and then makes up accessories in her eccentric and delicious prints. Scarves are the number-one item, but the new handbags of painted canvas and linen are sensational. There are other goodies as well; I bought a pair of gloves for £50 ($83) that are a piece of art. Very original and special. Not for the preppy set; a true British eccentric.

LIBERTY
210 Regent St., W1 (Tube: Oxford Circus).

Give me Liberty or give me death—a fabulous department store with great architecture on the outside and the inside, lots of charm, good clothing, good William Morris prints, good needlework department, good everything.

LUSH
123 Kings Rd., SW3 (Tube: Sloane Sq.), and other locations.

Set up like a deli with bath and skin-care items sold by the chunk or in a salad container—home of the bath bomb, Red Rooster soap, and many yummy and silly gift items for everyone you know. Original, creative, and exactly what you travel the world to find.

PICKETT
32–22 and 41 Burlington Arcade, W1 (Tube: Piccadilly Circus); also 149 Sloane St., SW1 (Tube: Sloane Sq.); and 6 Royal Exchange, EC3 (Tube: Liverpool St.).

One of the reasons I think Trevor Pickett is so clever is that the stores have been able to reinvent themselves each year and specifically make the pivot from purveyor of pashmina (so *last year*) to ethnic jewelry and a look that is sublime and special. There are a handful of shops all over town.

THOMAS GOODE
19 S. Audley St., W1 (Tube: Hyde Park Corner).

The fanciest china shop in the world with room after room of dishes, even some antiques. Also tabletop and design items; the tearoom is very expensive, but staring is free.

VICTORIA & ALBERT MUSEUM GIFT SHOP
V&A Museum, Cromwell Rd., SW7 (Tube: S. Kensington).

Besides the usual cards, books, paperworks, and museum souvenirs, there are wonderful reproductions from the decorative-arts collection of the museum itself. Everything from blue-and-white Spode dishes to Kaffe Fasset tin boxes and much, much more.

VV ROULEAUX
6 Marylebone High St., W1 (Tube: Bond St. or Marylebone).

A few years ago, VV Rouleaux was a fancy ribbons-and-trimming store at Sloane Square. While they still have a shop there (54 Sloane Sq. at Cliveden Place), the best shop to visit is the one on Marylebone High Street, where two levels of ribbons and stuff just knock you out with their colors, textures, and possibilities. Buy trims, artificial flowers, home style, and more.

BASIA ZARZYCKA
52 Sloane Sq., SW1 (Tube: Sloane Sq.).

This store is not for everyone, and it is unlikely that you will actually buy anything here unless you cashed out your tech stocks before the crash. But, but, but you must come here to simply gawk at the creativity, energy, high style, and whimsy in picture frames; accessories for fashion, home, and table; and all the lampshades, shawls, handbags, and so on. The prices are very, very high; the attitude is equally elevated—but it's still one of the best stores in London.

Ethan Sunshine's Five Best Buys in London

1. Diesel Jeans (£10/$17) at **Portobello Road Market,** NW11
2. Denim Royal Elastic sneakers (£20/$33) at **Free Spirit,** Kensington High Street, NW10
3. Born to Shop baseball T-shirt (£10/$17) at **Mendoza,** Brick Lane, E1
4. Smoking Kills necktie (£25/$41) at **Junky,** Brick Lane, E1
5. Ringspun Allstars T-shirt (£15/$25) at **Retro Man,** 30–34 Pembridge Rd., NW11

Jennifer McCormick's Five Best Buys in London

1. Four CDs (£10/$17) at **Portobello Road Market,** NW11
2. Vintage designer handbag (£22/$36) at **Retro Woman,** 30–34 Pembridge Rd., NW11
3. Adidas Mary Janes (£55/$91) at **Size? Sale Shop,** 145 Kensington High St., NW10
4. Painted cowboy shirt one-off (£35/$58) at **Laden Show Room,** EC1
5. Sex Bomb Bath Ballistic (£2.50/$4.15) at **Lush,** Kensington High Street, NW10

Chapter Two

·····················

LONDON DETAILS

WELCOME TO LONDON

···

On a recent visit to London, I was wincing from the cost of the taxi from Waterloo International to my friend Ruth's apartment, and mentally annoyed at the high cost of everything in the U.K. I was prepared to not like London that day, prepared to tell readers that other cities are more fun for less money. Yet within minutes of arrival, shortly after I hit the streets to begin my rounds and work, a doddering woman, resting on her walking sticks, came up to me and asked why Britain had changed so much, why it wasn't a "nation" as it had been before World War II. Then I got on the bus—to avoid those expensive taxis—and my bus driver took the fares of the passengers and then sang to us in a big, booming—quite professional— voice. While on the bus—heading toward Oxford Street—I passed a woman on her bike, her pink, fake-fur-covered bike.

And I had dared to grumble about the prices? What was wrong with me? Where else in the world do you get a show like this? As dear as it might be, London is a treat for the eye and the soul. Shop with care, look right, and "mind the gap." As a visitor, you're gonna have a ball. So welcome to London where a little Yankee thrift and some Yankee doodle-doo will get you a long way; where things are just different enough to make you want to shop, smile, and worry about the costs later.

15

Despite often-obscene prices and constant cock-ups (as *they* say) in the infrastructure, London is worth it. Brits more or less speak the same language as Americans, yet many of the products and brands are new and fresh. Prices may push you to cut your trip from 5 days to 3 or from a 1-week tour to 5 days, but I urge you to do so rather than let London prices send you scurrying to another destination.

There's a lot of energy in the stores, as well as some great things to buy at reasonable prices. Just tell me why I didn't get the garden gnome with a portable phone that actually rang . . . for £6 ($10)? Was I mad?

OH, GROW UP

Don't get depressed by the cost of living (or shopping) in London. Get even. Go for novelty and selection. Hone in on what you can't find in the United States or have never seen elsewhere. Spend time in grocery stores and street markets, buy vintage, go to outlets. Do the sales, shop off-season, snoop around museum stores.

I get enormous joy from stores such as **TopShop** and **Super-Drug,** which offer cheapie fun items at bargain-basement prices. I take a taxi to the **Tesco** on Cromwell Road, where I do a lot of gift shopping; it's far bigger than the easier-to-reach Tesco Metro stores and gives you great prices and grocery-store fun. They also sell bestsellers at discount prices and their own line of designer makeup.

America does bargain-basement very well, but the British do knockoffs of cutting-edge catwalk fashions that America isn't quite tuned in to. The British have also refined Power Shopping— you head out of town on a day trip to do big-haul purchases at lower prices. The most popular of such destinations is **Bicester Village,** a factory outlet mall, but there are others. Suburbs have their own **T.J. Maxx** stores, which for a reason I cannot explain are called **T.K. Maxx.**

Britain really wants your business, and here are some deals to look for:

- Airfares (both transatlantic and, in some cases, from London to other European points) can be lower than they were a few years ago. Even peak summer airfares average $500 or $600 per economy seat, round-trip; off-season seats go for less than $300 round-trip. Sometimes there are even $99 (one-way) tickets from New York to London. In a winter newspaper, there was an ad for American Airlines with airfares to London at $114 each way; today, I looked at the American Airlines website and found round-trip tickets from JFK in June for under $300.
- British Airways is offering round-trip airfares from JFK in New York to many cities in Europe—through London, of course—for about $600 round-trip with a free 3-night hotel stay in London. And this is during peak summer travel time.
- Hotels have rebates, promotional rates, deals in dollars, and all sorts of enticements to get you to come visit. I just read of an American Express promotion that offers free *limo* transfer to and from the airport to guests who arrange to stay just 3 consecutive nights or more in a certain hotel in London. **Thistle Hotels** (as well as other chains) often do a dollar-to-pound parity rate that's a rather welcome winter treat. I read about another deal (this one with **Millennium Hotels**) wherein you pay for 3 nights of hotel and get the fourth night free. In the American Airlines AAVacations advert (as the British say) that I mentioned above, two different hotel choices are given; each offers the fourth night for free.
- Package deals are becoming more flexible, so you can have the benefits of a fixed-price trip without being herded onto a bus and having to suffer with some first-timer who wants to know who Big Ben was named after. There are also combo deals that include Paris or a part of France, which brings down the prices a bit.

- Internet sites are the dumping ground for airlines and hotels; here you will find shockingly low deals that will free up many shopping dollars because you were smart enough to run all the angles. I had friends ask me to check out their London hotel choice from the online discount site they chose; they told me the four-star, name-brand hotel was going to cost them $159 per night for the room, not per person. I told them they were nuts; it was a good deal at £159 ($262). I went online and, behold, they were right! They found the deal of the century.

- This borders on bad taste, but it is a fact of life: Whenever something terrible happens in the world, and people are afraid to travel, prices go down and promotions prevail. Britain has had a string of bad luck since Mad Cow Disease and is still trying to get travelers into town. Use assorted websites to research bargains offered in such cases. I've found a segment of **www.travelbritain.org** with special deals including luxury hotels such as Savoy Group and Le Meridien, where rooms that normally cost about $500 a night are going for under $300 a night.

GUIDES TO LONDON

The number of guidebooks to London is staggering and can get expensive quickly. Because more and more information is available online (and is often free), I suggest you do a good bit of your investigation on websites, which also have the ability to be updated immediately.

Don't, however, miss *London A to Z* (say "A to Zed"), the map guide that everyone, absolutely everyone, uses—locals and tourists alike. It's an in-depth street-finder that will even tell you which Tube stop to use. Buy it at news kiosks on the street or in bookstores; most hotel gift shops also sell them.

There are a few specialty magazines for shoppers interested in a certain type of shopping, such as journals of art galleries, antiques shows, and so on.

Also note that the **British Tourist Authority** (BTA) has a few offices scattered around the United States that give away brochures. BTA has an excellent bookstore, but it also has maps and other goodies that are free in the U.S.—items you pay for once you walk into tourist centers in Britain.

GETTING THERE

. . . .

From the United States

There are a number of ways to get to England from the United States, but since there isn't yet a tunnel that connects Boston with Britain, you'll probably be best off in an airplane.

The *QE2* quits its transatlantic crossings to make way for a new sister ship, the *QM2 (Queen Mary 2),* in April 2004, which makes the crossing in 6 luxurious days at a variety of prices depending on size and location of the cabin you choose. Concorde has gone out of service—lose a plane, gain a ship . . . it all works out.

Her Majesty has just approved construction of three new runways—one each for Heathrow, Stansted, and Gatwick. Although they won't be ready for many years, these runways will bring even more traffic into the U.K., even though they are meant to alleviate congestion. Obviously, there's no slowdown in business and visitors.

You'll find that airfare prices from New York to London are particularly competitive because so many carriers want a piece of the action. There's also big noise about changing *cabotage* laws and merging E.U. carriers so that Lufthansa, for example, could fly the New York to London route. You may actually get price breaks from new gateway cities that are launching service, so New York is not your only way to London. Ask, depending on where you are coming from, and use some flexible thinking and map-planning to get the best deal you can.

If you find that all prices are the same, what do you base your choice on? I think about the airport itself (LHR—London Heathrow—is a zoo), safety, convenience, ability to change a ticket and the cost for doing so, frequent-flier mileage, overweight costs (I do a lot of shopping, remember?), and perks.

BRITISH CARRIERS

British Airways I make it simple by pretty much sticking with one carrier for the New York–London run: British Airways (BA). They've got use of Terminal 4 at LHR and a million amenities geared to their passengers in the terminal. Every trip finds new improvements onboard and within the terminal; there are a huge number of promotions and deals offered. I discovered that they now have express passport service, so you don't even have to stand in line at immigration in Heathrow.

In-flight amenities are extended to economy, which is not true on every other airline. They give you a free toothbrush and overnight kit, even in the "back" of the plane in the World Traveller section. There is also electronic check-in while you stand in line.

Prices vary with the seasons and the competition; there are all sorts of deals—today's paper has this stunner: "Buy a business-class ticket round-trip NY–LHR and get a free companion ticket!" I just booked and got 3 free nights of hotel in London—and in summer's high season!

Winter prices are always the best deal. Last winter they did a series of low-price fares that offered London with another city, and the list of cities included just about every major city in Europe. If you are thinking about adding on Paris via train, check out this kind of deal wherein flying costs less than a train ticket.

BA also has complete package tours with hotel rooms—in and out of London—and many specials. My best secret: BA doesn't always advertise its rates. Watch for an American Airlines airfare war; then call BA. They will match the current lowest fares. In the United States, call ℂ **800/272-6433**; find them on the Web at www.britishairways.com.

Don't forget to look for special deals online, directly through the airline and through discounters as well.

Virgin Atlantic I'll leave out the rivalry and rumors regarding BA and Virgin and let you know that Virgin is a strange creature that many consumers love and others are amused by. They still have three classes of service—sometimes four—so what you get is varied, but the Upper Class is amazingly creative and comfortable. Virgin has also recently bought slots at LHR. Could they eventually buy BA? Oh my heavens.

U.S. CARRIERS

American Airlines I sometimes book American Airlines, especially when I am in and out of Paris and London and will connect one-way via the Chunnel or when I am getting tickets for my son, who goes to school in Boston.

American Airlines does have weekend deals that are offered at the last minute—you get to stay for only a weekend (but it's a long weekend), and you can book through their website, www.aa.com. There are NetSaver Specials on this site, and they sometimes include London. I just checked the weekend specials: round-trip from JFK for $279 with 10 days' notice, which is more than I need. I booked my son a Boston–London round-trip in June for $348. The price was $348 to London from Los Angeles as well. But wait, I've had several reader complaints on inflexibility, so pay attention to the fine print. Call © 800/433-7300; www.aa.com.

Continental This one has a twist: Continental flies to Stansted, considered an alternative airport. They also have service from Newark to Gatwick, if you prefer a more traditional airport. Continental is also one of the airlines that offers business-first, a far more comfortable seat than on planes that still have three classes of service. Contact Continental at © 800/231-0856; www.continental.com.

Delta If you're saying you didn't know Delta flies from New York to London, here's the big news: They don't. Delta has regular London Gatwick service from Atlanta, or you can connect through Cincinnati. Delta has a special deal called Delta's Escape Plan from its major hub cities; it's a membership club (costing about $50 for you and $30 for each of your guests) that enables you to call a toll-free number in the middle of the week to get the weekend deals. Obviously, you have to be flexible here, but there are domestic and international deals. Delta also has business-first—far more value than regular old business class on airlines that have three classes. Contact them at © 800/241-4141; www.delta.com.

VIA CONSOLIDATOR

I don't fly on consolidator tickets because I am always collecting mileage, but if cash is short and you don't qualify for one of the winter rates that are so cheap, perhaps you'll want to try one of those brokers that specializes in tickets on major scheduled airlines. Note that rates are usually for peak travel or last-minute travel when you don't qualify for a low-cost ticket.

According to an ad in the *New York Times,* a firm called **Global Discount Travel Services** has London tickets at $136 each way! Not bad. Call © **800/977-7110** for domestic reservations; © 800/497-7132 for international reservations. Their website is at www.lowestfare.com. And yes, you get your miles!

There are a handful of other websites that offer bargains and discounts, some at the last minute.

STUDENT FARES

You need not be in school to qualify for a student fare; you just need to be under 26 years old. You often need an ID card.

STA   For travelers under 26, STA Travel (the world's largest student travel organization) provides very affordable airfares and package deals—and you don't even need to be a student! At **www.sta.com**, you will find a number of great bargains for a number of great trips. The only thing you need to reserve the airfares is an ISIC (International Student Identity Card), which comes with your picture, name of institution, and birthdate for $22. If you are not currently a student but are under

Web Warnings

I did try to do various bookings on prominent websites (especially the ones that offer deals) and always found myself thrilled by the initial offerings. Then when I got to actually booking the fare, I was furious that I was traded up and could never have the low fares I had been teased with.

26, you can get the IYTC (International Youth Travel Card). Both cards require proof (that is, a copy of your current class schedule and a copy of your birth certificate), but both can be your ticket to an inexpensive holiday. The cards can then be used throughout the world for deals on accommodations, museums, and theaters. The website also offers deals on hotels and hostels, rail tickets, and even travel insurance.

From Continental Europe

By Train   Remember that tickets and passes bought in advance in the United States through **Rail Europe** often offer the best deal. Call ✆ 888/382-7245. **Eurostar,** the train that travels through the Chunnel, which connects France, Belgium, and Britain, makes it a breeze to get to London from the Continent. Travel time has just been cut down to 2 hours and 35 minutes from Paris to London. There are promotional fares.

You can buy the tickets in the U.S. through Rail Europe or **BritRail** or while you are actually in London, although if time is short, you do not want to wait in line for an hour. Locations can be found online at www.britrail.com.

Note various quirks in the pricing, especially if you are buying the train tickets from Europe. Go online and do some homework so you are prepared for all the choices and all the different price possibilities. I just bought a round-trip, second-class seat on Eurostar from Paris for $100 by getting it in advance. The prices ranged from about $350 without a Saturday stay to $89

Meanwhile, Back at Luton

Many of the new, small carriers that serve continental Europe do not have offices in the United States and can be booked only on the Web, through your travel agent, or by making a long-distance call to London. Most of these airlines offer discounts if you book online. The largest percentage of them serves London-area airports, but remember that they usually use alternative airports and not Heathrow. Try the following (local U.K. phone numbers are listed):

- **BMI** (© 0807/607-0555); www.flybmi.com
- **EasyJet** (© 0870/60-00-000); www.easyjet.com
- **Ryanair** (© 541/56-95-69); www.ryanair.ie
- **Virgin Express** (© 020/7744-0004 or © 033/32-2-752-0505 in Brussels); www.virgin-express.com

with a Saturday-night stay. There are also youth and senior fares—if you qualify.

Air There's a new air war from continental Europe into London (and vice versa), partly because the train has cut travel time and prices and can be so attractive.

If you're flying, not only can you select from flights offered by **British Airways** and other international carriers, but more and more new regional airlines are getting into the fray and offering competitive prices and often alternative airports, which may not be as far away from London as Heathrow. *Trick:* Price round-trip as well as one-way tickets, even if you need only a one-way leg; often the round-trip ticket costs less than a one-way. Simply throw away the unused portion.

Also ask each airline about promotional deals—**Air France** had a fabulous deal whereby two family members traveling together got tickets at half price.

Work every angle; there's competition for your business, so fight for the best rates possible.

Alternative Airports

Almost all of the new, small airlines use alternative airports such as Stansted, Luton, or City Airport. City Airport is very close to Canary Wharf and is getting more and more of the business visitors; Stansted and Luton are north of the city.

EasyJet uses London's Luton airport. Before you jump on the Tube to dash to the airport, *know which one you're headed to!* Also try to get a brief understanding of transportation options once you get there.

Electronically Yours

Aside from all the travel information you could need (and far more) and all the deal-surfing you might want to do, please note that many London stores now have websites and even electronic shopping packages so that you don't even have to go on the trip in order to shop abroad. This doesn't beat a trip to London, but it's something to think about.

There are far too many addresses in the United Kingdom on tourist information to list here, but whether you need train schedules or theater listings, it's on the Internet. I've listed some of my favorite sites and some of the most unusual.

www.royal.gov.uk—Buckingham Palace website.

www.timeout.co.uk—*Time Out* Guide online.

www.tatler.co.uk—It's *Tatler* magazine, and I can't get through the month without it (also try www.excite.co.uk).

www.vogue.co.uk—Not to be outdone by *Tatler,* also through www.excite.co.uk.

www.officialLondonTheatre.co.uk—Official half-price and discount theatre ticket booth.

GETTING AROUND LONDON

• Buy an *A to Z*—it's a detailed street map in book form—
  it is essential for knowing where you are going and how to
  get there.
• Get free maps to the Tube and buses in major Tube stations.
  If you have always depended on the Tube, consider buses
  and begin to learn the major bus routes from your hotel.
  (The Tube has been having emotional problems and is not
  always reliable.)
• Walk whenever possible.

You can get information online: www.thetube.com.

Tube

The Tube—London's famous underground system—is the per-
sonification of the good news and the bad news. When it's working, it does get you just about everywhere you need to go. But
something goes wrong just about every day, and you can waste
a lot of time waiting for a train that's not coming or diverting
yourself through stations and lines you had no interest in visiting in an attempt to get somewhere while your precious time
is wastin' away.

More bad news. If you buy a single ticket for £1.60 ($2.65),
you must put it through the turnstile and enter the Never-Never
Land of the station before you find out if your train is running. You may waste a lot of cash this way. Some type of travel
pass will be your best buy if you plan an active visit with many
trips per day. A single trip usually costs £1.60 ($2.65) to £1.90
($3.15); if you travel more than three trips a day, a **Travelcard**
(for use on buses and the Tube, and British Rail services in
Greater London) becomes worthwhile. There are various types
of Travelcards; prices begin at £4.10 ($6.80).

You can buy Travelcards before you get to London. They
are available in the U.S. through RailEurope, through various
London hotel promotions, online, or in the Gare du Nord in

London Map Index

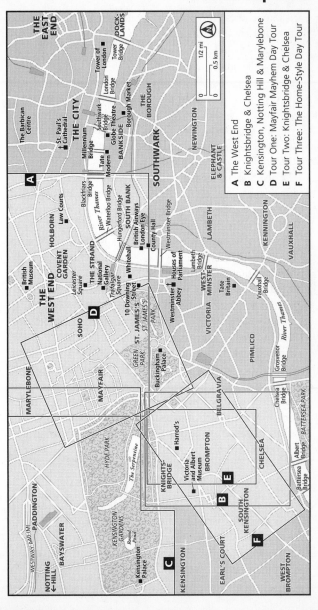

A The West End
B Knightsbridge & Chelsea
C Kensington, Notting Hill & Marylebone
D Tour One: Mayfair Mayhem Day Tour
E Tour Two: Knightsbridge & Chelsea
F Tour Three: The Home-Style Day Tour

Paris. Sometimes you can get a promotional airfare package that includes a Travelcard.

If you arrive in London without Tube tickets keep the following guidelines in mind:

- If you will ride the Tube only once or twice a day and possibly not every day, pay for individual tickets, as needed. If you can't figure out how to use the automatic machine, pay for the least expensive ticket and be prepared to pay up as you exit. You can also stand in line at the ticket window and ask questions before purchasing the ticket from the attendant.
- If you are on and off the Tube three or more times in a day, or if you're going to Greenwich, buy a 1-day Travelcard that includes more than zones 1 and 2.
- There is a **two-zone weekend pass.** It costs £6.10 ($10) and is good for travel Saturday and Sunday, and even on bank holidays that might fall on the Monday.
- If you are spending a week in London and plan to explore it from dawn till dusk and don't really know what you're doing—except that you want to do it all—purchase the London Visitor **Travelcard.** The cost varies with the zones; there is a weekly or monthly price. A six-zone weekly ticket costs approximately £30 ($50) (you can obtain it ahead of time in the U.S. through BritRail USA), and it gives you 7 days of unlimited travel on Tube and bus. You can also order 1-week Tube tickets online at www.oystercard.com or get information on all the prices and choices at www.transport forlondon.gov.uk.

Bus

Several of the tourist travel passes cover both the Tube and the bus; the best sales pitch I have seen anywhere, however, is published by London Buses, which remind you that the price of Tube passes goes up every year and the price of a bus ticket has not increased in 5 years.

Please note that you can no longer pay the fare once you're on the bus. This has just changed! There are little yellow machines that allow you to buy a single ticket at the bus stop before you board.

I buy a booklet of six bus coupons at newsstands; this makes the ride cost 65p ($1.10) instead of 95p ($1.60). I call these tickets the Tab Tix because they are small hexagonal pull tabs that come in a booklet; you pull one off for each ride. They cannot be used on the Tube. You buy them at newsstands and cigarette stores; this is the best bargain in Britain.

You can buy a bus map in any bookstore, or you can get a free neighborhood bus map in your local Tube station. My trick: If I can't find a bus to where I want to go, I hop a bus headed to Oxford Circus or Piccadilly and then Tube or cab it to my final destination from there, or even connect to another bus once I get oriented.

Taxi

Taxis are plentiful because they are so darn expensive. The flag drops at £2 ($3.30) and escalates quickly. I find that a taxi just always costs me a tenner or more, and when I am going to/from Waterloo International train station, we're looking at close to £20 ($33).

I also found that on days I tried to use the Tube, I ended up in taxis because the Tube wasn't working, and by then I was late and desperate.

Car

You do not want to rent a car in London. You may want to rent a car at the airport in order to drive around the countryside, but trust me: You do not want to drive in London.

If you want someone to drive you, that is an entirely different ball of wax. I keep on hand the brochure from **Capital Skylink,** which does airport pickups and transport, racecourse fares, and sightseeing around town at a flat rate. They do take credit cards, but there's a 10% surcharge for this, so have cash on hand. Phone © **020/7924-6556** or fax 020/7924-5513; drop the 0 if you are calling from the U.S.

CALLING AROUND

To call London from the United States, dial © 011 (the international code), 44 (Britain's country code), and the phone numbers, which include the codes automatically. Note that every single phone in Britain changed in 2000, and many mobile phones changed in 2001. Anything you may have in your Palm Pilot that begins with a "181" or "171" is the wrong number, but it can be easily updated.

To update: If the number was 171, it is now 207 plus the old number, so there are eight digits. If it was 181, it is now 208 plus the old number; again, eight digits—usually written in blocks of four numbers with a hyphen in between.

If you are calling these numbers from within London, they were 0171 or 0181 . . . now they are 0207 or 0208. *But* you can just dial the 7 or the 8 and then the local number.

If you are calling the U.S. from the U.K., remember:

- As in all E.U. countries, you dial 00, then 1, then the area code and number.
- Phone lines, especially from the U.S. and the U.K., are inexpensive these days if you have an international calling plan. Rates should be no more than 12¢ a minute. Ask your carrier before you leave home; it may pay to call home and then have them call you right back.
- Do be aware of the charges incurred each time you use one of those newfangled access codes that have been marketed as bargain phone fares. Yes, you get U.S. phone rates, which may be less expensive than British Telecom (BT), but you pay a per-call surcharge; so if you talk for only a minute, or get the answering machine of the party you are calling,

you're paying a very hefty price. (AT&T surcharge is $2.50 per call; MCI surcharge is $2 per call.) Also, they have varying rates, so that if you aren't on a promotional deal (10¢ a min.), you may be paying $1.20 a minute. You can have several rates depending on which branch of these services you use at the time.

I buy a £5 ($8.25) phone card upon arrival in London. (Any news agent will sell you one.) This card is good for calls placed anywhere in the world.

CONNECTING IN LONDON

Although many hotels have business centers where you can go online, London has scads of Internet cafes—there are even some in the department stores on Oxford Street. If you want to connect on your laptop from your hotel room, you will usually be charged for a local call. Local access numbers are:

AOL/CompuServe: 0845/080-7445
MSN: 0845/088-8181

The low point of one of my hotel bills was paying £15 ($25) for Internet use; I then went to **Easy Everything** on Oxford Street, where access costs £1 ($1.65) per 20 minutes. There are Internet cafes in every neighborhood.

SHOPPING HOURS

Shopping hours are downright unorganized in London. Tuesday seems to have later openings in the morning, while Wednesday, Thursday, and Friday have slightly later closings in the evening. Note that it can be all 3 of these days at some stores or only 1 or 2 of them. Some guidelines:

- If the store normally opens at 10am, on Tuesday it probably opens at 10:30am.
- Very few stores in London open at 9am. Almost all of the big department stores and multiples open at 10am. *Note:* If you have an early beauty-parlor appointment at a department-store salon, do not panic. One of the store doors is open at 9am with direct access to the hair salon.
- Canary Wharf stores do open early, as they want people coming to and from work.
- Covent Garden stores may not open until 11am.
- Very few stores close for lunch.
- All stores close early in London. They do not know the meaning of late. To a British store, a *late night* means they are open until 7 or possibly 8pm.
- There are Sunday retail hours, usually from noon to 5pm. Some stores, usually grocery stores or tourist traps, open at 11am on Sundays. (**Harrods** does not open on Sun except right before Christmas.)

HOLIDAY HOURS

The change in Sunday retail has created a huge wave of uncertainty about the rigid laws on holidays as well. Used to be, stores were closed on holidays. These days, no one really knows who will do what.

I am usually in London on Easter weekend because stores are sometimes open for Easter Sunday and Monday shopping, and this includes Harrods. Yep, **Harrods** was open on Easter Monday, but not Sunday. Also note that some branches of a store may be open while others will be closed, as with **Boots.**

Many an unhappy shopper has written to ask me to warn you about Christmas hours: Stores are closed for as many as 3 days in a row right at the Christmas season—they celebrate Christmas Eve, Christmas Day, and Boxing Day (the day after Christmas). Stores close again for New Year's Day.

Bank holidays are celebrated at regular intervals in the British calendar; they seem to fall around the same time as the feast of the Assumption of Mary (Aug 15), but ever since Henry VIII split from Rome, no one in England is big on the holiday. Bank holidays affect retail but in an odd way: Banks and smaller stores close; big stores and multiples are usually open.

CHEMISTS' HOURS

If you need an emergency prescription filled, or have a late-night personal need, there is always a chemist (drugstore) somewhere in London open later than usual. The **Boots** at Piccadilly Circus stays open until 10pm and is also open on Sunday; **Bliss Chemist** is open at Marble Arch on Sundays.

If your accommodations aren't anywhere near these addresses, don't despair: There are a handful of all-night or late-night chemists dotted around town—just ask your concierge for the one closest to your hotel. There's often a pharmacy or chemist at the train station.

Condoms are sold in vending machines in most restaurants and in hotel gift shops.

WARRANT SHOPPING

You may wonder where the Queen shops. She doesn't. Things are "sent 'round" to Buckingham Palace for her to consider. Money and price tags never touch her hands. However, she asks only certain stores and factories to send 'round goods—these stores have the royal seal of approval, which is called a "royal warrant." You too can shop these same resources, as they are always marked at the door.

Holding a royal warrant demands total discretion. The warrant holder may not talk about the royals in any way—especially to the press or public—or the warrant holder will lose the warrant. So if you walk into **Turnbull & Asser** and ask them what size pj's Prince Charles wears, you will be met with an icy stare and stony silence. Such stores are allowed to display the royal coat of arms and to use the words "by appointment." Because there is more than one royal family in Europe and there are several members of the Windsor family, you may see several coats of arms on the window of any given shop—appointments from various royals.

A warrant is good for 10 years and then must be renewed. If a merchant is dropped, he gets a sort of royal pink slip and has no means of redress. Every year, about 20 to 30 new warrants are issued and the same number of pink slips are passed out. To qualify for a warrant, you must provide a minimum of 3 years of service to the crown.

There are warrants on everything from royal laundry detergent (Procter & Gamble) to royal china, and even several warrants in the same category. For china, Her Majesty has as much trouble getting it down to one pattern as I do—she's got warrants at **Royal Worcester, Spode,** and **Royal Doulton.**

MUSEUM SHOPPING

London museums have really got it together and have come up with high-class gifts and reproductions from their collections. The tinny and tatty are out of style.

Bramah Tea and Coffee Museum   You know I could never resist a teapot; this museum traces the history of both tea and coffee and features many novelty teapots, as does the small gift shop. It's very close to the Design Museum. 40 Southwark St., SE1 (Tube: London Bridge or Tower Hill).

British Museum   Actually, there are seven different shops on the premises and two on the street outside that appear to be free-standing. Don't miss the reproduction gifts and the gorgeous books. This is a huge museum—it's free, it's across the street from a great sweater store (**Westaway & Westaway**), and you can walk to Covent Garden from here if you're strong enough. This is the perfect place for unique gifts and souvenirs if you aren't into kitsch and royal souvenirs. *Note:* As this museum is redone, it will offer more and more choices; the gift shop will be tucked under the stairs, according to Sir Norman Foster. Great Russell Street, WC1 (Tube: Tottenham Court Rd. or Holborn).

Design Museum   Sure, the museum is neat, and the part of town where it's located (Butler's Wharf) is worth taking a look at to get a view of Thames redevelopment, but don't forget the gift shop or the restaurant. Products are featured heavily in the collections and are sold, along with the postcards and visual arts, in the shop. This entire complex, including the restaurant, is an example of Sir Terence Conran's genius, and part of the new London. 28 Shad Thames, SE1 (Tube: Tower Hill or London Bridge).

Fashion & Textile Museum   This brand-new museum is sort of in the middle of nowhere but convenient to many places in the "nowhere" range, not far from the Tate Modern (but not really walking distance) or the Bermondsey Market (a flea market held early Fri morning). For that matter, you are near other London sights and the wonderful Borough Market, for foodies. It's all still being developed; doesn't compete with the Tate; but is bright pink and has permanent collections of, dare I say it, cutting-edge fashions. Some fashiony stuff. 83 Bermondsey St., SE1 (Tube: London Bridge).

London Transport Museum   Although Covent Garden is great on Sunday, this small museum is a treasure any day. Children will love shopping the gift area, which is also great for adults. There's a lot more here than you would expect; don't miss the thousands of postcards and posters of Transport Art (drawings that have decorated Tube and train stations since the early part of the century). Actually, the museum happens to be fun, too, but the gift shop is sensational. Covent Garden Piazza, WC2 (Tube: Covent Garden).

Madame Tussaud's   For a wax museum it is very expensive, and the lines out front can be heavy. You can quit the scene

and walk around to the side of the building, past the plane-
tarium, and gain access to the shop, but you'll have to knock
on the door to be let in. The tour ends in the gift shop; they
just aren't prepared for people who only want to shop.

The shop itself is rather large, with several rooms. Much
of the merchandise is standard London destination souvenir
stuff; however, there are some items that are unique to Madame
Tussaud's. My favorite line is the group of items with the slo-
gan "Some of the people I met in London"—pictures, shirts,
and coffee cups of the famous, and infamous, as created in wax.
Marylebone Road, NW1 (Tube: Baker St.).

Museum of the Moving Image   Part of the South Bank Arts
Center at Waterloo, this is one of London's best. It's also great
for kids weaned on TV and movies. Exhibits transport visitors from the earliest shadow plays to a 24-minute film that
covers all of Hollywood's famous faces, from Mickey Mouse
to Mickey Rourke. The gift shop has a huge selection of books
on movies, posters, videocassettes, notepads, postcards, Chap-
lin masks, movie-themed glassware, coasters, jigsaw puzzles,
lamps, aprons, and other cinema tchotchkes. South Bank Arts
Centre, South Bank, SE1 (Tube: Waterloo).

The National Gallery Shop   Cards and calendars are the real
finds, but the posters aren't shabby. The shop has been moved
around the corner as a free-standing shop. Although they do
great Christmas cards, they also have innovative products
based on the most popular works in the museum. For an original and witty gift, spend $50 for a Swatch-like watch created
from a great masterpiece by someone such as Vincent van
Gogh. Where does time Gogh? Hmmm. Trafalgar Square,
WC2 (Tube: Charing Cross).

The National Portrait Gallery   The Portrait Gallery is convenient for shoppers (there's a flea market at St. Martin-in-the-
Fields, next door) and has a lovely gift shop. For some reason,
they have just about the best Christmas cards in London. 2 St.
Martin's Place, WC2 (Tube: Charing Cross).

The Natural History Museum   Your kids will love the Natural History Museum and its many gift shops—from stars to dinosaurs, you can buy it all. Cromwell Road, SW7 (Tube: S. Kensington).

Royal Academy   Because of their tendency to do specialized shows that play for months, the Royal Academy also creates merchandise to tie in with their events—most of these items are made exclusively for the museum. I bought the Charlotte Salomon book during a recent exhibition; the museum told me they were the only store to sell it. Burlington House, Piccadilly, W1 (Tube: Piccadilly Circus).

Tate and **Tate Modern**   As you know, these are two different museums with different attitudes. The Tate Modern is the new kid on the block, even though the block is quite amazing and in an old power plant. The gift shop is large; some of the "modern" line is also sold at Selfridges, although why anyone would buy a coffee mug that just says MODERN on it is beyond me. Maybe that's British wit for you. I find myself thinking of my son's friend, Carver Tate, and wanting to buy all those T-shirts that say TATE on them. The postcard selection at the Modern is poor. Tate: Millbank, SW1 (Tube: Pimlico); Tate Modern: Bankside, SE1 (Tube: Blackfriars).

Tower of London Shops   Redone, reorganized, and more with-it since its upgrade in 2000, the shops not only have basic souvenirs and kitsch, but there's also an attempt at reproductions, serious items, and stylish gifts, including costume jewelry versions of the Crown Jewels. *Note:* The Tower of London is one of several properties managed by the Royal Palaces of London; each has brought in new merchandise and beefed up the gift shops. Tower of London, Tower Hill, EC3 (Tube: London Bridge or Tower Hill).

The Victoria & Albert Museum Shop   I adore the V&A gift shop—beats me why they keep reorganizing the space. The actual shop size is the same, but it has been reorganized so that there is 30% more selling space. There's also an additional shop for kids in the Henry Cole wing.

Although the usual postcards and paper goods are still for sale, the shop also sells jewelry, has some new lines created specifically to beef up the product range, and now even has a few items of clothing. They also do mail order.

A donation is suggested for museum admission; however, you can get into the gift shop without entering the museum. They have terrific shopping bags (the mark of good taste); they do a Spode blue-and-white coffee mug as a gift (GIFT FOR A FRIEND written on the mug); and they are simply the best place in town for one-stop shopping. Cromwell Road, SW7 (Tube: S. Kensington).

TUBE & TRAIN SHOPPING

Retail in train stations is already pretty sophisticated. People like to be able to grab what they need as they dash to and from the train; hence, there are always florists, candy stores, bookstores, and even shoe-repair or coffee-bean stores. I've even seen branches of **Knickerbox,** the lingerie chain, in several train stations.

Now then, what you really want to know about is Chunnel duty-free. I wish I could give an answer that made sense, but I can't because the laws in duty-free have changed. There is no duty-free shop in Waterloo International, where you take the passenger train, Eurostar, and there are no carts onboard the train selling duty-free perfumes. Technically speaking, the Chunnel backs the abolishment of duty-free.

SOUVENIR SHOPPING

The best place to buy London-specific souvenirs is from the street vendors who stretch across the "downtown" area—there are quite a few of them on Oxford Street from Marble Arch to Oxford Circus. There's another gaggle at Piccadilly Circus. The street vendors seem to have the best prices in town.

If you are traveling out-of-season, you can bargain a little bit with the street vendors, except at Buckingham Palace, where souvenirs are about the most expensive in town.

Royal commemoratives also make good souvenirs, but be warned that some of these things become collectors' items and are frequently very, very expensive. At the time of a royal event (such as a wedding or a coronation), the commemoratives seem to be a dime a dozen, but once they dry up, they are gone forever and become collectors' items.

If you are buying for an investment, buy the best quality you can afford (branded ceramic vs. cheap) and try to get something that was created in a limited edition.

On Saturday, Portobello Road has several vendors selling souvenirs. Although some of the antiques vendors may have royal souvenirs, beware: Most of what they're selling is the cheap and tacky kind that is not valuable.

Because the Harrods name has become synonymous with London, Harrods souvenirs are perfectly appropriate gifts. There are scads of them in every price range. Souvenirs are sold both on the street floor and in the lower level.

ROYAL MAIL: SHOPPING & SENDING

News agents sell books of royal stamps in cute little red packages. When you purchase a book, you must specify whether you want international stamps. Stamps do not have denominations printed on them.

If you do decide to mail items home, you can buy Jiffy bags in the stationery department of any department store or at an office-supply store. Then head for any post office or ask your concierge to do the deed. To avoid paying a duty fee, you may legally send one unsolicited package per day if its value is less than $50. So mark your package "Unsolicited Gift" and place its value at something unsuspiciously below the $50 limit (unless it actually *is* worth less, of course).

International mail through stores is not tricky, but it can be expensive. **Thomas Goode** agreed to send some cups and saucers to the United States; the charge was £25 ($41)! I'm sorry, but for that amount of money, I can carry them onboard. But wait, let's examine that cost without the first flush of passion. My purchase totaled £100 ($165). I would therefore qualify for a VAT (value-added tax) refund of more or less 18%. (More on VAT refunds in chapter 3.) The cost of the shipping was 25% of my total. If I didn't want the hassle of hand-carrying breakables or having to do the VAT refund myself at the airport, the price of the shipping isn't a bargain, but it offers a fair trade-off.

I sent a box of books to Paris, asking first about the cost. "The same as regular mail, madame." Well, it cost $25 to send maybe seven paperbacks that I could have put into my luggage. And to give you another comparison, I just sent through the Royal Post a package of bath bombs that I bought at **Lush** and packed myself, and it weighed almost 3 pounds and cost $13 to ship to the U.S.

A final note: If you plan to ship anything large or expensive or are considering reserving a container, see chapter 8, "Home Furnishings & Design Resources," for detailed information on shipping.

DUTY-FREE SHOPPING

Duty-free was abolished for travel between European Union (E.U.) countries but is legal for those of us who are departing the E.U. So if you go from London to Paris, no duty-free; if you go from London to the United States, there's duty-free.

The London airports have the best shopping in the world, but it may not be duty-free . . . or if it is, it might not be a bargain. Some thoughts:

- Know your prices on your favorite scents before you buy in London or in any duty-free shop.

- Keep the airline duty-free prices with you for comparison, as airplane prices are often less expensive than those at airport duty-free shops.
- Look for coupons and promotional deals. The duty-free shop at LHR frequently offers pound-off vouchers or does two-for-one promotions or price reductions if you spend a certain amount.

About the best thing about duty-free in the London airport is the huge selection, including big names such as Ferragamo and Hermès. The Ferragamo store doesn't carry my size, but I know several people who swear by their airport bargains. One last word: Anything you buy at a duty-free price is only free of *British* duty. You pay U.S. duty when you land.

Chapter Three

....

MONEY MATTERS

DOLLARS, POUNDS & EUROS

••

Will they or won't they?

Go to euros. That isn't only the question, but the topic of conversation with everyone, especially taxi drivers. Eventually, Britain will probably go "in," but for the time being, they are sticking to sterling. There is a good chance that the referendum on the subject has been held while this edition is on the shelves; but even if it passes, euros will not be in the U.K. before 2005. Most estimates: the year 2010.

Right now, you just care about the ratio of the U.S. dollar to the pound sterling. And how! The dollar-to-pound ratio fluctuates often and quickly; within a week it can go from $1.50 to $1.70 or vice versa. This will greatly affect your shopping . . . and your mental health. For the currency conversions in this book I've used the rate of £1 = $1.65.

Sterling Wisdom

I recommend using a credit card for your purchases while in Britain. Plastic is the safest and provides you with a record of your purchases (for Customs as well as for your books). It also makes returns easier. Credit card companies also give the good exchange rates.

Conversions to Euros

If you are going into an E.U. country that uses euros and have already converted dollars to sterling, you will lose more money if you convert that sterling into euros (or another currency). Instead, spend all your sterling or save it for another trip and convert to euros (or assorted currencies) directly from dollars.

The bad news about credit cards is that you can overspend easily. However, making purchases on a credit card offers the potential for delayed billing.

Traveler's checks are good—especially if you buy them in sterling and lock in a good rate. Cash them in your hotel. On my last two visits to London, I had terrible problems cashing traveler's checks in stores. My checks were in sterling and from a major name-brand. Stores have really cracked down on their cash flow and have many strange rules. For the most part, the purchase price had to be over one half of the denomination of the check itself.

Best plan: Stop at an ATM and take out money directly in sterling as needed, although your bank in the United States will charge you a flat fee (usually $5) for each hit. Jenny McCormick has the kind of MasterCard that does not charge a fee for international withdrawals. One bank in particular advertises no ATM fees worldwide (and even pays you back if another bank charges a fee) if you keep a minimum balance in the account: **First Republic Bank** (www.firstrepublic.com). Since it costs nothing to join, the ATM deal might be worth signing up for if you do any serious travel.

Make sure to check out the cost of ATM transactions from your credit card companies and banks before you leave town.

Currency Exchange

Currency exchange rates vary tremendously. The rate announced in the paper (it's in the *International Herald Tribune* every day) is the official bank exchange rate and does not particularly apply to tourists. Even by trading your money at a bank or ATM, you will not necessarily get the same rate of exchange that's announced in the papers. Here are some tips for your monetary transactions:

- You will get a better rate of exchange for a traveler's check than you will for cash, because there is less paperwork involved for banks, hotels, and so on.
- The rate of exchange can be fixed if you buy traveler's checks in the U.S. in sterling. There will be no fee for cashing them in Britain, and shopkeepers are happy to take checks in sterling, whereas they rarely know what to do with checks in U.S. dollars—or won't touch them.
- Expect a bank to give you a better rate than your hotel. I've found the best rate of exchange at the American Express office. Usually they give an exchange that's close to the bank rate, and they do not charge for changing traveler's checks or personal checks.
- Don't change money (or a lot of it, anyway) with airport vendors because they will have the worst rates in town— yes, higher than your hotel.
- Have some foreign currency on hand for arrivals. After a lengthy transatlantic flight, you will not want to stand in line at some London airport booth to get your cab fare. Your home bank or local currency-exchange office can sell you small amounts of foreign currency so that, when you arrive in London, you have enough change to take care of immediate needs. Do keep this money readily available on landing—you don't want to have to undress in the taxi to reach your money belt, nor do you want the money packed in a suitcase.
- If you are arriving at London Heathrow and plan to take a taxi into "town," have £50 ($82) minimum on hand. If you

are arriving at Gatwick and plan to take a taxi into London, have a minimum of £100 ($165) on hand. If you are taking the bus, the train, or the Tube, £20 ($33) will be sufficient.

- Have your bank card with you; this is by far the easiest way to get money and to control how much foreign currency you have left over. Find out how much your bank charges for each international withdrawal.

- Do not exchange money with friends or take/make loans in dollars to sterling (or vice versa) as you will not only lose money but possibly lose friends; one side of such a negotiation always loses out.

- Make mental comparisons for quick price reactions. Know the conversion rate for $50 and $100 so that you can make a judgment in an instant. Also know them in reverse: Can you cope with an item priced at £10, £20, or £50? Have your reflexes honed to know where your price barriers are. If you're still interested in an item, slow down and figure out the exact price.

- Expect to pay a commission (often hidden) each time you change money—even at banks. That commission is commonly £3 ($4.95), but can be £5 ($8.25) per transaction! Compare the cost of the commission (if you have to pay one) with your hotel rate; sometimes convenience is the lesser of two evils. There is no commission for card members at American Express.

- If you want to change money back to dollars when you leave a country, remember that you will pay a higher rate for them. You are now "buying" dollars rather than "selling" them. Therefore, try not to change more money than you think you will need, unless you plan to stockpile it for another trip.

Citicorp Offices: Citicorp has made a big dent in the banking services in the United Kingdom and has a very convenient office for shoppers right on Oxford Street (no. 322). You can exchange money, get an advance against your card, get electronic money, or buy traveler's checks in sterling. They have tons of services.

Odd Exchange

I had various experiences at assorted cash-point machines (ATMs) throughout town. In all cases, I asked for £200 ($330). In some cases, I got it. In other cases, I was told that my request was rejected; yet the same machine gave me £100 ($165). If at first you don't succeed, don't freak—just skin the cat a few different ways.

SAVINGS STRATEGIES

English-made ready-to-wear should be less expensive in England, but don't get caught assuming anything—especially if the dollar has been dancing.

- European designer fashions can work to your advantage, mostly depending on the dollar. You can usually score on European designer fashions at sales times or at the end of the season. That's because everybody in Britain, if not still broke, is being very careful about purchases or is buying *used* designer clothing.
- Even the sale prices on highfalutin designer clothes may be too outrageously high for Sloane Rangers; so if other international jet-setters haven't beaten you to the punch, you can get lucky at a sale. Note that, although there are no bargains on regularly priced designer items, you need to run the numbers carefully, as there may be concessions due to VAT and state sales tax.
- If you are investing a few hundred pounds, perhaps you want to seriously think about a conversation piece that travels, something from the new St. Martins designer set. Whether you buy clothes or accessories, anything from the cutting-edge kids will give you something to brag about.
- Even with the cost of shipping to the U.S., you will save money on china and crystal if you buy it on sale or in outlet stores.

Bad Buys in London

With prices as high as they are, and the tendency to mentally go to parity, watch out for some of these items, which only on examination and reflection can turn out to be bad buys. Things to watch for:

- **"Moderately priced" clothes.** These are not moderately priced in England—they are downright expensive. If you expect to find both fashion and quality for less than £30 ($50) or so, forget it. *However, if you are willing to give up quality, you can find some great trendy items.* Note that they seem inexpensive when they cost £10 or £28, but in fact that's a $16 T-shirt and a $46 skirt—prices you can find in the United States.
- **Origin and quality.** The £17 ($28) adorable handbag I once bought in a middle-class department store lasted exactly 1 week before the shoulder strap pulled out and snapped. Before that, I was prepared to tell readers to rush into this department store and snap up all the cheap handbags. Junk wears like junk. Don't waste your money.
- **Sweaters (or jumpers).** Although these may be pushed at you from every direction, think twice. Unless you buy from a factory outlet, get seconds or discontinued styles, or get a big markdown, you may not find the savings you expected on lamb's wool or cashmere. You can count on finding a two-ply cashmere sweater in any big U.S. department store on sale for $129, maybe even $99. Take my word for it: Brits come to the United States to buy cashmere. British sale prices on a cashmere jumper are rarely below £99 ($163.35).
- **American brand names.** Clothes from Gap have their American price code on them, and the price in dollars is merely translated into pounds sterling. Honest. I'm not making this up. Something on the sale rack for "$20" means £20, or about $33.

- More specifically on the home-decor front: fabrics. If you crave the cabbage roses or the toile, locally made fabrics cost less in London. Know your yardage and allow for the repeat. Few dealers will ship your order because they don't want to compete with their U.S. showrooms.
- Regular high-fashion shoes or even moderately priced high-fashion shoes are a bad buy, since the British don't know from moderately priced. In Britain, they sell cheap shoes at high prices.

But wait—if you are the parent of a child 12-years-old-on-the-way-to-20, or if you are a 'tween-to-20 yourself and you or your kin wouldn't be caught red or dead (you'll only get that reference if you're young and hip, so don't sweat it) without **Doc Martens,** here's the deal: These shoes are a good bit cheaper in London. If you get them on sale, you may even snag a pair for £30 ($50).

Big Brand Savings

Forget it. Luxury brands purchased in the U.K. are a bargain only when the dollar is strong against the pound. When times are tough, British brands can be cheaper in the U.S.

TIPPING

When you travel, it works better if you plug into the local rules and denominations for tipping, because the amounts are pegged to local coins. If you normally tip $1 per suitcase at a hotel, you are not going to stand there with your calculator and tip 73p ($1.20) in London. You need to go with the local standards.

- If you don't have sterling for tips, U.S. dollars are preferred to euros.
- As shocking as it sounds, the dollar and the pound actually work on parity pro rata when it comes to tipping—spend a pound the same way you would spend a dollar. If you

normally tip $1 per suitcase, now you tip £1 ($1.65). As expensive as that is, that's the system.

- In restaurants, ask if VAT and service are included in the bill. In most cases it is clearly stated on the bill. I had a dreadful experience where I made an expensive miscalculation and lost £20 ($33) because the tip was already included. However, in the U.K. this matter is not as flat and dry a rule as in continental Europe. In most cases in London, you add a tip at a restaurant.
- Check to see the deal with room service; you may add a tip onto the bill, only to find that a service charge and a tip have already been included.
- If the doorman of the hotel gets a taxi for you, tip him 50p (83¢).
- At the hairdresser, tip a total of 15% on the whole—that usually means £1.50 ($2.50) for the shampoo person and £3.50 ($5.80) to the stylists.
- In taxis, round up the bill to the nearest number that is somewhere around 10%. If the driver has been particularly helpful, round up a bit more.
- If the concierge staff has been helpful, tip £10 ($17) on checkout—more if they have been incredibly helpful.
- At the airport, I do not tip the skycap unless he has really helped me out. Should you need a skycap, there is a fixed price of £7 ($12), which to me includes the basic tip. Since they have free carts at London airports, you are encouraged to use them.

THE EXPORT TAX SCHEME (VAT)

When you bring an item to a cash register in the United States, sales tax is added to the sticker price of your purchase. In Europe, the tax is added before the item is stickered, so that the price on the sticker is the total amount you are charged.

This system is called value-added tax. It's known in Britain as VAT. Businesses that make over £37,000 ($61,050) a year must pay VAT. The cost is therefore passed on to the consumer.

If you are not a British subject and if you take the goods out of Britain, you are entitled to a refund on the VAT. You may also get a refund on VAT for hotel rooms and car rentals, but only if you are on a visit.

The VAT for purchases is 17.5%, and you should be getting that refunded to you on purchases; however, that is a major oversimplification of the system. You will most likely get back 15% or even 13%, and you may even pay a cash fee.

The value-added tax system works pretty much like this:

- You are shopping in a store with prices marked on the merchandise. This is the true price of the item, which any tourist or any national must pay. (I'm assuming you are in a department store with fixed prices, not at a flea market.) If you are a national, you pay the price without thinking twice. If you are a tourist who plans to leave the country within 6 months, you ask a salesperson, "What is the minimum expenditure in this store for the export refund?" before shopping.
- The rate varies from shop to shop—usually touristy neighborhoods and drop-dead, chichi stores have a higher quota. The law states that a refund can come your way with a minimum expenditure of £50 ($83). However, in some shops you may be asked to spend £75 ($124) to £100 ($165) before you qualify.
- More and more stores, especially the fancy ones, charge a commission for issuing the VAT refund. Expect to lose £5 ($8.25) of the refund.
- But wait! It gets worse! There are now three different companies paying out VAT refunds for shop subscribers. All three have different types of forms, but the system works the same way. The one I hate the most uses a formula on a chart. The clerk gets out the chart, sees how much you have spent, and writes down the automatic refund amount, according to the chart. Although I spent almost £100 ($165) at Culpeper the

Herbalist, according to the chart my refund was £3.50 ($5.80)! I was outraged. For $5, it wasn't worth my trouble to show those goods to the Customs officer in London and schlepp them on the plane with me. I bought £75 ($124) worth of goodies at Next and the refund was even more insulting.

- Check out the size of the refund before you get stars (or discounts) in your eyes, especially if you are going to many cities in the E.U. and are expected to show the goods at Customs at the point of departure.

- Once you know the minimum, decide whether you will make a smaller purchase, or come back another time for a big haul. Only you know how much time you have for shopping. Remember that on a £60 ($100) purchase, the 17.5% minus a £5 ($8.25) fee may mean the savings are too little to make the VAT meaningful. The lines in summer at the VAT desk at LHR can be fierce.

- Judge for yourself whether you are certain the store that you are about to do business with will actually give you the refund after the paperwork is done. If you are dealing with a famous department store or a reputable boutique, there should never be a problem. However, I have had considerable problems with several big-name boutiques in both London and the countryside. More and more stores are switching to Tax-Free Europe, a firm that does the tax-back for them. This is a reliable firm with a desk at the airport to give you an instant cash refund.

- Sometimes the only savings you get when shopping abroad is the VAT discount. Don't knock it.

- If you go for the VAT, budget your time to allow for the paperwork before you leave the country. It takes about 5 minutes to fill out each form, and you must have them filled in when you present them upon exiting the country.

- Along with the VAT forms, you will be given an envelope. Sometimes the envelope has a stamp on it; sometimes it is blank (and you must provide the postage stamp before you leave the country). Sometimes it has a special government frank that serves as a stamp. If you don't understand what's on your envelope, ask.

- When you are leaving the country, go to the Customs official who serves the VAT papers. Do this before you clear regular Customs or send off your luggage. The Customs officer has the right to ask you to show him or her the merchandise you bought and are taking out of the country. He or she may not even look, but by law you are supposed to have the goods with you.

- If you have too much stuff to carry onboard, you must allow plenty of extra time, as you'll have to exit immigration with your baggage while a security guard stands by, then get rid of your checked luggage. I dare say 17.5% just isn't worth this kind of aggravation.

- Right after you've done passport control in Heathrow, go to the VAT desk (to your right if passport control is to your back) to show your goods and get your paperwork taken care of. All of the paperwork takes some preparation (filling in your name, address, passport number, and so on), which you are expected to have completed before you stand in the VAT line. It gums up the works for everyone else if the officer has to explain that you should have already done the fill-in-the-blanks part and would you please step over to one side.

- Whether the officer sees your purchases or not, he or she will stamp the papers, keep a set (which will be processed), and give you another set in the envelope. You then mail the envelope (which usually is preprinted with the shop's name and address or has been addressed for you by the shop). There is a mailbox next to the officer's desk. Or use the Tax-Free Europe desk for an instant refund.

Sailing Away

If you are on a ship that departs from Southampton and are worried about your VAT, fret not. Have everything prepared and ready and watch carefully for the VAT postbox, which is on a wall somewhere near the gangplank and after immigration. There usually is no Customs agent and no inspection, so just put the papers in the box and you're off.

U.S. CUSTOMS & DUTIES TIPS

To make your re-entry into the United States as smooth as possible, follow these tips:

- Know the rules and stick to them!
- Don't try to smuggle anything.
- Be polite and cooperative (up until the point when they ask you to strip, anyway . . .).

Remember:

- You are currently allowed to bring in $800 worth of merchandise per person, duty-free. Before you leave the U.S., verify this amount with one of the Customs offices. Each member of the family is entitled to the deduction; this includes infants. You may pool within a family.
- You pay a flat 10% duty on the next $1,000 worth of merchandise.
- Duties thereafter are based on a product-type basis. They vary tremendously per item, so think about each purchase and ask storekeepers about U.S. duties. They will know, especially in specialty stores like china shops.
- The head of the family can make a joint declaration for all family members. The "head of the family" need not be male. Whoever is the head of the family, however, should take the responsibility for answering any questions the Customs officers may ask. Answer questions honestly, firmly, and politely. Have receipts ready, and make sure they match the information on the landing card. Don't be forced into a story that won't wash under questioning. If they catch you

in a little lie, you'll be labeled as a fibber, and they'll tear your luggage apart.

- Have the Customs registration slips for your personally owned goods in your wallet or easily available. If you wear a Cartier watch, be able to produce the registration slip. If you cannot prove that you took a foreign-made item out of the country with you, you may be forced to pay duty on it.

- Remember the duty on ready-to-wear and stay within the $1,800 U.S. Customs limit, on which you will pay only $100 duty. After that, you'll get into higher duties on clothes, and your bargains may be tarnished. Generally speaking, you can save on U.S. prices if you buy British when it's on sale or if you get the VAT refund.

- The unsolicited gifts you mailed from abroad do not count in the $800-per-person rate. If the value of the gift is more than $50, you pay duty when the package comes into the country. Remember, it's only one unsolicited gift per person for each mailing. Don't mail to yourself.

- Do not attempt to bring in any illegal food items—dairy products, meats, fruits, or vegetables. (Coffee is OK.) Generally speaking, if it's alive, it's *verboten*. I don't need to tell you that it's tacky to bring in drugs and narcotics.

- Antiques must be 100 years old to be duty-free. Provenance papers will help (and so will permission to export the antiquity, since it could be an item of national cultural significance). Any bona fide work of art is duty-free whether it was painted 50 years ago or just yesterday; the artist need not be famous.

- Dress for success. People who look like "hippies" get stopped at Customs more than average folks. Women who look like a million dollars, are dragging their fur coats, have first-class baggage tags on their luggage, and carry Gucci handbags, but declare they have bought nothing, are equally suspicious.

- Laws regarding ivory are new and improved—for elephants, anyway. You may not import any ivory into the United States.

Not to worry, there is little new ivory for sale in London; antique ivory should have provenance or papers to be legally imported.

- When the papers get back to the shop and the government has notified the shop that its set of papers has been registered, the shop will grant you the discount through a refund. This can be done by issuing a credit on your credit card or by check, which will come to you in the mail, usually in 3 months. (It will be in a foreign currency. Please note that your bank may charge you to change it into dollars.) If you are smart, you will indicate that the refund should be credited to a bank card or American Express so that you end up with a refund in dollars.

- If you used a Europe Tax-Free voucher, after it is stamped you can go to the Europe Tax-Free desk in the airport and get your money. You can ask for it in a variety of currencies, but the conversion rate will not be very favorable. You'll do best to take the cash in sterling and save it for your next trip, or spend it at the news agents on wonderful British magazines.

U.S. Customs Warning: If you arrive in the United States by ship, note that the ship's store personnel report to the U.S. Customs which passengers are the big onboard shoppers and what they bought! Don't try to run anything past Customs when you arrive because they are waiting for you with your name on a list. Let the buyer beware.

Chapter Four

························

EATING & SLEEPING IN LONDON

LONDON OR BUST

···

There's no need to go bust in order to get to London—or in order to enjoy your stay. True, London is one of the most expensive destinations in Europe these days, but smart shoppers are taking more care with their trip planning and can get lots of value from their travel funds. A penny saved is a penny to spend at Liberty, I always say.

SLEEPING IN LONDON

···

It's not hard to find a fabulous hotel in Mayfair—or elsewhere in London—but you may want to give some thought to what combination of location, price, and ease of making reservations suits your budget and sensibilities. Hotel prices are sky high, so without a deal or a secret find, you may find that a weekend in London is all you can afford.

I've found that a hotel is the single greatest factor in ensuring whether my trip has been a dream or a nightmare. I believe in luxury hotels, but I also believe in getting the most for my money, which is why I like London in the winter so much. Luxury hotels have deals! Please keep in mind:

- Prices for London hotel rooms are pretty uniform and are based on the rank of the hotel—all five-star hotels cost almost the same amount per night; the same holds for all four-star hotels, and so on. Therefore, one hotel with a fancier reputation is not necessarily more expensive than another. In other words, you may actually be able to afford a hotel that you thought was out of reach.

- Promotions are not uniform. You can better your life with a hotel you didn't even know you could afford if you get the right promotion, or you can be miserable. Many hotels have special promotions and rates; some do winter deals where they strike the pound and U.S. dollar at parity (you'll save a bundle). Almost every hotel discounts rooms in January until March when business is down, but they'll discount during other time periods as well, often in July and August. When hotel rooms are empty, management gets creative. Use this fact to your benefit, and don't be shy about places with hoity-toity reputations. It behooves you to spring for an international call to the hotel of your choice and negotiate directly with them; it's unlikely that a computerized reservation service will have as much flexibility as a live person smelling a deal. Some hotels have year-round rates guaranteed in U.S. dollars. Ask!

- Aside from non-peak travel discounts, there may be disaster discounts. The foot-and-mouth disease epidemic brought out the best in this system, with hotels and airlines working together to make London too good to pass up. My son's airline ticket to Paris included 3 free nights at a London hotel.

- If you are a regular at a specific hotel but want a break, don't be afraid to write to the hotel and say what you want. Direct your letter to the general manager.

- Look to the chains for promotions for which you may qualify. **Hilton, InterContinental, Savoy Group, Thistle,** and **Forte** all run price specials, even in the summer season. Often, you can prepay for a room in U.S. dollars. Also, as hotel groups merge, there may be hotel members that you are not familiar with; again, ask. Even **Four Seasons** has deals.

- Look for oddball locations or special events, such as luxury hotels that have just been opened, bought, or sold, or are rumored to be in financial trouble—frequently, they have deals just to bring in cash or to gain new clients.
- Check out chains and/or hotels in a chain that you have never before heard of so that you know for next time. My friend Ruth suggested that I try the **Hotel Britannia,** to which I said "pooh-pooh"; then I walked by it and realized I was a jerk. Explore, broaden your horizons, and drop down a star. Spend time during your next trip to line up possible hotels for subsequent trips. The Britannia is a member of the Millennium chain; they have bought up several hotels recently and offer many good hotels in great locations, including a hotel right on Sloane Street.
- To thine own self be true: If you're the type who really doesn't care where you stay or if you're someone who spends little time in the hotel room, book a dump—or at least a less-than-well-known hotel. I know plenty of people who have traded down from five-star hotels to three-star properties in order to keep coming to London.
- Check out concierge floors or executive deals at hotel chains that offer "free" breakfast and possibly drinks or tea; breakfast can be downright expensive these days. You may pay more, but you'll also get a lot more.
- Consider sharing a luxury room with a friend or bulking up the number of people in the room so that you can giggle together in style. I have two girlfriends on their way to London along with one 11-year-old son—they are sharing at **The Dorchester** because they thought it would be more fun to go for the gold and be cramped than to spread out in less-fine digs. It's only for 3 nights and they plan to laugh a lot and really enjoy it.
- Watch out for parity deals—some hotels offer these during the winter season, some year-round. By parity, I mean they trade the sterling price for an equal dollar price, saving you about 60%! Many hotels do this, but **Thistle,** a chain of mostly middle-class hotels in the three- and four-star range,

is famous for it, and they offer a lot along with their promotions: taxes, service, and full English breakfast. Children
under 16 board free in their parents' room.

- For heaven's sake, go online! No, you won't find The Dorchester dumping any rooms online, but you will find many,
many four-star hotels that are just fine—and prices are
often in U.S. dollars, not sterling. Do make sure you are right
on the currency issue, as well as the per-person or per-room
issue—mistakes in either category can get you in trouble.
If you don't have a favorite discount source online, try
www.hoteldiscounts.com.

Luxury Lowdown

Although no one can beat the prices offered by mass tourist
hotels on a package, if you crave the comforts of luxury hotels,
you may be surprised by the promotions some of them offer.
Certain luxury hotels, including the ones with the most famous
names, can be more affordable than you might think.

Resist the little voice inside that says you shouldn't even try
to stay at "a place like that." The last time I checked, The Ritz
and the Holiday Inn a half-block away were priced at the
same amount per room. Wouldn't you rather stay at The Ritz?

Don't be afraid to call around, use toll-free numbers, fax
the general manager of a fancy hotel, or ask for a deal from
all of your resources. You just may be pleasantly surprised. Don't
be intimidated!

- Big chains may have gem hotels that you've never heard of—
check them out on a reconnaissance trip, then book for your
next stay. Think about the InterContinental's **Churchill
Hotel** and the many Hilton hotels that are members of the
Hilton family but may not be well known, such as **Hilton
Mews,** a true gem (although the rooms are very small). Also
note that Hilton has rebranded itself and has all sorts of new
offers so that you can test their new boutique hotels.
- Weekend package deals are popular. Usually called "weekend breaks" in Britain, they are meant to generate business

when businesspeople and their expense accounts have not filled the ranks.

- Single rooms in fancy hotels sometimes cost a lot less than you would expect. These rooms may be tiny, but they are fancy, and if it's just you and your shopping bags, you may get one of London's most plush hotels for a song.

- Combination city/country deals are sometimes offered. If you are traveling around Great Britain, consider arranging your schedule so that you spend the first weekend in London at one hotel, travel during the week (rates are lower in the countryside and in Edinburgh), and then return to London for the second weekend—maybe even to a different hotel, depending on the deal. Forte has a good program for combining destinations. Also note that Four Seasons Canary Wharf has a "country" feel in that it's on the river and near Greenwich and in a very non-London environment. The hotel is only 12 minutes from the heart of town, and you can get fabulous weekend deals.

Apples & Oranges

When you begin to gather information and make price comparisons, be sure that you are comparing apples with apples. I just had a terrible experience wherein I stayed at two so-called luxury hotels with rooms at about the same price. One of the hotels (from Leading Hotels of the World) was a dream come true; the other (from Hilton) had two tour groups and gave me a room so bad that I rejected it on first sight and had to spend an hour looking at rooms before I found something decent. They lost my luggage within the hotel and took 24 hours to change a light bulb. Niceties such as turndown service and plush towels were not to be found. Yet the difference in price between these hotels was small.

While we are comparing, I have a small list of rack rates of assorted deluxe hotels so that you can compare what you get. Few people pay rack rate—most get deals or discounts and upgrades, but since these are all rack rates, they serve to offer an interesting comparison basis.

The Berkeley	$650 per night, room only
Claridge's	$600 per night, room only
The Dorchester	$450 per night, room only
Four Seasons	$600 per night, room only
Hilton (Hyde Park)	$410 per night, room only
The Ritz	$650 per night, room only

Note that most of these hotels can be booked for 30% less, and with breakfast included.

The Game

I made a series of telephone calls to all of the hotels listed in this chapter. In all cases I told them my real name, Suzy Gershman, and identified myself as "an American journalist." I called London directly and said I was calling long-distance. I asked for the price of a double superior room for the next night at rack rate (official listed rate) and one for the night of December 15, asking for a promotional rate on a similar room to the one I would get in the first quote. I specifically chose December 15 because it is before Christmas and a time of the year when hotels often have special rates or offerings.

Best Luxe for Shoppers

All hotels in London are expensive. Surprisingly, there is a large range in choices wherein a perfectly nice room can be £212 ($350) a night or £394 ($650). Name-brand luxury hotels can easily cost £303 ($500) a night for a double room; some of them cost a lot more than that.

Sometimes I ask myself why anyone would spend that kind of money . . . then I survey the best London hotels and realize that when you book one of these hotels, you are not just getting a roof over your head and clean sheets for the night . . . you are plugging into art. The top hotels always have the latest trends, the most creative people, the breaking news, the last word on the first word. The decision to stay at one of these hotels means that you have to divide the cost in half—one half is what a hotel room costs and the other is rent on a window into the world of what's happening and who is part of the scene. Note that the three hotels I have chosen below all have a very specific identity.

THE BERKELEY
Wilton Place, SW1 (Tube: Knightsbridge or Hyde Park).

First off, be sure that you can pronounce this properly—it's *Barkley.* Now you're ready to be converted. The hotel is the secret find of a secret sect of fine shoppers and businesspeople who settle into the rather plain-looking building to a world of comfort, including one of the most famous spas in town (with rooftop swimming pool and retractable roof) and The Blue Bar, which is not only chic but also the hangout of many movie stars. But the scene is not just in the bar—there are restaurants galore, including the new Petrus, which has been designed by a man named David Collins to showcase the latest style trends.

The hotel is so dedicated to shopping that they give you your own shopper's map and directions to hidden and nearby shops that aren't your average chains or multiples. You are within walking distance of all the best shopping in town (1 block from Harvey Nichols and Sloane St.) and can even book a shopping or after-shopping spa package at the hotel. Ask specifically about their Retail Therapy Weekend Break.

Best yet, there are promotional deals: I found a super room with a bathroom to die for, all for under £181 ($300) per night through a special online promotion. But I lucked out. See "The Game," below, for more average rates.

Also note that, as well situated as the hotel is for your well-known shopping areas, it prides itself on guiding you to the little-known shopping spots hidden in Belgravia. Until I stayed here, I had never had a way to connect the dots before and always got lost roaming around the little streets off Sloane. Now I am found.

The Game: In a polite and straightforward manner, The Berkeley quoted me a superior king at £375 ($619) and a promotional rate in December of £249 ($411).

For U.S. reservations, call the Savoy Group at © 212/220-8960 (New York office) or © 818/754-3775 (Los Angeles office); local phone © 020/7235-6000. Fax 020/7235-4330. www.savoy-group.com.

THE DORCHESTER
Park Lane, W1 (Tube: Marble Arch).

I first met The Dorchester while writing an article for *Newsweek* on European value. Before then I would never have gone near this temple of luxury and celebrity, fearing for my life's savings. Yet here's the best part: Of all the fancy schmancy hotels in London—all of which are very expensive—The Dorchester has the least-expensive rack rate. So if you are wondering which of the palaces provides the best value, voilà.

I've since become a regular, but on my own terms, which means I can't afford to stay too long. Still, the experience is worth it, if only for a night or 2. They have new amenities; the spa is free (treatments are extra); teatime is one of the best in London. The hotel has been totally redone and has brought itself online and in-line to such an electronic pedigree that there is now an E-butler, who will teach you how to get your e-mail from your bed.

If you can't stay here, come for breakfast or tea. For £15 ($25), you can have the time of your life. Don't forget to look at the ceiling in the Grill Room, where they serve breakfast.

Oh yes, also check out their little news agent/gift shop. They sell some Dorchester logo gifts and the house brand of private-label champagne.

The Game: I was offered a superior room for £375 ($619) plus VAT; when I asked what that was I was told to add 17.5% to the total. The rate for December was the same.

Member of the Leading Hotels of the World. For U.S. reservations, call © 800/727-9820; local phone © 020/7629-8888. Fax 020/7409-0114. www.dorchesterhotel.com.

FOUR SEASONS
Hamilton Place, W1 (Tube: Hyde Park Corner).

Once I got hooked on The Dorchester and the Park Lane neighborhood, it wasn't long till I found my way to Four Seasons. The truth here is that I have fallen in love with the chef; I used to stop in for all my meals at the Lanes Bar, where they specialize in bar snacks—finally I just moved in.

The hotel is closer to Green Park and Piccadilly than The Dorchester; it also has a raft of shopping services for those too busy to make it to a store or too rich to mingle with those who shop. In fact, this hotel prides itself on making things come to you.

You can have a Savile Row tailor come to your room, fit you, and leave your suit for your next visit. (It will be hanging in the closet of your room.) You can also buy dishes through Thomas Goode when they have special teatime promotions, or you can even order a shopper's pick-me-up menu created to give you energy. To top it off, the chef will pack you a traveler's meal in its own little cardboard box—great if you are flying home or driving off to Southampton to catch the *QM2*.

The Game: They were quite friendly here and offered a superior room for £345 ($569) plus VAT. For December 15, there was a promotion that included breakfast for two and tea for two each day at £251 ($414) plus VAT.

This hotel is the original Four Seasons on which all others were patterned. Member of the Leading Hotels of the World. For U.S. reservations, call © **800/223-6800**; local phone © 020/7493-1895. Fax 020/2499-0888. www.fourseasons.com.

Fabulous Finds

THE RADISSON EDWARDIAN MAY FAIR
Stratton St., W1 (Tube: Green Park).

This is one of my better secrets, so get out your highlighter. The May Fair (sometimes written as "Mayfair," but the hotel awning says "May Fair") is a luxury hotel—not in the same class as the palace hotels, but a find nonetheless. It has recently changed hands and is now a member of the Radisson group. This is a hidden hotel on a Mayfair back street, half a block from The Ritz and the Green Park Tube station and unknown to most tourists. It is now a member of the Radisson Edwardian chain.

The Game: For a double superior room with a queen-size bed, the rate was £215 ($355) including full breakfast. The rate in December was the same. For U.S. reservations, call © 800/333-3333; local phone © 020/7629-7777. Fax 020/7629-1459. www.radissonedwardian.com.

THE ROYAL GARDEN HOTEL
2–24 Kensington High St., W8 (Tube: Kensington High St.).

For the research on this edition, I have moved away from my usual hotel haunts and into this part of London, often staying with my friend Ruth. Through her, and through several readers, I discovered this hotel, which I made headquarters for our family visits and research trips, partly because of the location and mostly because of the price . . . or the value afforded me between the fabulous location and the reasonable prices. There's a Tube stop half a block away and all the buses I need right outside the front door.

This hotel is neither the cute little charming type nor a palace of unspeakable luxury. It's simply a nice hotel at the top of the four-star range with very fair prices and all the services you need.

The Game: This was perhaps the most interesting and the least fair in the reporting because they recognized my name when I called. After I asked my questions, I was put on hold. When the man I had been speaking to came back on, he called me "Suzy," which I found somewhat shocking since he didn't know me. He turned me over to a press-relations person, who reported that rack rate is £305 ($503) plus VAT; the average rate is £170 ($281) plus VAT. In December I could get a special rate of £160 ($264) plus VAT, which included breakfast.

Local phone © **020/7937-8000.** Fax 020/7361-1991. www.
royalgardenhotel.co.uk.

The Chains

My favorites among the many chain properties:

HILTON

Believe it or not, Hilton has shocking news in rebranding. You
can sample it yourself, just by booking the Hilton Trafalgar—
the first hotel in the chain to go the unbranded Hilton route.
It feels more like a boutique hotel and you can't even tell it's
a Hilton since it only has a sign with a small H on the door.

There are plenty of other Hiltons in London—in all sizes,
shapes, and flavors. They differ enormously but do offer some
advantages such as family rates, executive floors, some hotels
with spas, and so on. With the theatre break package, you get
show tickets. I used to stay rather regularly at the **Langham
Hilton** (1 Portland Place, Regent St., W1; Tube: Oxford Circus), but it has changed so much that it no longer competes in
the luxury category. However, there are plenty of others to test.

First on my list is the **Hyde Park Hilton,** which seems like
a perfect weekend hotel—it's small, very low-key, within walking distance of Portobello Road, and not fancy. Note that it's
more at Queensway than Hyde Park. **The Trafalgar Hilton** is
a boutique-style hotel—so different from the Hilton image, your
head will spin. This is the new future.

Warning: It seems to be corporate policy to give Hilton hotels
snazzy names that imply certain locations, but in fact, their
locations are a tad bizarre—the Hilton Kensington is not truly
in Kensington. The Hyde Park hotel does overlook Hyde Park,
but is nowhere near other businesses that call themselves Hyde
Park. Use a map if need be or ask a lot of questions before you
book. For U.S. reservations, call © **800/HILTONS.** www.
hilton.co.uk.

HYDE PARK HILTON
129 Bayswater Rd., W2 (Tube: Lancaster Gate).

This hotel is very small and not too fancy, but I happen to like the location, although it's easier for the bus than the Tube—transportation wise.

The Game: The reservations clerk called me "Suzy" so many times I thought I would burst out laughing. Then I thought perhaps this was a Monty Python sketch. I was asked a lot of questions, such as did I belong to frequent-flier programs and Hilton Honors. They explained that rates varied due to availability. Finally I was offered a superior room overlooking the park for £129 ($213) plus VAT, room only. The same room would be £149 ($246) plus VAT if I booked ahead for the December date. I asked for the least-expensive room in the house and was offered a single for £109 ($180) plus VAT. Local phone © 020/7221-2217. Fax 020/7229-0559. www. Hilton.com.

TRAFALGAR HILTON
2 Spring Gardens, SW1 (Tube: Charing Cross Station).

This hotel prides itself on being top-notch and cutting-edge. You sure can't beat the location, right on top of Trafalgar Square.

The Game: When I asked for the reservations desk, I was asked if that would be individual or group bookings. Uh-oh. I was offered a room at £189 ($312) plus tax and then traded up to a deluxe room at £219 ($361) plus tax. The reservations agent was polite but a bit pushy. When I asked for promotional rates in December, he cheerfully suggested they might be "a whole lot better for you, mum"—£159 ($262) plus tax, and the deluxe room at £189 ($312) plus tax. No brekkie. Local phone © 020/ 7870-2900. Fax 020/7870-2911. www.Hilton.com.

INTERCONTINENTAL

Stand by, folks, have I got a winner. Aside from the corporate news—Interconti has rebranded and added a whole lot of luxury and value at very good prices—these two hotels offered terrific deals. In the U.S., call **800-HOLIDAY;** for weekend promotional rates, go to www.ichotelsgroup.com/weekends.

INTERCONTINENTAL THE CHURCHILL
30 Portman Sq., W1 (Tube: Marble Arch).

The Game: I was offered a double superior for £340 ($561) plus VAT, at rack rate. I was offered the same price for December. Then I asked for a promotional rate; the woman seemed confused at first, then said I could have more or less the same room for £229 ($378) plus VAT and full English breakfast. Local phone ✆ **020/7486-5800.** Fax 020/7486-1255. www.London-churchill.intercontinental.com.

INTERCONTINENTAL HYDE PARK
1 Hamilton Place, W1 (Tube: Hyde Park Corner).

The Game: This was the only reservations agent who called me "Mrs. Gershman" and addressed me by name throughout our conversation. She gave me totals—no other agent did—and figured out which offers were the best, to spare me any confusion over somewhat conflicting deals. Furthermore, her prices beat the band. I was offered a double superior with full breakfast at £199 ($328) plus VAT. She then provided the total for me: £234 ($386). For December I had my choice of several promotions, including a room for £159 ($262) or one for £129 ($213), but the more expensive room included full English breakfast for two, making it the better deal. Hats off! Local phone ✆ **020/7409-3131.** Fax 020/7493-3476. www.intercontinental.com.

MARRIOTT

Marriott's hotel near the American Embassy in Mayfair has been well known for years, but there is now a newer property right near the London Eye and not too far from Waterloo International or The City; or you can get into a great shopping location at Marble Arch (see below). You can often use frequent-flier miles. For U.S. reservations, call **888/ 236-2427**. www.marriott.com.

MARRIOTT LONDON PARK LANE
140 Park Lane, W1 (Tube: Marble Arch).

An older hotel that has just been redone in the sleek modern style that makes it stand out in the new hotels division. The hotel has only 157 rooms, making it about the same size as The Ritz, but prices are lower. There's a pool, spa, and club.

The Game: Christmas rates were offered at £169 ($279) plus VAT and included full English breakfast. Rack was twice that.

Local phone © **020/7493-7000**. Fax 020/7493-8333. www. marriotthotels.com/lonpl or www.140parklane.com.

RADISSON

With a half dozen hotels in London and one at the airport, Radisson offers excellent value for the money in a four-star hotel. Furthermore, you can often find Radisson rooms online at great prices. Locations tend to be in the Covent Garden area, which is convenient for museums, theater, and browsing. In the United States, call © **800/333-3333**. www.radisson.com.

Flat News

If you don't want to be anyone's guest at all, you may want to consider renting a flat, which not only works out cheaper on a nightly basis, but also gives you the option of cooking some of your meals. Although prices vary tremendously, you can get a nice flat with two bedrooms and two bathrooms in a slightly suburban London neighborhood in the £300/$495-per-week range. Expect to pay £500 ($825) minimum for a small luxe flat with a fine location.

The Barclay International Group is a U.S. firm that will book you into any of its apartments in London. A two-person studio starts at £220 ($363) for an entire week (including VAT). There are properties in Kensington and Mayfair; you can even arrange for their limo to pick you up at the airport. Their Grosvenor House apartments come with the use of health-club facilities. In the United States, call © **800/845-6636.**

The Apartment Company is a British firm that seems to work much like Barclay, with similar properties. Their hottest locale is Dolphin Square because Princess Anne is a tenant there. Draycott House is a prestigious address where flats are frequently rented by celebrities; you're looking at £700 ($1,155) to £2,000 ($3,300) a week (depending on size), plus VAT. Call © **020/ 7835-1144.**

Naturally, there are now online sources for bookings as well; try **NoMoreHotels** (www.nothotels.com). Most of their clients are corporate clients who bring in their top people for social events during the season. Rates start at about £100 ($165) per night; they too book Draycott House. For a copy of their brochure, you can go online or call © **020/8600-7470.**

Coach House London Vacation Rentals offers short-term status in private homes. They also own a Victorian Coach House, for $50 per person, per night—this includes full English breakfast. Contact them online: www.chslondon.com/vr for rentals, and www.chslondon.com/ch for the guesthouse.

Airport Hotels

If you are connecting through LHR and need an airport hotel, you won't have trouble finding one. Many airlines have links with a specific hotel that will offer you a price break or other amenities and privileges. I stayed at a Holiday Inn at the airport once and was lent a Virgin Atlantic bathing suit! Indeed, I often pick my hotel based on the spa and pool services and often go for a swim and have a massage.

However, if I am using Terminal 4, I only stay at **The LHR Hilton,** since it is the only hotel inside that terminal. Well, it's not really inside, but it's connected by a very long walkway. But you don't have to spend a half hour on the shuttle to get there.

What you may not realize is that the airport is very close to the town of Windsor, and it isn't that far from a few other

English country-house mansion-style hotels. So if you want luxury and convenience (or charm and convenience), you don't have to stay at the airport to be close to it. Many of these nearby hotels will include airport transfer in the price; ask.

Also note that many airport properties provide shuttle service into London for free or a small cost. Airport hotels usually cost less than London hotels per night, so they may be a worthwhile alternative if you have only half a day to explore London as you connect elsewhere.

And speaking of shuttles, the airport system for the immediate-area airport hotels has changed in the last year or so. There is now what's called the Hotel Hoppa. (Hey, don't shoot the messenger; I didn't make this up.) You do not call your hotel directly on arrival, but instead buy a shuttle ticket, find the proper zone number for your hotel, and go outside to await the next shuttle. Round-trip tickets are discounted.

LONDON EATS

More, please. Since Oliver Twist had the nerve to ask for a second helping, British food has improved to the point where it is hard to get reservations at certain restaurants, and the French are actually coming over just to try the cooking at a few fine kitchens that have earned extra Michelin stars.

If you don't want to spend all your money on food and want to save a little for shopping, do not despair. London has more meal deals than almost any other city. Even the hotshot places have deals.

Those with small appetites or small budgets can rejoice: This is the city where the "jacket potato" (baked potato) constitutes an entire meal and can be eaten in any of the numerous potato fast-food joints, where it comes with a variety of toppings that turn it into quite a hefty meal.

I also like to have at least one picnic when I visit London. I usually buy prepared food at **Marks & Spencer** for an alfresco lunch of my own devising—or a hotel-room picnic, depending on the weather. M&S has a new chain of food stores, but there are now so many grocery stores that sell prepared meals in the key shopping areas of London that you'll have no trouble finding something to please your palate and your purse. The hardest part may be selecting just the right bench or stretch of lawn on which to plop yourself.

Big-Time Meal Deals

The secret to dining in style in London on a budget lies in knowing about the two basic tricks that have been added to almost every upscale eatery's repertoire: the pre-theater meal and the fixed-price meal. A la carte prices may kill you, but a deal will enrich you.

Pre-theater meals are usually served around 6pm; note that curtain times in London vary by the production and are usually earlier than in New York. A 7:30pm curtain is the general rule. Therefore, pre-theater dinners are available only at an early hour. If this doesn't bother you (you are American, right?), you can dine like a king at some of the best tables in London for the price of a song. A little night music, anyone?

Fixed-price meals are offered in all the major hotel dining rooms (dancing and/or entertainment is usually included) and at the hautest of tables, including London's most famous Michelin-star chefs. *Note:* Many of London's fancy tables take some getting into, so the browse-and-book method will not work for you. You may want to fax ahead for a reservation, or several reservations, hold them until you can check out the situation, and then cancel once you get to town. Do give 24 hours' notice when you cancel; this is a very polite town and manners matter.

Shoppers Who Lunch

All of the restaurants below serve dinner (except **Nicole's**); many are considered both hot spots and places to be seen in London. I care more about location, size of the portion, and size of the bill. Still, it's nice to be comfortable and chic all at the same time.

MEDITERRANEAN KITCHEN
127–129 Kensington Church St., W8 (Tube: Notting Hill Gate).

For those who could care less how chichi a place is or whether Princess Diana ever ate there, this is my regular haunt for the Kensington High Street, Church Street, Portobello Road area, and where my friend Ruth and I often go to eat because her son is the chef. The food is delish; the prices are quite fair, and the atmosphere is easy and open. Full meal for £20 ($33) per person. Brunch is the scene and costs less. ✆ **020/7727-8142.**

NICOLE'S
158 New Bond St., W1 (Tube: Bond St.).

The place of the moment is actually inside a store (see below) and offers expensive but stylish lunch—or tea. It is the place to say you've been; you can snack or nosh and not do a whole big meal. Prices begin around £15 ($25). Wear beige. No hat. ✆ **020/7499-8408.**

SAN LORENZO
22 Beauchamp Place, SW3 (Tube: Knightsbridge).

The *in* place before Daphne's opened—and still not shabby; it was the fave of Princess you-know-who and gets a jet-set and celeb crowd still; it's right on Beauchamp Place in the middle of one of London's fine shopping streets and walking distance from Harrods. It's expensive; expect to pay £30 ($50) per head. ✆ **020/7584-1074.**

Shoppers Who Save

With the high cost of everything in London, you will often find me cutting corners or looking for fun places to eat that aren't too expensive.

I buy ready-made foods in the grocery store at **M&S** (try the chicken tandoori). I eat at any of the many new noodle bars, such as **Wagamama** (branches all over town, including the lower level of Harvey Nicks) or **Nyonya** at Pembridge Road, right at the start of Portobello Road (Tube: Notting Hill Gate). I have found Pizza Express much changed and crossed it off my list (it's a chain; I haven't tested them all), but still swear by **Pizza at the Park,** between the Lanesborough and Berkeley hotels on Hyde Park (Tube: Hyde Park Corner). I still believe in the picnic, with foods bought at Borough Market (p. 113), from any grocery store, or in the food section of the Portobello Road Market, Saturdays only.

In-Store Meals

Eating inside a store has become very trendy in London. **Emporio Armani** serves Italian food at a really super cafe, while **Nicole Farhi** offers her signature fare downstairs in her Bond Street flagship shop. **DKNY** has a snack bar that serves bagels and cream cheese, brownies, and other American-style foods. Even **Sotheby's,** the auction house, has a cafe now.

The big department stores have always had restaurants, and some have several. Now, many of these store restaurants have spiffed up and are quite hip; some use big-name chefs as consultants. Note that they also use one of the restaurant venues to show shoppers how "with-it" they are, so at least one venue in a store is usually new and devoted to a concept.

The best thing for shoppers about eating in a store is the convenience—you're already there, so put down your bags and take a seat. Arrive early if you don't have a reservation.

BIBENDUM/CONRAN'S
Michelin House, 81 Fulham Rd., SW3 (Tube: S. Kensington).

Nobody combines food and shopping like Sir Terence Conran. His state-of-the-art masterpiece is still the rehabilitation at Michelin House, which features his store and its companion restaurant, Bibendum. Book way in advance and hope that someone else is paying. © 020/7581-5817.

DICKINS & JONES
224 Regent St., W1 (Tube: Oxford Circus).

Part of the store's remake is a restaurant/cafe from the Roux family—one of the most famous names in food in the United Kingdom. You can actually eat lunch here for around £10 ($17); I had a blackened-chicken Caesar salad that was perfect. © 020/7439-0112.

FENWICK
63 New Bond St., W1 (Tube: Bond St. or Oxford Circus).

A trendy branch of Carlucci's is downstairs; the Italian deli concept offers great food, many salads, and a fun crowd. You probably don't need a rez, but if you want to, call © 020/7629-9161.

FORTNUM & MASON
181 Piccadilly, W1 (Tube: Piccadilly Circus).

They have several restaurants, and although I've done the silver-cart and roast-beef bit, I prefer The Fountain, where I can get in and out rather quickly. They don't take lunch reservations; if you are alone, team up with a stranger to be served more quickly. I do it all the time. The upstairs restaurant, very fancy and formal, has been redone and is worth doing at least once in your life. © 020/7734-8040.

HARRODS
87–135 Brompton Rd., Knightsbridge, SW1 (Tube: Knightsbridge).

London's most famous department store has several restaurants, including the famed food halls. In fact, there are several food bars, great for those who are alone in the food halls. And this just in—for that sweet American fix you're craving—Krispy

Kreme doughnuts are now on sale as well. Note that they charge to use the loo at Harrods, but if you flash your food receipt, you get to have a wee for free.

HARVEY NICHOLS
Knightsbridge (corner of Sloane St.), SW1 (Tube: Knightsbridge).

The fifth floor of this Sloane Square institution is a gourmet restaurant where reservations are a must. There's also a small sushi area in front of the restaurant, complete with conveyor belt, and across from the food products. ✆ 020/7235-5250.

Bar Meals

The latest craze to sweep London is the taking of meals in posh bars. This accomplishes many things: You get to visit a swish place; it's okay to be alone; it costs less than a full sit-down, gourmet-style, old-fashioned meal; you meet divine people; and you can stare all through your meal. The trendiest are Claridge's Bar (separate entrance from Claridge's), Lanes Bar inside Four Seasons, and The Berkeley.

Even if you don't drink, you can still have the bar meal— you get very fancy miniature meals, like lobster burgers and foie gras on potato pancakes and other morsels you wouldn't have at home. You can eat for as little as £10 ($17).

Teatime

I am a longtime believer in the English custom of taking tea for two very simple reasons:

1. After you've been shopping all day, plop down, drop the packages, and get off those feet at 3 or 4pm.
2. If you want to save money, you can have a big tea and go light on (or skip) dinner. Conversely, if dinner isn't until 8pm or later, you won't last without a good tea break.

All the big, fancy hotels have tea service; you can make it your job to try a different one every day. I have discovered, however, that there are several ins and outs to getting full value from teatime, so get out your highlighter. If you're British, don't blush—I'm going to talk about money.

Generally speaking, tea comes at a set price per person and includes the tea (or coffee) of your choice and a three-round selection of sandwiches, scones, and sweets. There is also tea with sherry or tea with champagne.

Tea is usually served from 3 to 5:30 or 6pm. If sherry is served, it is called high tea. "Teatime," as a time of meeting someone or fixing your schedule, is usually meant to be 4pm; by 5pm, it is socially acceptable to start drinking. I've never heard of anyone going to tea at 6pm.

Now for the tricky part: the finances of taking tea. At grand hotels, you pay a flat fee for the total tea service, and that price is not cheap. Expect to pay an average of £12 ($20) per person, although some are £10 ($17) and prices do go higher than £12 ($20)—often £15 to £25 ($25—$41) per person at a very elegant place.

It is very unusual, especially at an elegant hotel, for tea to be served a la carte. However, at a few addresses, you may buy the full tea service for one and a second (or even third) pot of tea a la carte, thus saving about $20. Furthermore, one or two hotels allow for total a la carte tea service. Since very few people can eat all of what is provided at teatime, this is a money-saving device—don't be embarrassed to make it clear that you don't want to pay for what you won't eat.

BROWN'S HOTEL
Albemarle St., W1 (Tube: Green Park).

For years I've been sending people to Brown's Hotel for tea: There's no question that it's one of the best teas in London, with scones that are among the best. You may request one setup (tea for one) and additional cups of tea, or you may request a platter of scones to replace the tea setup (but at the same cost) and individual pots of tea. Jackets and ties for the gentlemen; be prepared for a long wait if you aren't early. © 020/7493-6020.

CLARIDGE'S
Brook St., W1 (Tube: Bond St.).

I sometimes go for tea at Claridge's simply because it's so fancy and I crave to be part of the scene. Rather than pay the price of the whole package, I ask for a la carte service. This is still pricey, but a big savings over the set price. Of course, for less money you get less food—still, for two you can have the famous Darjeeling tea, a small plate of four sandwiches, and a large plate of eight scones (four plain and four sultana), and the bill is about £40 ($66). And that's the bargain price. Sultana is Britspeak for a big, fat, golden raisin, but once cooked they are no longer golden. © 020/7499-0099.

FOUR SEASONS
Hamilton Place, Park Lane, W1 (Tube: Hyde Park Corner or Green Park).

This is one of the best teas in London because it's different from everyone else's—and reasonably priced as well! You can do a scone-tasting tea service, or simply order a scone a la carte at £3 ($4.95) per scone. The three kinds of scones in the tasting are peach, mango, and sultana. And I needn't tell you that, like at all Four Seasons hotels, the service is sublime and the room is in traditional English style. © 020/7493-1895.

Note: Tea is not served at Four Seasons Canary Wharf as guests tend to be there on business and do not take tea. They have cocktail service.

THE RITZ
Piccadilly, W1 (Tube: Green Park).

Tea at The Ritz is a "Ritzual" that few people want to pass up. Although I recommend it as a once-in-a-lifetime thing to do, I have several Ritz secrets for you. Tea at The Ritz is so popular that management doesn't even like to publicize it—the place is packed. You may not even get to sit in the main court, but could end up in one of the fancy halls, and you must have a reservation.

Tea is a lavish affair; if gentlemen do not have their ties on hand, they may borrow one from the cloakroom.

The trick at The Ritz is to come for either lunch in the Palm Court or breakfast. Breakfast is served in the most beautiful dining room in London (this is general knowledge, not just my opinion) and is not as crowded as tea, so you can really relish your surroundings. © 020/7493-8181.

Teen Time

I've made it rather clear that I don't come to Britain to do business with American brands, but if you're with teens, you may want to at least note the location of several of the big American teenage haunts that have recently invaded Piccadilly, such as **Fashion Café** and **Planet Hollywood. Hard Rock Cafe** actually began in London; it's over near Four Seasons. I'm fonder of **Rainforest Cafe** (20 Shaftesbury Ave., W1), which actually started life in the Mall of America and now has branches all over the United States—it's a jungle out there (with shopping), but it's cute and amusing if you or your kids have never been there before.

Inside the **Miss Selfridge** department of the flagship Selfridges, there's a tiny cafe geared to teens.

McDonald's and **Starbucks** can be found everywhere.

Coupons/Conran's

I buy the *Evening Standard* newspaper every afternoon that I am in London; I love this paper for dozens of reasons. One of those reasons is that they often have promotional deals for various things that you want—such as a meal at one of the many Conran restaurants. Terence Conran, as you surely remember, is the home-style king of the planet who has been opening restaurants all over the world and has several in London—all interesting to look at, eat in, and be part of the scene in.

There were meals offered at £10 ($17), £15 ($25), £20 ($33), and £30 ($50) at the various restaurants. You got three courses and a glass of champagne; tip was not included. Call whichever restaurant you are interested in; ask if they currently have the *Evening Standard* offer. You hand in the completed coupon (which you clip from the paper) and that's all there is to it.

Chapter Five

....

SHOPPING NEIGHBORHOODS

YOURS IN A ZIP

Zip codes in London are called postal codes. They are made up of letter and number combinations. The code actually indicates the precise part of town where the address is located, and it makes a good indicator for shoppers who want to organize themselves by neighborhood.

If you study the map, you'll see that the metropolitan area is divided into quadrants that have a few subcategories, such as southwest, southeast, and so on. There is a central core; those central zones have the letter C in them for—you guessed it— "central." You can look up the general area of a store or shopping neighborhood just by using this map.

As you get more sophisticated at using this method, you'll learn the few overlapping places. For instance, Mayfair is W1, but Jermyn Street, at the edge of Mayfair, is in SW1. Practice, practice, practice.

LONDON BY NEIGHBORHOOD

London is one of the best cities in the world in which to pick a neighborhood and wander without specific goals. Each neighborhood is distinctive because of the way the city grew out of many individual towns. Some famous names overlap (Chelsea and Knightsbridge); some are actually separate cities, such as the city of Westminster.

Do note that it is inappropriate to refer to London or the portion of London an American might deem to be "downtown" as "The City." In Brit-speak, The City truly means The City of London, which is a teeny-tiny 1-mile area; it is where the financial institutions have their offices and the banking people—and insurance people and the other suits—do their business. (Not much shopping here.)

Now then, it behooves you to know the areas of town more than ever because of the congestion tax, which does indeed limit noncommercial traffic but may also affect where your local friends want to meet you.

Connect the Dots by Neighborhood

If you work with a daily schedule or a list of shopping goals, you'll soon see that certain neighborhoods lead directly to each other, usually by foot but often by bus. The tours in chapter 10, "London Shopping Tours," are organized to move you through London in an orderly neighborhood sequence.

I have tried to organize this neighborhood section by interconnecting neighborhoods related to a larger area. To me, as a person who listens to the vibes of the sidewalk, a shopping neighborhood may hold a specific mood for only 2 or 3 blocks before changing into something else. I've tried to indicate the changes and segues.

Note: There are "new" neighborhoods popping up all the time; people are getting tired of moving farther and farther out of town, so they are taking over older areas and gentrifying them. We all know about Notting Hill, thanks in part to Julia Roberts, but the next Notting Hill is said to be Shepherd's Bush. Meanwhile, the East End is getting hotter and hotter. First it became semi-residential; then some service businesses came on board. Now even retail is blooming there.

London Postal Codes

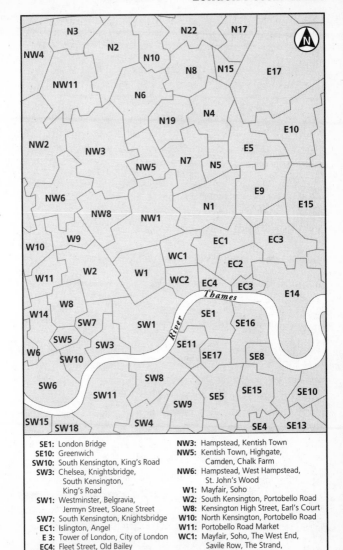

SE1: London Bridge
SE10: Greenwich
SW10: South Kensington, King's Road
SW3: Chelsea, Knightsbridge,
     South Kensington,
     King's Road
SW1: Westminster, Belgravia,
     Jermyn Street, Sloane Street
SW7: South Kensington, Knightsbridge
EC1: Islington, Angel
E 3: Tower of London, City of London
EC4: Fleet Street, Old Bailey
N1: Islington, King's Cross
NW1: Camden, Chalk Farm,
     King's Cross, Euston
NW2: West Hampstead

NW3: Hampstead, Kentish Town
NW5: Kentish Town, Highgate,
     Camden, Chalk Farm
NW6: Hampstead, West Hampstead,
     St. John's Wood
W1: Mayfair, Soho
W2: South Kensington, Portobello Road
W8: Kensington High Street, Earl's Court
W10: North Kensington, Portobello Road
W11: Portobello Road Market
WC1: Mayfair, Soho, The West End,
     Savile Row, The Strand,
     Oxford Street
WC2: Covent Garden, Trafalgar Square,
     Charing Cross Road, Piccadilly

London Neighborhoods at a Glance

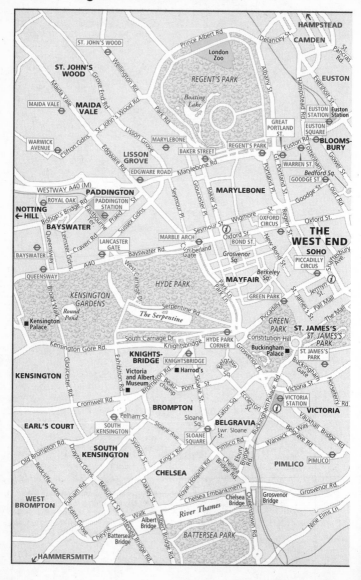

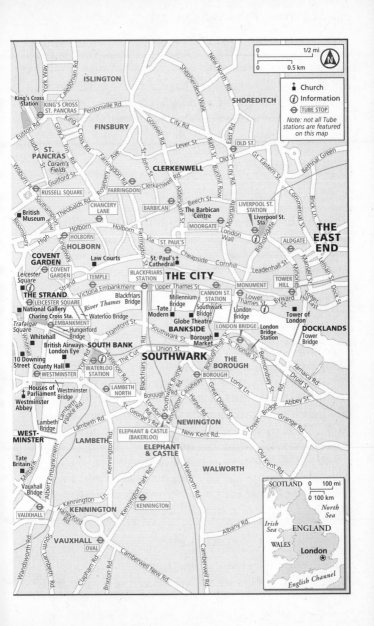

THE WEST END

The West End is the name for a large portion of real estate; a W1 address is very chic—for a store or a residence. The major shopping areas in the West End are Oxford Street, Oxford Circus, Regent Street, Bond Street (Old and New), and Piccadilly. While they are well established, there are enormous changes in the vibe from time to time.

Oxford Street

To enjoy Oxford Street, you have to settle into the right frame of mind (or be 22) and begin to groove on the street vendors selling Union Jacks printed on T-shirts and underpants, the fruit and flower stands, the locals in search of a bargain, and the street fashions that pass by in hurried profusion.

The beauty of Oxford Street is the fact that most of the moderately priced big department stores are lined up in a row between Marble Arch and Regent Street. There are also a lot of teeny-bopper stores, trendy but cheap chains, and plenty of cheap eats; in fact, many popular stores are so popular they have branches toward the Marble Arch end of Oxford Street and toward the Oxford Circus end as well. But here's the big news: **Bally** just moved from Regent Street to Oxford Street at the Marble Arch end, and many more upscale stores are expected to follow. Watch this space.

Meanwhile, the more upscale department stores are on Regent Street, just around the corner, but a million miles away. But wait, the Oxford Street department stores are reinventing themselves, and the new, improved **Selfridges** is plenty upscale.

Oxford Circus

To me, Oxford Street is the stretch from Marble Arch to Regent Street. End of story. Oxford Circus (and it *is* a circus) begins at Regent Street and continues along Oxford Street for a block or two toward Tottenham Court. In Roman-speak, a circus is a circle.

Oxford Circus has a decidedly more hip and hot atmosphere to it than plain old, vanilla Oxford Street. The stores are still cheap, but they are selling high-fashion street looks to young people on the cutting edge of the cutting edge. My favorites? **TopShop** and **SuperDrug. NikeTown** moved in a few years ago.

Note: Teenyboppers may want to eventually segue over to Carnaby Street (see below) from Oxford Circus—it's just a few blocks away. Follow Regent Street toward Piccadilly until you see the sign for Carnaby Street.

Marylebone High Street

I can barely even pronounce this area. I find that I prefer to say *Marleybone,* but if I could afford it, I'd move here in a flash—although I'd still hang on to my Paris flat. Marylebone High Street has a wonderful neighborhood feel and a ton of stores. It goes from Oxford Street (more or less) right to a big, snazzy branch of Conran's, complete with good eats.

The highlight of shopping this street is **VV Rouleaux,** which used to be a simple ribbon-and-trim shop at Sloane Square (it's still there); but the company has expanded to about five different stores and has knock-your-socks-off style.

Regent Street

I love to walk Regent Street from Piccadilly to Oxford Circus. It's a little less than 1.6km (1 mile) in distance, and each side of the street is packed with stores; but only one side of the street appeals to me—the **Hamley's** side (if Oxford is behind you, you're on the left-hand side of the street toward Piccadilly). Also, the Piccadilly end is a little tacky and in need of dressing up, so it's fun to watch out for changes.

Among the big chains are **Zara** (the Spanish chain that makes low-cost women's clothes for the office) and **Mango** (another Spanish chain). Regent Street still hosts the British institutions that make London retail so glorious. If there's only one store on your tour, it's got to be **Liberty,** which has now reopened

The West End

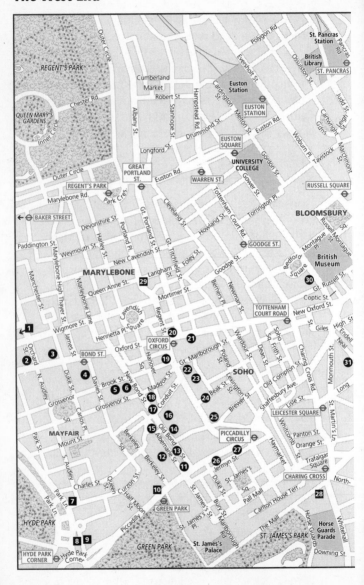

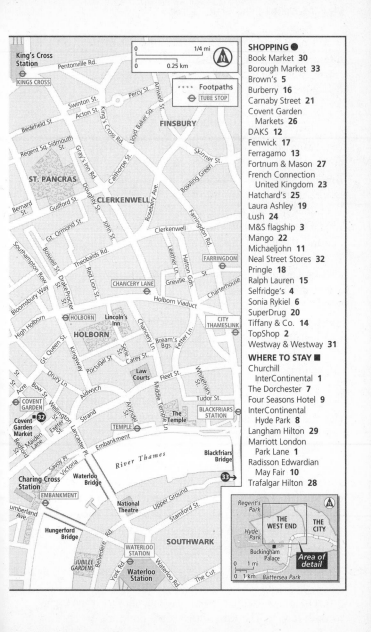

SHOPPING ●

Book Market **30**
Borough Market **33**
Brown's **5**
Burberry **16**
Carnaby Street **21**
Covent Garden
  Markets **26**
DAKS **12**
Fenwick **17**
Ferragamo **13**
Fortnum & Mason **27**
French Connection
  United Kingdom **23**
Hatchard's **25**
Laura Ashley **19**
Lush **24**
M&S flagship **3**
Mango **22**
Michaeljohn **11**
Neal Street Stores **32**
Pringle **18**
Ralph Lauren **15**
Selfridge's **4**
Sonia Rykiel **6**
SuperDrug **20**
Tiffany & Co. **14**
TopShop **2**
Westway & Westway **31**

WHERE TO STAY ■

Churchill
  InterContinental **1**
The Dorchester **7**
Four Seasons Hotel **9**
InterContinental
  Hyde Park **8**
Langham Hilton **29**
Marriott London
  Park Lane **1**
Radisson Edwardian
  May Fair **10**
Trafalgar Hilton **28**

with a totally redone Regent Street store. There are also traditionalists from **Jaeger** to **Lawley's** (china). Not far away is a small branch of **Lush,** the bath and beauty store that is a must-do—unless all those scents make you sneeze.

Bond Street

Bond Street has rebonded and rebounded, and everything is coming up roses, from **Dolce & Gabbana** to the flagship **Burberry** store to **Alexander McQueen.** Whereas Regent Street is big department stores with big names, Bond Street is small boutiques with big names. **Louis Vuitton** has a swanky new store; **Donna Karan** has what looks like a museum for her fancy line and another, more casual shop for the DKNY line. **Ralph Lauren** has two shops also, one for infants and kiddies and also his flagship. Chanel has totally remodeled and has opened a separate jewelry shop.

You won't find any bargains in these stores (especially the American ones), but do remember that most of them have prices that will automatically qualify you for a VAT refund.

Now then, this isn't tricky, but since I frequently get mixed up, you may too. Bond Street is divided into two parts: Old Bond and New Bond. Both are chockablock with big-name designer boutiques from all over the world selling clothing, jewelry, and gift items for the tabletop—you know, your basic **Baccarat** and **Lalique** stores.

What's amazing is that in the last year or so, many stores picked up and moved from one end of Bond to the other. If you're a London regular but haven't been here in a couple years, don't convince yourself that you've been here and done that. Bond Street feels very fresh and new with a lot of new faces; the energy is contagious, and you will love coming back to see what the old neighborhood has been up to.

Piccadilly

To get to the good stuff, cut over onto Piccadilly itself and begin to walk toward **The Ritz,** where you'll find some patches of retail heaven. This is part of the Regent Street experience to me, since it is home to some special British institutions that make London the shopping mecca it is. Some of my favorites include **Fortnum & Mason, Burlington Arcade,** and **Hatchards,** the bookstore, just a few doors from the enormous **Waterstone's** bookstore in what was once a department store.

Carnaby Street

The street itself has artistic banners and flags to welcome you to the rebirth of this tourist trap, and there are a number of head shops selling black-leather clothing (much with studs); funny, floppy hats; T-shirts; and imports from India—with and without tie-dye. You get the picture. But wait: The picture is changing. This real estate is now so valuable that the head shops are being torn down and brands such as Diesel and Miss Sixty are moving in. The teens hang out in droves.

- The kids and the people are fabulous to stare at.
- There's a lot of energy here, and it feels like a foreign destination, which is exactly what you want from a trip to Europe.
- There are tons of postcard shops.

For my own shopping taste, there's a branch of **Boots,** there's a **Body Shop,** and there's **Lush.** Of particular note is a teeny makeup store called **Pixi.** Don't miss Newburgh Street, the tiny back street where the expensive new-wave designer shops of Soho are located.

Soho

Just past Carnaby, Soho has been a seedy neighborhood known for its porn shops. But here and there among the tattoo places and the massage parlors, there are some hip stores, and the area is somewhat transformed (but not completely). The most expensive hip stores are strung together in order to improve the real estate and make shopping easier for the customers.

Newburgh Street is such a venue—it's chockablock with places such as **Gaultier Junior. Workers for Freedom** on Lower John Street looks small and uninviting, but has a reputation for high fashion.

Jermyn Street

These few short blocks of a shopping neighborhood run 1 block from Piccadilly and end at St. James's. Most of the stores here are small, with the exception of **Alfred Dunhill,** and the back of **Fortnum & Mason.** Jermyn Street represents a world that has almost ceased to exist—most of the stores are devoted to serving the private world of the upper-crust London gent. It's the home of exclusive shirt shops, such as **Turnbull & Asser, Hilditch & Key,** and **Harvie & Hudson.**

Press your nose against the glass of all the shops; take in the dark wood and the aroma of old money. There are several stores famous for toiletries, from **Czech & Speake** to **Trumper's** (which is in Simpson's and is actually a place for milord to have a shave and a haircut for more than two bits); and there's **David-off** for the right smoke. Cuban cigars cannot legally be brought into the United States, but it is not a crime to smoke them in London. Besides these men's haunts, there are old-fashioned suppliers such as **Paxton & Whitfield,** cheese merchants to the royal family.

The Jermyn Street Association publishes its own map and directory to all stores in the area, which is given away free at area stores.

St. James's

St. James's Street stretches from St. James's Place near Pall Mall to Piccadilly and is lined with some of London's most famous stores, many of which are 100 years old or more. It all adds to the charm of the stroll.

Most of the stores have their original storefronts or have been restored to make you think they are original. Don't miss

John Lobb (no. 9) for custom-made shoes (you can look; you needn't plunk down a thousand bucks); **James Lock & Co.** (no. 6), a hat maker for men and women; **William Evans Gun & Riflemaker** (67A St. James's Place); and **D. R. Harris** (no. 29), an old-fashioned chemist whose brand of toiletries is considered very chic and where I buy almond oil, Skin Food, and other necessities of life.

Dorchester

There's a private part of Mayfair that you will never find unless you prowl the streets or happen to be staying at **The Dorchester** or possibly **The Connaught.** South Audley Street is the main drag of this niche of good taste and fine retail, but you will also want to wander Mount Street and end up at Berkeley Square before taking Bruton and connecting to Bond Street; or you can go across from South Audley to Davies to Oxford.

Mount Street and Bruton are known mostly for their very fancy antiques stores. South Audley has a hodgepodge of delectable goods, from one of London's better spy shops (honest) to **Thomas Goode,** London's most exclusive address for china and tabletop. This shop now runs a museum service so that you can bring your coat of arms out of retirement and have it painted on your next set of dishes. Yes, it's that kind of neighborhood.

This is a part of town frequented only by rich people, which is just what makes it so much fun. Don't miss **Shepherd Market,** which is closer to Curzon Street—it's a hidden medieval alley with a few shops and pubs that looks like it hasn't changed in 300 years.

KNIGHTSBRIDGE & CHELSEA

Fashionable and "with it," Knightsbridge crosses into a few different neighborhoods and borders Chelsea to such an extent that it can be confusing for a tourist to grasp the difference.

Once you've passed Hyde Park and are heading toward **Harrods,** you'll be on a street that is first called Knightsbridge but then changes its name to Brompton Road. This makes it especially confusing if you are watching addresses or street numbers because Knightsbridge doesn't really change its name; it just disappears into a nowhere turn. Chances are you won't realize you've turned a corner at Sloane Street and ended up on the beginning of Brompton Road. Never mind. Pay no heed to street names, and you'll be fine.

Knightsbridge

The part around **Harvey Nichols** is decidedly different than the part that comes after **Harrods.** At the Harvey Nichols end, aside from wonderful Harvey Nichols itself, there are branches of all the multiples and a number of high-end retailers such as the new **Burberry,** which replaced **Scotch House.** The closer you get to Harrods, the less tony the retailers become. Once you pass Harrods, you are on your way to Beauchamp Place and then the Victoria & Albert Museum.

Harrods and Harvey Nichols are only a few blocks apart, so we're talking chockablock shopping here. Also note that Sloane Street (which has its own atmosphere and tempo; see below) leads off from Brompton at the corner where Harvey Nichols is standing. So you have to be organized and know where you're going because there are many directions and many, many choices to make. If you head in the other direction, you will end up at Beauchamp Place and maybe even Museum Row.

Sloane Street

The juicy shopping part of Sloane Street is only about 2 blocks long. Yet it is 2 blocks of cheek-by-jowl designer chic. You could glance down the street and just rattle off an international who's who in big-name retailing, from **Chanel** to **Valentino**— and much, *much* more. **Jo Malone,** the skin and scent queen,

Knightsbridge & Chelsea

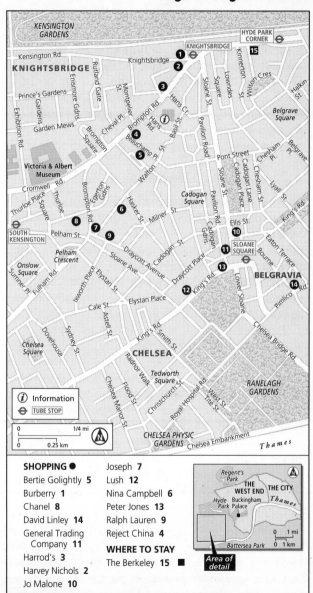

KENSINGTON GARDENS

HYDE PARK CORNER

KNIGHTSBRIDGE

15

Kensington Rd.

Knightsbridge

1

2

KNIGHTSBRIDGE

Prince's Gardens

Rutland Gate

Ensimore Gdns.

Gardens

Garden Mews

Exhibition Rd.

Montpelier St.

Cheval Pl.

Brompton Square

Brompton Rd.

3

Hans Cr.

Sloane St.

Lowndes St.

Kinnerton St.

Wilton Cres.

Halkin St.

Belgrave Square

Brompton Rd.

Beauchamp Pl.

Hans Rd.

Basil St.

4

5

Hans St.

Pavilion Road

i

Pont Street

Chesham Pl.

Belgrave Pl.

Victoria & Albert Museum

Cromwell Rd.

Thurloe Place

Thurloe Square

Thurloe

Brompton Rd.

Egerton Gdns.

Walton

6

Hasker St.

Milner St.

Cadogan Square

Sloane St.

Cadogan Place

Chesham St.

Lyall St.

King's Rd.

Belgrave Pl.

SOUTH KENSINGTON

Pelham St.

8

7

9

Draycott Avenue

Cadogan St.

Cadogan Gdns.

Pavilion Rd.

Ellis St.

10

SLOANE SQUARE

11

Eaton Terrace

Bourne

EVERYTHING

Pelham Crescent

Sloane Ave.

Draycott Place

13

King's Rd.

Lower Sloane

BELGRAVIA

14

Onslow Square

Summer Pl.

Fulham Rd.

Ixworth Place

Elystan St.

Cale St.

Elystan Place

12

Pimlico

Chelsea Bridge Rd.

Sydney St.

Astell St.

Dovehouse

Chelsea Square

Radnor Walk

Flood St.

King's Rd.

Smith St.

CHELSEA

Tedworth Square

West Sloane

RANELAGH GARDENS

Chelsea Manor St.

Christchurch St.

Royal Hospital Rd.

West St.

Tite St.

CHELSEA PHYSIC GARDENS

Chelsea Embankment

Thames

i **Information**

⊖ **TUBE STOP**

0   1/4 mi

0   0.25 km

SHOPPING ●

Bertie Golightly **5**

Burberry **1**

Chanel **8**

David Linley **14**

General Trading Company **11**

Harrod's **3**

Harvey Nichols **2**

Jo Malone **10**

Joseph **7**

Lush **12**

Nina Campbell **6**

Peter Jones **13**

Ralph Lauren **9**

Reject China **4**

WHERE TO STAY

The Berkeley **15** ■

Regent's Park

THE WEST END

THE CITY

Hyde Park

Buckingham Palace

Thames

Battersea Park

0   1 mi

0   1 km

Area of detail

has a large flagship here (at the far end, closer to Sloane Sq.), and David Tang opened a branch of **Shanghai Tang.** Other brands with stores here include **Browns, Gucci, Joseph Pour La Ville, Hermès, Cartier, JP Tod's,** and **Louis Vuitton.** Browns is a branch of the South Molton Street icon.

Sloane Street leads to Sloane Square, and then you're on King's Road. Tucked into a side street off Sloane Square and before you amble off onto King's Road is the new **General Trading Company,** as well as a shop called the **White Store.**

Belgravia

I used to call this area Sloane Street Adjacent, but now that I know it better, I am going with the local name: Belgravia. In the old days, you moved from Sloane Street to King's Road without too much detour, but now that everyone is building and expanding and opening shops, well, the residential area here is blossoming with stores. Pont Street is one such nook, which always has had a few stores on it and is now home to the new **Anya Hindmarch** store and the Knightsbridge branch of **Agent Provocateur** for lingerie. **Liza Bruce** has a shop on Pont Street and one in Los Angeles.

Around the corner on Motcomb Street, there's **Jimmy Choo Couture** for couture shoes, which is almost next door to **Christian Laboutin,** the French shoemaker that sells red-soled shoes; one street over on West Halkin, there's **Belinda Robertson** for top-of-the-line Scottish cashmere.

Do look at your *A to Z* for these side streets—Pont is on one side of Sloane Street (the Beauchamp Rd. side), and the other two are on the Belgravia side of Sloane. Better still, book into the Berkeley Hotel, where you get a map and a tour, and can even sign up for a Retail Therapy package.

King's Road

If you continue along Sloane Street, you will end up at Sloane Square. Here, surrounding the square, are numerous stores and many choices for your happy feet. On your way to the square, make sure you take a look at **Jane Churchill** and **General Trading Company,** now located right off Sloane Street on Symons Street, right across from Peter Jones as mentioned above. Indeed, the focal point of Sloane Square itself is the medium-size department store **Peter Jones,** which has totally renovated itself but is still best for bed linens and fabrics.

Just as Sloane Street dead-ends and disappears, you hit Sloane Square (there's a Tube stop here) and have two choices for two different retail experiences: Pimlico Road (below) and King's Road. Totally different choices, believe me.

King's Road became famous (or is that infamous?) in the 1960s as the hot street for the bell-bottom people. Now it's mostly a congregation of multiples, but it is having a renaissance and has a lot of fun addresses, including the original branch of **Lush** (no. 123).

King's Road also possesses a few of London's best antiques arcades as well as **Steinberg & Tolkien,** a free-standing shop selling vintage clothing that is a fashion junkie's version of paradise. Much Pucci! High prices! Who cares?

The worst thing about King's Road is its lack of Tube transportation, since there is no convenient Tube station along the way. You can either go up one side and down the other and end up back at Sloane Square, or put on your hiking boots and march all the way to the 500 block, since it is kind of interesting all the way up. There is also a bus, so you can bus to the far end and pick and choose what interests you, and then walk back to Sloane Square.

Pimlico Road

If you were in Knightsbridge, you did Sloane Street, and you got to Sloane Square but decided against King's Road (see above)—this is the other choice, the design and antiques-prowler choice. *Note:* This is not the neighborhood of Pimlico as laid out in your *A to Z,* but rather a *street* called Pimlico Road (SW1), which comes right before the real Pimlico district. To reach it by Tube, use the Sloane Square stop.

For those interested in interior design, this street is filled with shops of trimmings, fabrics, and antiques. Working designers or those with a decorating need should find some useful resources here; gawkers will simply want to stare at the goods in **David Linley's** incredible store.

From the Sloane Square Tube, if the station is to your back and you are facing toward Peter Jones, make a left on Holbein Place. This will lead you to Pimlico Road within a block; there are some shops here along the way. When you do both sides of Pimlico Road, return to Sloane Square via Lower Sloane Street, which runs parallel to Holbein Place.

KENSINGTON

This neighborhood is a must if you are in the fashion business, want to see the young hip looks, or have teens and 'tweens. It's also a must for those interested in antiques, and it includes Portobello Road market.

Kensington High Street

Like any other high street, the thoroughfare that stretches before you as you emerge from the Kensington High Street Tube station is chockablock with multiples and real-people stores. This has become our new family headquarters neighborhood, with our regular hotel, the **Royal Garden,** located smack dab in the middle of all this and next door to **Urban Outfitters.**

Just about every British multiple is between the hotel and the Tube station or just past the Tube, including **M&S, Beauty Boots** (the Well-Being Centre; p. 196), and—directly across the street—a branch of **Lush.**

Kensington Church Street

Leading up the hill from the high (or main) street is Kensington Church Street. It leads directly to the Notting Hill Tube. Kensington Church Street hosts a few multiples, a branch of a **Portmeiron** china store with some seconds and off-price pieces, as well as several designer resale shops.

Shortly after you swing onto Kensington Church Street from Kensington High Street, there's **Lancer's Square,** a sort of mini-mall, which has a branch of the famous Belgian chocolatier **Pierre Marcolini** as well as the wool and tapestry shop **Ehrman.**

The street curves uphill toward Notting Hill Gate; hopefully you aren't carrying too many packages. Upper Kensington Church Street is home to many, many antiques shops of the high-end type, but not so high-end that they are too stuffy to enjoy. Many of these dealers do the big shows, so watch out particularly for the month of June when there are a lot of fancy shows in town—the stores may be closed or open only at weird hours.

Note: There are several cafes and bistros as you get closer to Notting Hill Gate; they make the perfect place for a shopper's snack. I always stop at **Mediterranean Kitchen** (p. 73).

Notting Hill Gate

This is actually more of a residential address than a tourist-shopping district, but it is also a major segue to various areas. Right around the Tube stop you can find the usual suspects—fast-food joints, cash machines, **Boots, WHSmith, Waterstone's,** and so on. The area is important simply because of its location as the center of a universe. The real shopping fun of the area is the corner of Pembridge Road, which leads to Portobello Road Market but is chockablock with vintage-clothing stores.

Ledbury & Westbourne Grove

This is not very near the Notting Hill Gate Tube station, which is at the top of Kensington Church Street, but it's not very far either—and is in walking distance. You may want to take a taxi to the corner of Ledbury Street and Westbourne Grove, explore this area on foot, and then end up at Notting Hill Gate.

Kensington, Notting Hill & Marylebone

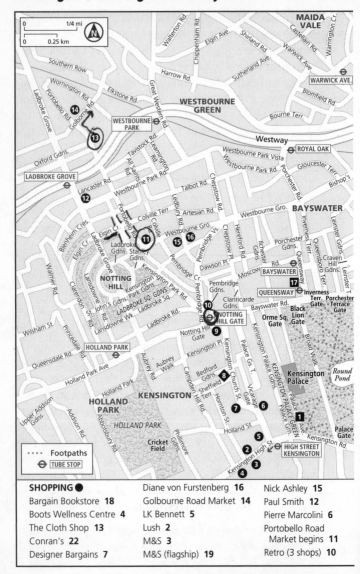

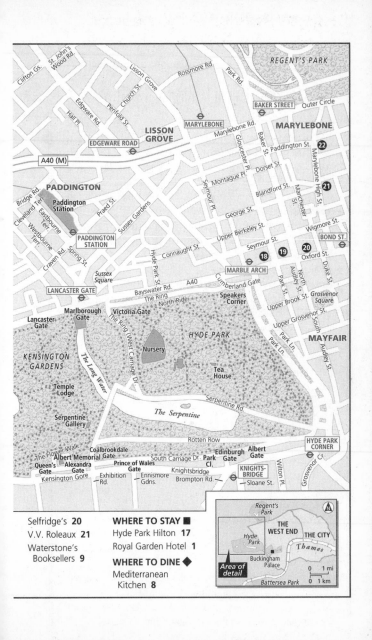

St. John's Wood Rd.
Clifton Gs.
Lisson Grove
Rossmore Rd.
Park Rd.
REGENT'S PARK
Church St.
Edgware Rd.
Penfold St.
Hall Pl.
BAKER STREET
Outer Circle
MARYLEBONE
LISSON GROVE
Marylebone Rd.
MARYLEBONE
EDGEWARE ROAD
Gloucester Pl.
Baker St.
Paddington St. 22
A40 (M)
Montague Pl.
Dorset St.
Marylebone High St.
Manchester St.
PADDINGTON
Blandford St. 21
Bridge Rd.
Paddington Station
Praed St.
Seymour Pl.
George St.
Wigmore St.
Cleveland Ter.
Eastbourne Ter.
Westbourne Ter.
Sussex Gardens
Upper Berkeley St.
BOND ST.
Craven Rd.
PADDINGTON STATION
Spring St.
Connaught St.
Hyde Park Sq.
Seymour St.
19 20
Oxford St.
North Audley St.
Duke St.
18
Sussex Square
MARBLE ARCH
LANCASTER GATE
Bayswater Rd.
A40
Cumberland Gate
Lancaster Gate
The Ring
North Ride
Speakers Corner
Upper Brook St.
Grosvenor Square
Marlborough Gate
Victoria Gate
The Ring West Carriage Dr.
HYDE PARK
Upper Grosvenor St.
Park St.
Park Ln.
MAYFAIR
KENSINGTON GARDENS
The Long Water
Nursery
Tea House
Audley St.
Temple Lodge
The Serpentine
Serpentine Rd.
Serpentine Gallery
Rotten Row
HYDE PARK CORNER
The Flower Walk
Coalbrookdale Gate
South Carriage Dr.
Edinburgh Gate
Albert Gate
Grosvenor Cr.
Albert Memorial
Queen's Gate
Alexandra Gate
Prince of Wales Gate
Park Cl.
KNIGHTS-BRIDGE
Wilton Pl.
Kensington Gore
Exhibition Rd.
Ennismore Gdns.
Knightsbridge
Brompton Rd.
Sloane St.

Selfridge's **20**

V.V. Roleaux **21**

Waterstone's
Booksellers **9**

WHERE TO STAY ■

Hyde Park Hilton **17**

Royal Garden Hotel **1**

WHERE TO DINE ◆

Mediterranean
Kitchen **8**

Regent's Park
THE WEST END
THE CITY
Hyde Park
Thames
Buckingham Palace
Area of detail
Battersea Park
0   1 mi
0   1 km

Heeeere's Jenny:
Shopper's Tour of Kensington High Street

Ladies, lace up those trainers and prepare yourself for a half day of trendsetting stores on one of London's most practical shopping streets. Comprised of international names along with local London shops, Kensington High Street is just the avenue to find the latest catwalk styles at (semi-) affordable prices. The street has so much to offer, even your fella will want to come along!

Starting at Palace Avenue (easily landmarked by the **Royal Garden Hotel**), the main shopping area runs only .8km (½ mile) and ends at **Phillmore Gardens**. At half the size of its rival King's Road, Kensington High Street offers much the same in the way of fashion, yet is much easier on the feet, and therefore is fancied over King's anytime. Begin your tour after lunch and be done by high tea.

For hot looks from major European brands (these ain't your mum's jumpers), there is many a shop to hop. **Diesel** (no. 38A), **Miss Sixty** (no. 42), and **FCUK** (no. 168–170) all offer of-the-moment looks for those not afraid to show off their assets. Though these looks are great for hitting the London nightlife, the price tags may hit hard on your wallet.

No need to go to the ATM; just hit up the **H&M**, a much more cash-conscious solution. At H&M (no. 103), all the hit/now looks are available at super-low prices—whatever your style. From flirty to classy, to punky and trendy, you'll find your look without losing your mind. This particular location has a wide selection of clothes not found in other European or U.S. locations.

Another quid-friendly option is **Zara** (no. 48–52), the Spanish brand with shops across the continent (and the States, too). Zara carries a vast selection of urban-chic fashions at reasonable prices.

Other international names to check out are the international multiples, such as **Morgan** (no. 88–90), **Kookai** (no. 123), **Muji** (no. 155), and **Sisley** (no. 131). Muji, a Japanese import, has clothes as well as things for home and office.

If it's American names you are after, at no. 196 you'll find a **Levi's** brand store. I've found the prices are higher than in the States. Also, the jeans here are less cool and more expensive than the vintage Levi's found throughout London.

A better bet for selection (if not price) is **Urban Outfitters** (no. 36–38). As the only London location, this store is a five-level mecca for runway dresses, ironic T-shirts, and funky shoes and sneakers. Check out the housewares section on the top level for kitschy accents for the home (where else will you find those Che Guevara coffee mugs?). This Urban also carries forever-hip vintage clothes for guys and gals—aptly named Urban Renewal.

If it is solely shoes you are after, two of London's greatest shops are right at your feet. **Sacha** (no. 80) and **Size? Sale Shop** (no. 145) both sell footwear, but are vastly dissimilar. See below for more on Size? . . . from me and from Ethan Sunshine.

Sacha has great sandals, boots, and dressy shoes in a wide range of colors and flirty styles. Designs range from fashionista funky to feminine frilly. A wide selection for a small shop. The store also offers a smaller variety of unique and artsyurban handbags.

Size? is a young and hip sneaker shop with locations all over London. The Kensington address, however, is the city's Sale Shop. The sneakers are still the latest "now" brands and the current styles, but with severe reductions in price. You'll find brands including Adidas, Puma, and Royal Elastic, at the cheapest prices in the city.

After all this shopping, you need a break! With two **Starbucks**, a **Café Nero**, and **Crussh** (a super-yummy smoothie bar), there is something to satisfy everyone's taste and to rest everyone's tootsies.

As you head off back to your hotel, don't forget to stop into the **Lush** (no. 96) to get some products to pamper yourself as you relax and rest while dreaming about your purchases.

The heart of the development is Westbourne Grove, running from Chepstow Road (try **Bill Amberg** for leather goods at 10 Chepstow Rd., W2) to Portobello, where the market is

The Sunshine Report: Kensington High Street

Aside from the usual big names that you will recognize on this street, there is a plethora of cool British shops selling everything from skateboards to hiking gear to my personal favorite, sneakers. For all my fellow sneaker-freakers out there, I strongly recommend the following shops in this 'hood.

FREE SPIRIT
178 Kensington High St., NW11 (Tube: Kensington High St.).

When I went into Free Spirit, they were having a huge sale on Royal Elastics and Onitsuka Tigers, two of my favorites for their unique designs and originality. The American-based Royal Elastics were actually cheaper here, running (no pun intended) at about £20 to £30 ($33–$50). But the Onitsukas were the cheapest that I've ever seen in five countries worth of Tiger hunting.

SIZE? SALE STORE
145 Kensington High St., NW11 (Tube: Kensington High St.).

There are quite a few of these shops in London and they are arguably the coolest and most well-stocked sneaker stores in the city. This particular store offers huge discounts on almost all of its inventory, as does Free Spirit, making them the only two shoe stores where you're likely to find better prices than you will in the States, as long as you buy only items on sale and avoid American imports like Converse.

Note: Two of the three shoe stores listed below have branch stores near Covent Garden on Neal Street (Tube: Covent Garden or Leicester Sq.), but they are not discount branches like the ones listed below.

SOLE TRADER
96A Kensington High St., NW11 (Tube: Kensington High St.).

Sole Trader has the similar high-end Pumas, Nikes, and Adidases that you would find in Size?, but they also feature a large selection of designer-label sneakers. If you're willing to spend a little more, you can find some really exciting trainers here. Among the best are offerings from Armani, Boss, and Evisu. The Evisus are a must for any serious denimhead, but considering that Evisu Genes (actual spelling) start around £150 ($250) and almost reach the £600 ($1,000) mark, the shoes aren't cheap (£100/$165).

held on Saturdays. It need not be market day for these stores to be open or happening.

Note that, as Ledbury continues to fill and spill to Westbourne Grove and vice versa, Chepstow Road will become the last holdout for lesser rents and the up-and-coming, so consider walking over the extra 2 blocks.

The really cute part is Ledbury Street, with 2 blocks of town houses painted pastel colors, all devoted to retail. Westbourne Grove has several blocks of boutiques, cafes, and antiques stores. Some of the side streets are beginning to have interesting tenants, such as Denbeigh Street.

If you're there on a Saturday, you can move on to Portobello Road Market after you've done this area and enjoyed **Vent**, a leading vintage-clothing store, open only on weekends. If Vent's hours make you nuts (Fri–Sat, 11am–6pm), visit nearby **Virginia** (p. 183) for yet more vintage . . . and Sheila Cook, on Portobello Road itself.

But back to Ledbury. Check out those boutiques, including a branch of **Ghost;** as well as **Nick Ashley** (son of), an interesting shop for men's weekend clothes. Ghost has a new designer and I do not love it as I used to, but it stays in these pages for now. I much, much prefer a shop called **The Wall,** located 1 block over (1 Denbeigh Rd.). The clothes here represent the droopy-chic look that I find so easy to wear and easy to collect.

You can seriously browse or even hang out at **Tom Conran's Deli**—yes, son of *that* Conran (226 Westbourne Grove, NW8)—where you can buy groceries or sit down and eat a light lunch (try the spinach and feta quiche) or have a coffee . . . and stargaze. In fact, there are a few cafes and pubs for hanging out and some specialty bookshops, including **Books for Cooks** (4 Blenheim Crescent) and **The Travel Bookshop** (13 Blenheim Crescent).

Portobello Road

There is indeed a Portobello Road, and it is the home of the Saturday market; it is also the home of many genuine antiques dealers who are open during the week. It's actually easier to enjoy the shops during the week when the Saturday throngs, the tour buses, the German tots, and the organ grinder are not in place.

Considering how famous Portobello Road is, it's not that easy to find. Please note that on Saturdays there is a chalkboard at the stairwell inside the Notting Hill Gate Tube station giving specific directions for how to get to Portobello Road. The fun starts as soon as you turn right onto Pembridge Road from Notting Hill Gate, and continues as you wend your way to Portobello Road. Follow the crowd.

If indeed the market is just too much, work your way through part of it and then tuck into Elgin Crescent Road, which has several cute boutiques (including four branches of **Graham & Greene** for clothes and home-style gift items) and some market spill. This leads to Kensington Park Road, which is filled with cafes and bistros. Then you can walk over to Holland Park, where I promise there will not be a flock of German tourists hopping off a motor coach (see below).

Golborne Road

This is a street that is the twilight zone of neighborhoods, one of the last truly funky and fabulous finds in Europe. You get here by walking on Portobello Road much farther than you thought possible. After you walk beneath the overpass of the highway, you are getting warm. The street is marked, and you simply turn right.

You will walk into a road filled with antiques stores, architectural-building-parts shops, some street stalls, some fabric stores, a few cutie-pie boutiques, and several Portuguese cafes. You will be in the middle of nowhere and will have to walk back to Portobello Road in order to get out, but this is heaven, filled with true charm and no tourists.

Holland Park

Holland Park is actually an extremely chichi residential area of London, on the other side of Portobello Road from the Ledbury Grove district. It has not had much retail over the years; but suddenly, in the middle of a bunch of row houses, there is a tiny enclave of sensational shops that are wildly creative (and expensive) and exciting—the fashion editors are mad for the area. You can walk from Portobello, although it's about 10 minutes of boring residential sidewalk.

If you don't want to walk, just take a taxi to 100 Portland Rd., W11, the address of **Summerhill & Bishop** and the center of the big cluster of hotshot chic.

Check out **Virginia** for vintage clothing (no. 98), **Summerhill & Bishop** (French and tabletop, imports from France and Morocco, and just great stuff in a homey-chic environment), and **The Cross** (no. 141), for cutting-edge pieces from up-and-coming designers—I was gaga for the cutout felt shawls, but they were very expensive. If you pride yourself on seeing the newest shops, this is your find for the day.

Now then, The Cross is on the corner of Portland Road and Clarendon Cross (hence the name). Clarendon Cross is a small street, mostly residential but with about three little boutiques when I was there and possibly three dozen as you read this because you know how it goes once an area gets hot. Among the cutest, **Cath Kidson** (8 Clarendon Cross).

TRAFALGAR, WESTMINSTER & COVENT GARDEN
....

The Strand

This isn't a warm and fuzzy neighborhood, but it leads to Covent Garden. The midpoint of The Strand is the Charing Cross train station, a few hundred yards past Trafalgar. There are some multiples around here; in fact, there's one of everything you might need, including a **SuperDrug.**

Covent Garden

The area I call Covent Garden is actually a parcel of real estate that includes Covent Garden among a handful of other neighborhoods. This part of town begins at Trafalgar, but actually backs up on one end at Mayfair and at Soho on the other.

The entire area around Covent Garden is filled with fabulous little shops and pubs that make the whole place a super shopping area. It's also an officially designated tourist area, so stores are open on Sunday (not all are open, but unlike other parts of London, many are). Prowl everywhere, not just the festival marketplace.

The Covent Garden Market is made up of several markets and several buildings, so don't get confused. The original market buildings are red brick and they have been turned into a series of stores and restaurants, like a strip mall. In between the two buildings is an outdoor market of stalls. There is a glass covering over the market so you won't get wet in the famous English rain, but it is essentially outdoors. There is a brick pavement that surrounds this market; it is referred to as **The Piazza.** Behind all this, in what isn't much more than a corrugated tin warehouse, is the **Jubilee Market,** which is not nearly as classy as everything else, but is there . . . so you might as well take a look.

Several multiples have branches in the redbrick mall stores; two of the most interesting entries are **Twilight,** a division of Monsoon, and **Accessorize** (technically also a division of Monsoon). I will admit that I flipped out when I discovered that a mere wisp of nothing but Thai silk and wire to wrap around the hair was selling for £18 ($30), but the clothes themselves are more moderately priced. **Lush,** my beloved bath-bomb supplier, is also in Covent Garden's main piazza. I like their King's Road store better (and Carnaby St.), but if you can't get there, be sure to stop in here. There's also a branch of **Culpeper the Herbalist,** smaller than the one in Mayfair but stocked with the same great stuff.

Neal Street

Walk out the front end of Covent Garden (the non-Jubilee Market side) and pass the Covent Garden Tube. There, you'll see Neal Street, a pedestrian area that's home to several hip stores and lots of funky fun. A mall (**Thomas Neal's,** Earlham Court) adds to the excitement, and there are pubs and people and stores galore with a funky, friendly feeling that makes the whole Covent Garden adventure more complete. The stores here are mostly open on Sundays as well. Inside the mall there's **SpaceNK,** the local cult makeup shop—they sell a lot of American brands (don't buy 'em—very expensive) but also some cult British and French brands.

Leicester Square

Get here—to the heart of the theater district and not much of a shopping district—via New Row, so you can take in a few more charming shops. New Row is only a block long, but there's something very quaint and very Old World about it that makes its combination of bookstores, antiques shops, and crafts stores thrill you with a sense of discovery.

Charing Cross & The Strand

This is a so-so tourist area where there are branches of the big-name shops (**Chinacraft, Next,** and so on), but where everything seems to have been in its prime in 1960. The Strand begins at Charing Cross and stretches along in the direction of St. Paul's Cathedral and The City. The Strand actually changes its name in a few blocks and becomes the infamous Fleet Street (where trashy tabloid newspapers were once published), but no matter.

The heart of The Strand as a shopping district is near Charing Cross and Covent Garden; here you've got **The Savoy Hotel, Simpson's in the Strand** for roast beef, and a handful of multiples. Stamp collectors know the area well because several famous dealers are located here; there are also a lot of sporting-goods stores. You can connect to Covent Garden or Charing Cross (by walking), so the location can't be ignored, and it's certainly not as intimidating here as it can be for some in Mayfair.

THE EAST END

Pick up any magazine with an article about London in it and you are bound to read about the renaissance of London's East End. A neighborhood that immigrants fought their way out of is now becoming gentrified and even chic. Right now it's the London version of Manhattan's Meat Packing district, so not a whole lot is happening, but you can see the potential and smell the future. If you like it funky, rush there now.

You may want to have a taxi drive you around to look at **Hoxton Market** so that you can feel like you are part of it. You'll do your shopping in more fun zones, but this is the heart of the new world. The truly fun stuff is in Brick Lane nowadays, but this whole area should be explored.

The Sunshine Report:
Brick Lane Area & Market

For the most part, this market—as a market—is a bust, but the stores in the area more than make up for it. If you do want to do it on a market day (Sun), make a day out of it and find Cheshire Road (off of Brick Lane) and then go to the nearby and indoor **Spitalfields Market,** which is pretty good for vintage clothes and new designers. No matter what anyone tells you, stay away from the Petticoat Lane market, which is also nearby. It's a big waste of time.

When you're prowling the Brick Lane area, don't miss these shops and stops. The Tube for all of these destinations is Liverpool Street Station.

THE LADEN SHOWROOM
101–107 Brick Lane, E1.

This place is amazing! It features separate booths by different indie designers such as Red Mutha, Your Majesty, Charles of London, and many more. Some of the booths have cheesy stuff, but most of it more than makes up for it. Many clothes feature one-of-a-kind cut-ups, sew-ons, and paint-and-marker additions. A little pricey, but well worth it.

MENDOZA
158 Brick Lane, E1.

Mendoza has a great selection of vintage clothes and modern styles. Among their best were painted trucker hat one-offs and rare Nike Dunks. But the ultimate prize of the trip was to be found lying helplessly on the £10 ($17) rack . . . a red-and-white baseball tee sporting the slogan "Born to Shop," with a dollar sign for an s.

OLD TRUMAN BREWERY
91–95 Brick Lane, E1.

The highlights here are **eatmyhandbagbitch, Public Beware Co.**, and **Junky**; there are also a few worthwhile vendors with vintage clothes in the alley. Junky was by far my favorite; their classic Mr. T prints were priceless, but the custom-made neckties won me over. The ties are old thrift-store finds that are sliced up and stuffed with packs of rolling papers, or glued with plastic cigarette butts, and come complete with the anti-smoking labels ripped off of cigarette packs (England's labels are much more direct than ours in America, stating simply, SMOKING KILLS).

ROKIT
101–107 Brick Lane, E1.

Rokit is like the vintage-shopping conglomerate or almost-high street multiple. Aside from this string of stores right on Brick Lane, they have a store on Camden High Street, a store on Kensington Gardens in Brighton, and a store that is being built now in Covent Garden. They have quite a stronghold on the local vintage scene and are able to raise prices pretty high. I saw a dirty pair of used Nikes selling for £125 ($206). In the Brick Lane Rokit complex, note that there are two separate Rokit stores and the "Laden Showroom" sandwiched in between them (see above for Laden info).

The bad news is that **Spitalfields Market** is not as great as it used to be and is the sort of thing that I will no longer require you to visit.

Instead, go around the corner to Brick Lane. The most sophisticated stuff is in the **Truman Brewery,** but the short 2 blocks are filled with fun stores. If you turn onto Cheshire Road on a Sunday, you end up in a free-for-all street market. Those DVDs are illegal, but there's much else to buy.

Before you pooh-pooh it, grab onto the fact that Alexander McQueen came from this area. The **Columbia Road Flower Market** is also held only on Sundays, from 9am to 2pm. You can use Liverpool Street, the same Tube stop you use for Spitalfields and Brick Lane, or the Old Street station and walk. If you splurge for a taxi, you have the benefit of no traffic on Sundays; I went via taxi from Piccadilly for £10 ($17).

If the Columbia Road Flower Market were just a flower market, I would have a lot of trouble sending you there, since few tourists are looking to buy flowers or trees. However, this is a scene, and there are boutiques that sell home style (furniture and furnishings), antiques, and whimsy. The boutiques, like the market, are open on Sundays only. The flower market is in full swing by 8:30am, but most of the stores open at 9am. There are plenty of places for a coffee or even breakfast. We had bagels and loved it, although these were not New York bagels.

OTHER NEIGHBORHOODS

The City

The City is the business and financial district located in East London near St. Paul's—not too much shopping here, although there is a trend for big-name boutiques to open tiny boutiques in order to snag the FTSE (Financial Times Stock Exchange, the British stock market) dough and the business folk that are too busy to shop.

Borough Market/London Bridge

The highlight of my last trip to London was my first visit to Borough Market. It is a work in progress, so it can change from what I write here—but the basics will stay the same. Around the corner from the London Bridge Tube stop, this market is under cover as well as partially under railroad tracks, so the trains go rumbling through and add to the carnival atmosphere.

Market days are only Friday (noon–6pm) and Saturday (9am–4pm) . . . Saturday has the real action crowd-wise. Twisting around green-painted Victorian-style arches is a series of lanes with dealers offering wines, local farm products, flowers, produce, and fresh foods just brought over from France for the weekend. You can have a terrific sit-down lunch at Fish (guess what they serve) or stand in line for world-famous chorizo sandwiches.

The market is adjacent to Southwark (say *Suttock*) Cathedral—this is a nice place to visit, but you may just enjoy shopping while the bells are pealing. This part of London is also near the Tate Modern and the Globe Theatre.

Camden Town

If you are over 10 and under 30 (hmmm, maybe you need to be under 25 . . .), you just may adore it here; I admit to having a change of heart and finding some real finds here. This is an entire neighborhood dedicated to clothes and crafts and hippies, and talented immigrants and those who just came back from holiday with an extra suitcase filled with Lord only knows what. The main street seems to be about black T-shirts and having your nose pierced, but when you get around The Lock (as in canal) and into some of the markets (don't miss The Stables), it's more crafty and funky and fun. It's particularly busy on Saturday, as this is the day to shop and socialize among the many markets that line the high street.

You may have the urge to hold on to your handbag and to take a bath after you've been here, but your kids will consider this a very awesome part of town. Take the Tube to Camden Town and walk to your right.

Islington

The Tube stop for Islington is Angel, and you will be in heaven, especially on a Wednesday or Saturday, when you wander for awhile through fair Islington. You see, Wednesday and Saturday are market days, and there's an alley filled to overflowing with vendors—talk about charm galore. There's an indoor antiques market open every day, but the extra street (alley) action is what makes this fun. However, the population increase in nearby Clerkenwell (see below) has made Islington really boom. The high street has a branch of each multiple; there are plenty of pubs and cafes, from Mexican food to pizza; and then there's lots of real-people stuff (like pantyhose, Band-Aids, and sunscreen) as well.

The antiques market is sort of the tag-sale type with people setting up tables, even in the rain; there are also some shops. Prices are not giveaway. There are several vintage-clothing shops that may interest collectors. (Try **Cloud Cuckoo Land,** 6 Charlton Place, Camden Passage; and **Annie's,** 10 Camden Passage.)

I also like the **city market,** which is for real people and is no different from any other market, except that this is where I buy my **Arsenal** team luggage. If you are looking for anti-status luggage, you too may want to stock up on the lines offered by the football vendors.

All of these marvels are within walking distance of the Tube, so go and take cash. You're gonna love it.

If you are looking for more than the flea market, walk from the Tube station along Upper Street—there are many shops on Upper Street and in the area around where Upper Street gets to Cross Street.

Clerkenwell

Clerkenwell (say *Clarkenwall*) is breaking through as a neighborhood now and will be happening in the next few years—the area is now in transition and is part blue collar and ethnic unchic and part hot architecture and movin'-on-up money. It is still a commercial district where industrial buildings are being rehabbed for nonindustrial usage. Pick up any magazine that has a feature on the hot new areas of London, and you're certain to bump into news about Clerkenwell. Lots of photographers have moved in; there are restaurants such as **Stephen**

Bull Bistro—it's all very downtown New York. Retail is just beginning. Watch this space. *Note:* There isn't really any handy Tube stop. If you have a car and want to drive around to see the lovely brick architecture and what's happening—great. Otherwise, you can give it a miss until the shopping comes onboard.

Nonetheless, if you want to be part of it, you can book into a boutique hotel (**The Rookery,** Peter's Lane, Cowcross St., London EC1M 6DS; © **020/7336-0931;** fax 020/7336-0932).

Hampstead

To the north, and in a totally different frame of mind from the Docklands (below), is the wealthy suburb of Hampstead, charmingly located right off its own heath. For those who want to see what upper-middle-class London suburbs (with good shopping) are like, and for those who may be browsing for just the perfect neighborhood to move to, Hampstead is a must. Note that Hampstead had Sunday shopping long before everyone else, so it used to be a big Sunday-brunch kind of village, but now it's more of an insider's place.

Hampstead still has the feel of an English country village. The Tube station is very deep and sort of ugly; I have found it frightening. You'll fall in love only once you get to street level. Trust me on this.

After all, if it was good enough for Blake and Keats, it'll probably have something to please you, too. Beyond the immediate shopping area lies the famous Hampstead Heath. In nearby Highgate Cemetery, a number of famous folk are buried.

The Docklands

The term *Docklands* has come to refer to all development along both sides of the Thames, below Tower Bridge and stretching to Greenwich. However, the development on the south side of the river, where the Design Museum is located, is not actually in the thick of what is generally known as the Docklands; this is confusing if you are an out-of-towner.

Canary Wharf is the heart of the true Docklands, and it has changed enormously in the last few years—back from the dead, filled with a series of malls and all kinds of good shopping, especially of the local nature. This branch of **Tesco** has the makeup sponges I adore, which to me makes it worth the trip. The shopping has been developed in phases, so don't think you are limited to one building; oh no, this is shopping with attitude and altitude.

To get here, take the Jubilee line of the Tube; this is the most fun line because it's clean and everything works. *Note:* Do not get off at Canada Water because you are not paying attention— you want Canary Wharf.

Four Seasons has opened a second London hotel here, so the area is back in style and is going to bloom. Many people come here for the weekend in order to have a river view, be near the markets at Greenwich, shop the multiples without the London crowds, and enjoy the health club/spa.

Across the river from the Docklands and Four Seasons, at **Butler's Wharf,** there is a lot to see and do and think about. Meanwhile, **Oxo Tower** has happened, with its fancy-dancy restaurant and—someday—some shops. **Gabriel's Wharf** is a community of craftsmen (studios open Tues–Sun, 11am–6pm), although I found it dismally depressing. Someday, my love.

The best way to see it all is to go to the **Design Museum,** eat lunch at one of the several restaurants or cafes there (take your choice—they are all Conran establishments and something to behold), pop into a few of the hot new galleries, check out the **Oil & Spice Shop,** see the museums and their shops, and then take a boat and see the rest from the water.

Greenwich

Greenwich is more a suburb than a neighborhood. The Sunday retail used to be fabulous, but now that Sundays have changed shape in London and so much is available, it's not the fun it used to be. But flea-market freaks may enjoy the outing. There are also a good museum, some historical buildings, and a chance to walk under the River Thames.

Greenwich is on the regular tourist beat because the clipper ship *Cutty Sark* is anchored here. Probably as a result, there are many upscale places to eat and even branches of **Pizza Express** and **Starbucks.** There are other significant sights—such as the **National Maritime Museum** and the one-time royal residence, the **Queen's House,** designed by Inigo Jones and restored rather recently.

Do not take the Jubilee line to North Greenwich, thinking this will be the right place. Instead, take the Docklands Light Railroad to Cutty Sark, clearly marked, and you will be right where you want to be.

Chapter Six

....

LONDON RESOURCES A TO Z

ACCESSORIES

....

You don't need to be born to shop to know that the ground floor of any department store sells all the lines of accessories, or that just about every boutique brand sells some accessories . . . or that accessories are in the eye of the beholder.

That understood, this is a list of those stores or brands you might not know or may find particularly well stocked or well priced. Some specialize in one sort of fashion accessory or another. Hugh Grant, the ultimate British fashion accessory, is currently available, but not listed.

ACCESSORIZE
The Market, Covent Garden, WC2 (Tube: Covent Garden); and assorted trading areas all over London and the U.K.

This chain is a division of Monsoon and sells only accessories (duh) that are quite fashionable, quite well priced, and quite certainly going out of style in a year or two. Who cares? The colors and textures alone are enough to drive you wild with greed. Please note, a branch of Accessorize is often next door to a branch of Monsoon. Sometimes, Monsoon or Twilight (another division, all about evening wear) will have their own accessories. The tiny beaded handbags are to drool for.

DE BEERS
50 Old Bond St., W1 (Tube: Green Park).

Just to let you know that I haven't lost my sense of humor and I still think that dogs are a girl's best friend, then diamonds. And what an accessory.

LULU GUINNESS
3 Ellis St., SW1 (Tube: Sloane Sq.).

Lulu Guinness is one of a handful of handbag mavens in the cult heroine role in the British social ranks; she made her name with evening bags topped with flowers and has continued to produce clever and whimsical designs ever since. Prices are high; some of the line is sold in Bergdorf's in New York. This is the statement handbag that tells the world how clever you are. Also sold at Liberty in London.

MICHAELA FREY
62 Burlington Arcade, W1 (Tube: Piccadilly Circus).

This Viennese artist is known for her enamel bracelets and accessories and is rumored to make the enamelware for Hermès. Her specialty is historic art styles translated into cloisonné; the works are also sold at several museum shops.

OCTOPUS
130 King's Rd., SW3 (Tube: Sloane Sq.).

For all the latest in kitsch and oddities, Octopus is open for business in the name of art and nonsense. From frog-painted toasters to far-out watches and jewelry, this store has everything the imagination could muster, and a lot it couldn't. The handbags are truly unique designs with a fun edge. The bags cost about £15 ($25) and up depending on size. A great place to go for gifts, or just to stop in and marvel at the eccentric stock. *Note:* Other locations all over London.

BALLET

FREED OF LONDON LTD.
94 St. Martin's Lane, WC2 (Tube: Leicester Sq.).

If you are a ballet freak, you have long known of Freed of London, one of the most famous names in slippers and stuff. They also carry a dance and exercise line. The store is old and musty and not that charming, nor is the selection of leotards too great, but they do come with the hallmark of the Royal Ballet imprinted on them.

BEAUTY

See chapter 7 for an entire chapter devoted to London bath, beauty, and spa sources.

BIG NAMES (BRITISH)

What's a British big name? It's either a major designer or a manufacturer whose name connotes a look that others imitate, yet it's based in the United Kingdom and may not be known outside of London. Note that some of the major names do not have their own stores and are sold either at Browns (see below) or at department stores.

ALEXANDER MCQUEEN
4 Old Bond St., W1 (Tube: Green Park or Piccadilly Circus).

I'd like to tell you that Alexander McQueen is a creative genius and nut case who does not make wearable clothes and whose prices are so high that you may as well forget him. When I got to his new store, however, I almost fainted from the wave of creativity and the inspiration I received just from gazing in the windows. McQueen has joined the Gucci team—yes, he did leave Givenchy—but he keeps this line as his own little plaything.

AMANDA WAKELY
80 Fulham Rd., SW3 (Tube: S. Kensington).

Big for locals with moola; known for wedding dresses and special-event do's. Modern and not frou frou.

AQUASCUTUM
100 Regent St., W1 (Tube: Piccadilly Circus).

The "other" **Burberry,** Aquascutum has hired a young designer (Michael Herz) and is hopeful that he knows how to bring classic flash to this old-fashioned classic house.

Established in 1851, Aquascutum has grown from a tiny cottage industry to a major international name. Most people who go to London for the first time want to come home with an Aquascutum or Burberry raincoat. The Aquascutum line includes skirts, sweaters, and any accessory you could imagine. Instead of a plaid like Burberry's, Aquascutum is known for its checkered pattern.

ASPREY
167 New Bond St., W1 (Tube: Bond St. or Green Park).

Asprey has always been the place to go to buy a gift that needed some status behind the brand name. However, it was losing market share to Tiffany & Co. and more modern brands, so it did the only thing it could do: pinched execs from Tiffany's, closed the store for a year, and completely recast it. Now they sell designs by Jade Jagger.

BILLY BAG
This is a brand, not a store. I discovered it at **Selfridges,** but you may see their handbags in any fashion magazine. The look is hot; the price is even better—around £60 ($100) per.

BROWNS

23 S. Molton St., W1 (Tube: Bond St.); Browns Focus, 38 S. Molton, W1 (Tube: Bond St.).

Anytime you get the urge to pooh-pooh British fashion as dowdy, walk yourself right into Browns—the store, not the hotel—for a look-see at what has been London's temple of high fashion for decades. Browns is filled with a ready-to-wear selection from the top designers in Europe: **Sonia Rykiel, Jil Sander, Jean Muir,** and **Missoni** are all represented. Calvin Klein and Donna Karan were launched here before they went on to open their own stores in London.

This very chic and with-it shop is patronized by a very prestigious clientele that includes celebrities and movie stars.

Browns Focus is a shop to spotlight younger and hipper designers; a few of these lines are American (Lilly Pulitzer), but most are local.

Browns usually has a sale shop that continues to move, depending on where empty storefronts turn up in the area. Ask at the store. I visited a sale store and was horrified that they considered £78 ($129) for a blouse to be a bargain.

BURBERRY

Flagship store: 21–23 New Bond St., W1 (Tube: Bond St.); 165 Regent St., W1 (Tube: Piccadilly Circus); 3 Brompton Rd. (Tube: Knightsbridge); factory shop: 29–53 Chatham Place, E9; factory outlet shop: Bicester Village (p. 288).

In keeping with their new image, Burberry has begun to take over the world. A few years ago it was the new flagship store on New Bond; now they have Scotch House in Knightsbridge. Both stores are large and modern, made of layers of glass and levels of display; and feature everything known to man (or woman) that could be made in plaid. I happen to think the lavender braces (that's Brit-speak for suspenders) in the trad plaid are incredibly chic and well priced at £75 ($124), but the stores sell everything for you and your dog. For the factory store, take bus 55 (it's a long schlepp); also note that many old-fashioned Burberry styles—especially in traditional rain gear—are available in flea markets.

CAROLINE CHARLES
170 New Bond St., W1 (Tube: Bond St.).

Think taffeta and silk, dress-up, and veddy-veddy-but-still-gorgeous, and you've got the edge on Caroline Charles. Think Ascot and The Season and just the right hat-and-suit combination. You're back at Caroline Charles. There is an unwritten rule with British women that you can't go wrong with Caroline Charles, so if you're trying to impress the natives, one-stop shopping will do it.

CONNOLLY
41 Conduit St., W1 (Tube: Bond St. or Oxford Circus).

Connolly provides the leather to Rolls-Royce. It opened its first and only shop a few years ago but has now been bought by one of the most important style makers in the United Kingdom (which was able to expand the line into other leather categories, such as shoes).

DAKS
10 Old Bond St., W1 (Tube: Bond St.); 32–34 Jermyn St., SW1 (Tube: Piccadilly Circus).

Daks is the third of the plaid trio (along with Aquascutum and Burberry, above) that comes from a veddy, veddy old tradition but has modernized in order to survive. Its plaid is beige with a rust, taupe, and charcoal-grayish black tattersall. You will faint when you see how with-it this store is—eat your heart out, Miuccia Prada!

EATMYBAGBITCH
6 Dray Walk, 91–95 Brick Lane, E1 (Tube: Shoreditch).

Forgive me, I could not resist. This is a brand with limited distribution, although they have a store on Brick Lane near the Truman Brewery and a space in **Selfridges** in the lower level. It is not a handbag resource, despite the name. They sell antiques and fun stuff for the home, mostly from the '70s. Frankly, I like the name better than the merchandise, but I want you to feel plugged in, to be up-to-date on the latest. They take their stuff seriously and I must do so also.

FROST FRENCH

This is a brand—and one that gets so much press I thought I should mention it, although frankly my dears, I don't get it. It's underwear. As far as I am concerned, that's it. It's underwear. But the creators of the line are famous and everyone seems to think the creations are sexy and risqué and worth it. Carried in major department stores.

GEORGINA VON ETZDORF
Burlington Arcade, W1 (Tube: Piccadilly Circus or Green Park).

With hand-painted silks and scarves and items so yummy that they've caught on with the upper classes, von Etzdorf is now the darling of all with her own shop in Burlington Arcade. Her new line of handbags and totes are to swoon for; like all her prints, they are very colorful, swirly, artsy-fartsy, and wonderfully delish. Not for the shy.

JAEGER
204 Regent St., W1 (Tube: Piccadilly Circus or Oxford Circus).

If you have despaired that Jaeger had lost its touch, fret not— the line has been bought, has a new designer, and is going for a new look. The inspiration to it all is Audrey Hepburn.

The shop on Regent Street is almost a department store, with all the house lines, of which there are many. The newest is a knits range. Not only is this shop easy to find, but it also has everything.

One of the good things about the Jaeger line is that it is totally color-coordinated each season, so you can buy a complete wardrobe of interchangeable pieces, which is great for travel. The bad news is that if you don't like the color palette for a season, you're out of luck.

One warning: Jaeger may cost less in the United States! Shop carefully.

JOHN SMEDLEY
24 Brook St., W1 (Tube: Oxford Circus or Bond St.).

This is actually the first John Smedley store ever, despite the fact that this cult maker of fine knitwear is very well known in the U.K. The mills make great knits—woolens and cottons and cashmeres—but Smedley is most famous for its Sea Island cotton shirts. The store is very tiny and not too exciting visually, but there's more stock downstairs. Prices are high.

JOSEPH
74 Sloane Ave., SW3 (Tube: Sloane Sq.); 26 Sloane St., SW1 (Tube: Knightsbridge); Brompton Cross flagship store: 88 Peterborough Rd., SW6 (Tube: S. Kensington); 130 Draycott Ave., SW3 (near Brompton Cross; Tube: S. Kensington); 17 New Bond St., W1 (Tube: Bond St.); 23 Old Bond St., W1 (Tube: Green Park).

Not all Joseph stores were created equally, so attempt to see them all. Joseph Pour La Maison and various other Josephs around town have survived hard times and reflect the glory of their creator, Joseph himself. The man is incredibly inventive and creative. His nest of stores in Brompton Cross can still give you a visual stimulation that defines the best in hot British fashion, even though a raft of international labels is for sale. It's the look and the mix that make the show, and sometimes the copies from more expensive brands. The home style is zen-ish, before Armani Casa got there. And the cafes are a good place to hang. It's a lifestyle, man.

LAURA ASHLEY

7–9 Harriet St., SW1 (home furnishings only; Tube: Knightsbridge); 35–36 Bow St., Covent Garden, WC2 (Tube: Covent Garden); 256–258 Regent St., W1 (Tube: Oxford Circus); MacMillan House, Kensington High St., W8 (Tube: High St. Kensington); 449–451 Oxford St., W1 (Tube: Marble Arch or Bond St.); 120 King's Rd., SW3 (Tube: Sloane Sq.).

Goodbye little flowers, hello vamp with feathers. This firm is fighting to survive—so please, buy something. Regular prices at regular retail in London are substantially less than in the United States. Some of this stock is not sold in the United States. The line encompasses everything that has to do with the home and also a complete line of dresses, kids' wear, and sleepwear. Oh yes, they even have hats.

In the **Regent Street store,** which is the single best store, there is clothing on the street level and home furnishings upstairs; the store on **Harriet Street** (right off Sloane St.) is devoted entirely to home furnishings.

Note: The new look for those who do vintage and thrift is Laura Ashley from the 1970s.

MARGARET HOWELL

29 Beauchamp Place, SW3 (Tube: Knightsbridge).

Margaret Howell offers—to me, at least—the epitome of British-casual classy dressing. The clothes are expensive but so chic and elegant, so much the real subtext of what Ralph Lauren has always been able to capture and re-create. There are London dress-up clothes, but this resource is best for more casual, everyday clothes and for weekend chic—casual sweaters (hand-knit), twin sets, jackets, and coats. There's menswear at 34 Wigmore St., W1 (Tube: Bond St.).

MARY QUANT

3 Ives St., SW3 (Tube: S. Kensington); 7 Montpelier, SW7 (Tube: Knightsbridge).

It was a mod, mod world when Mary Quant came to fame in the swingin' '60s. When her clothes lost their cutting edge, her makeup line lived on, although it eventually went off the shelves in the United Kingdom. Now, Mary Quant makeup is back, and you can stop by to visit and stock up, or call for mail order (✆ 020/7581-5181).

Don't be thrown by the addresses—they are convenient. Ives is a tiny street right near Brompton Cross; it runs parallel to Walton Street. Montpelier is half a block from Harrods and on the way to Pandora's Alley, in the direction of the V&A museum.

MULBERRY

41–42 New Bond St., W1 (Tube: Bond St.); 171–175 Brompton Rd., SW3 (Tube: Knightsbridge or Brompton Cross).

They're at it again. Once upon a time you knew what this firm stood for, but they have re-invented themselves so many times I am flat out dizzy. When I last went in to check out the changes, I was floored. Everything is modern and the handbags have a distinctly Gucci feel—and price tag. Shop at your own risk.

NICOLE FARHI

158 New Bond St., W1 (Tube: Bond St.); 25–26 St. Christopher's Place, W1 (Tube: Bond St.); 193 Sloane St., SW1 (Tube: Knightsbridge); 27 Hampstead High St., NW3 (Tube: Hampstead); 11 Floral St., WC2 (Tube: Covent Garden).

This British designer does the elegant-working-woman look with New York panache and would fit well into the American scene. The tailored clothes are rich and simple, always elegant, but with sporty comfort. Branch stores are popping up so frequently that she may soon be considered a multiple. For those who like Armani but can't afford it, this line is less expensive than Armani, and can serve the same purpose.

Farhi's Bond Street showcase is in the modern style; her restaurant is the place to eat while on a shopping spree. They even serve breakfast!

Around the corner (17 Clifford St.) is the home-furnishings store, which does not impress me enormously. Still, if you need to give a gift to someone in the United Kingdom, this is a cult fave. There's a men's store at 11 Floral St., WC2 (Tube: Covent Garden).

PAUL COSTELLOE
156 Brompton Rd., SW1 (Tube: S. Kensington).

The flagship shop has opened, and expansion throughout the United Kingdom in free-standing stores is underway. Can global acceptance be far away? This Irish designer does wearable clothes that are suitable for work but have a nice sense of humor that's soft and pleasant. Good color palette.

PAUL SMITH
Westbourne House, 122 Kensington Park Rd., W11 (Tube: Notting Hill Gate).

That's Sir Paul to you. Although he began as a menswear designer offering funky chic before it existed, Smith was recently knighted for all his contributions to fashions and style, including women's wear and kid's styles, too. His main store is in a funky little house near Portobello Road, although his designs are sold all over the United Kingdom and in most London department stores.

The stores in Covent Garden (40–44 Floral St., WC2) sell menswear and children's wear. There is an outlet store (23 Avery Row, W1) for men's clothing, but I've never found it worth the visit.

STELLA MCCARTNEY
30 Bruton St., W1 (Tube: Bond St.).

Hard to imagine Stella without some of the big-name luggage that goes with her—she's Paul's daughter and is financed by **Gucci.** Tom Ford and **Madonna** are her best friends. Yet she's got her own four-story shop complete with a VIP salon and a separate scent room for her perfume. Worth taking a whiff, if only to see how the other half lives.

VIVIENNE WESTWOOD
41 Conduit St., W1 (Tube: Bond St. or Green Park); 6 Davies St., W1 (Tube: Bond St.); World's End, 430 King's Rd., SW10 (take the bus).

When American fashion lion John Fairchild made up his list of the most influential and important designers of our time, Vivienne Westwood headed it up. She invents shapes, moods, and concepts of dressing and produces slightly way-out clothes that age well, although they are more for the young and moneyed.

The Conduit Street shop is right in the heart of your Mayfair shopping time, so pop in. They do sell off the samples at the end of the season, and prices can be reasonable. This is Viv's version of a markdown shop or factory outlet. The new fragrance, Boudoir, is super.

VOYAGE
50–51 Conduit St., W1 (Tube: Bond St.); 33 Monmouth St., WC2 (Tube: Covent Garden).

For those of you who keep score on the most important "it" looks, Voyage was once riding high, especially with a little £360 ($600) cardigan sweater that was a must-have. The sweaters are out and can sometimes be found in resale shops, but the beat goes on. Voyage has closed their old shop in Fulham and opened this new one. The Portuguese couple who have created and designed the line from the beginning are still at it. Surely they have the next next thing.

BIG NAMES (INTERNATIONAL)

No shopping mecca is more international than London; no international resource can consider itself in the big time if it doesn't list a London address on its shopping bags. There are very few bargains in international merchandise here unless you hit a big sale. Prices may even be seriously better in the U.S.— think selection, not price.

Although American retailers and chain stores are opening right and left in London, don't think for a minute that you might save on American goods abroad. With very few exceptions, these stores offer merchandise that is much more expensive in the U.K. than in the United States. I go to **Gap** stores all the time just to laugh. The prices in pounds are the same as the prices in U.S. dollars at home. (If you want to bring a gift to someone in Britain, buy it at Gap in the U.S.)

I must also report that in **Harvey Nichols,** I did see merchandise from a major U.S. designer that I'd never seen in a U.S. store. Granted, I don't live in the shipping department of a major mall—but it seemed incredible to go to London to fall in love with an American outfit (at full British retail, no less). Academics may want to note that one of the ways Harvey Nichols likes to differentiate itself from other London department stores is that they are heavily committed to American designers and American brands.

ADOLFO DOMINGUEZ
129 Regent St., W1 (Tube: Piccadilly Circus).

AGNES B.
111 Fulham Rd., SW3 (Tube: S. Kensington); 235 Westbourne Grove, NW11 (Tube: Notting Hill Gate); 36 Floral St., WC2 (Tube: Covent Garden).

ALBERTA FERRETTI
205–206 Sloane St., SW1 (Tube: Knightsbridge).

BOTTEGA VENETA
33 Sloane St., SW1 (Tube: Knightsbridge).

CELINE
28 New Bond St., W1 (Tube: Bond St.); 27 Brompton Rd., SW3 (Tube: Knightsbridge).

CHANEL
173 New Bond St., W1 (Tube: Bond St.); 167–170 Sloane St., SW1 (Tube: Knightsbridge); Heathrow Departure Terminals 3 and 4.

CHLOE
152–53 Sloane St., SW1 (Tube: Knightsbridge).

CHRISTIAN DIOR
31 Sloane St., SW1 (Tube: Knightsbridge).

COMME DES GARCONS
59 Brook St., W1 (Tube: Bond St.).

DOLCE & GABBANA
6–8 Old Bond St., W1 (Tube: Green Park).

EMANUEL UNGARO
150 New Bond St., W1 (Tube: Bond St.).

EMPORIO ARMANI
187–191 Brompton Rd., SW3 (Tube: Knightsbridge); 51–53 New Bond St., W1 (Tube: Bond St.).

ERMENEGILDO ZEGNA
37 New Bond St., W1 (Tube: Bond St.).

ETRO
14 Old Bond St., W1 (Tube: Bond St.).

FENDI
20–22 Sloane St., SW1 (Tube: Knightsbridge).

FERRAGAMO
24 Old Bond St., W1 (Tube: Bond St.).

FOGAL
36 New Bond St., W1 (Tube: Bond St.).

GIANNI VERSACE
80 and 92 Brompton Rd., SW3 (Tube: Knightsbridge).

GIORGIO ARMANI
37 Sloane St., SW1 (Tube: Knightsbridge).

GUCCI
34–36 Old Bond St, W1 (Tube: Bond St. or Green Park);
17–18 Sloane St., SW1 (Tube: Knightsbridge).

HERMES
155 New Bond St., W1 (Tube: Bond St.); 179 Sloane St.,
SW1 (Tube: Knightsbridge).

ISSEY MIYAKE
52 Conduit St., W1 (Tube: Oxford Circus).

LOEWE
130 New Bond St., W1 (Tube: Bond St.).

LOUIS VUITTON
17–18 New Bond St., W1 (Tube: Bond St.).

MARINA RINALDI
39 Old Bond St., W1 (Tube: Bond St.).

MARNI
16 Sloane St., SW1 (Tube: Knightsbridge).

MAX MARA
32 Sloane St., SW1 (Tube: Knightsbridge); 153 New Bond St., W1 (Tube: Bond St.).

MIU MIU
123 New Bond St., W1 (Tube: Bond St.).

MOSCHINO
28–29 Conduit St., W1 (Tube: Bond St.).

PRADA
15–16 Old Bond St., W1 (Tube: Bond St.); 43–45 Sloane St., SW1 (Tube: Knightsbridge).

RODIER
106 Brompton Rd., SW3 (Tube: Knightsbridge).

SONIA RYKIEL
27–29 Brook St., W1 (Tube: Bond St.).

VALENTINO
160 New Bond St., W1 (Tube: Bond St.); 174 Sloane St., SW1 (Tube: Knightsbridge).

YOHJI YAMAMOTO
14 Conduit St., W1 (Tube: Oxford Circus).

YVES SAINT-LAURENT/RIVE GAUCHE
32–33 Old Bond St., W1 (Tube: Green Park); 33 Sloane St., SW1 (Tube: Knightsbridge).

BIG NAMES (NORTH AMERICAN)

Paul Revere's ghost could well be riding the Tube and shouting "The Americans are coming! The Americans are coming!"

Indeed, American brands have their own stores and are sold in the big department stores as if they were unique.

Tiffany & Co. and **Ralph Lauren** act like they have been here forever; **Gap** is everywhere. What is London coming to? There are now so many American retailers in London that I am not going to waste space listing them. I've already made it pretty clear how I feel about this shopping option.

For the architecturally curious, the **Donna Karan** store is drop-dead chic and gorgeous—possibly the most beautiful, spare-style store in London. You may also want to poke into the flagship **Ralph Lauren/Polo** (1 New Bond St., W1) because it's decorated in true Brit Ralph-style and is something to behold; there is a new and separate Ralph Lauren kids' store. But please, we didn't come here to buy American brands. For the curious, both Ralph and Donna have two different shops on Bond Street, so don't get confused.

BOOKS

Below are listings of booksellers who sell recently published books, bestsellers, and other titles in print. If it's first editions, rare or antiquarian books, or out-of-print titles you seek, please see chapter 9, "Antiques, Used Books & Collectibles," for antiquarian- and used-book sellers. For business books, try the major multiples or **Foyle** (see below). Note that there are also bookstores at LHR's Terminal 4. The only time you would be saving money, or even breaking even, on a British book is through an international edition (sold at airports and international train stations) or at discount shops, where you can sometimes get bestsellers in hardback for £11 ($18); see below. The real reason to buy in Britain is selection.

BORDERS
203 Oxford St., W1 (Tube: Oxford Circus).

Despite this being an American chain, they have a wide selection and fair prices—and this branch is located right next to SuperDrug, so you can kill a few shopping birds in the same tote bag. In the rear on the ground floor there are magazines, calendars, wrap, and small gift items. They seem to have the best prices (aside from the discount source below) on bestsellers.

BRITISH BOOKSHOPS & SUSSEX STATIONERS
530 Oxford St., W1 (Tube: Marble Arch).

This is a rather average-looking bookstore from the street, but it's a real find. They sell hardcover bestsellers at excellent prices (about 40% less than regular retail) . . . and at the same time as the major booksellers, so there's no wait to read your favorites. Many international authors (such as James Pattern, Michael Crichton, and so on) are printed in English in a U.K. edition and a U.S. edition; you may save on the U.K. edition when bought here. There's also nonfiction; some stationery items.

THE BUILDING BOOK SHOP
The Building Centre, 26 Store St., WC1 (Tube: Goodge St.).

For design freaks, this is the last word. Just camp out and order in. This is a bookstore for the design trade, with specialty books for architects, designers, do-it-yourselfers, and the like. It's more industrial than crafts, but you'll find something for everyone. On Saturday, it closes at 1pm.

DILLON'S
82 Gower St., WC1 (Tube: Goodge St.).

In London, Dillon's is to new books what Harrods is to everything else; they've also taken some American lessons from Barnes & Noble and even added cafes here and there. Consider that each year approximately 40,000 new titles are published in the English language. Dillon's has approximately 250,000 titles on hand at any one time. Dillon's lays no claim to being a discounter, but its policy has led to rapid expansion. There are now about 50 shops in the United Kingdom.

FOYLE
119 Charing Cross Rd., WC2 (Tube: Leicester Sq.).

Foyle is the largest bookstore in London, with more than 4 million volumes in stock. It's as crowded as ever, but the somewhat lackadaisical staff has been replaced by earnest and mostly helpful college students. There are large children's and fiction sections on the main floor, while upper floors are devoted to technical books, a small antiquarian library, and huge sections on hobbies, art, and commerce. The business section is particularly noteworthy.

HATCHARDS
187 Piccadilly, W1 (Tube: Piccadilly Circus).

Looking for me in London? Stop by Hatchards at Piccadilly. I spend part of almost every visit to London here. Far and away the most complete of the modern booksellers, the main Hatchards is in a town house near **Fortnum & Mason** and is filled with just about everything. The store is owned by **Dillon's** as a sort of boutique bookstore. There are bigger stores in London, but I like the size of this one, and I love its travel section.

WATERSTONE'S BOOKSELLERS
88 Regent St., W1 (Tube: Piccadilly Circus); 99–101 Old Brompton Rd., SW7 (Tube: Knightsbridge); 193 Kensington High St., W8 (Tube: High St. Kensington); 121–125 Charing Cross Rd., WC2 (Tube: Tottenham Court Rd.).

A chain—but with a large selection of everything and many locations near the shopping areas to which you gravitate. This is simply a good basic source for extra guidebooks (no one can survive in London without an *A to Z*), books for airplane reading, and art books.

ZWEMMER
Oxford University Press Bookshop, 72 Charing Cross Rd., WC2 (Tube: Leicester Sq.).

ZWEMMER ART (FINE ARTS)
24 Litchfield St., WC2 (Tube: Leicester Sq.).

ZWEMMER BOOKSHOP (GRAPHIC ARTS)
80 Charing Cross Rd., WC2 (Tube: Leicester Sq.).

Zwemmer has three stores in Charing Cross: (1) the Oxford University Press Bookshop, company store for one of the most respected publishers in the world; (2) a shop across the street devoted to the graphic arts—illustration, photography, and so on (there were three different books on Issey Miyake the last time we looked); and (3) a shop devoted to the fine arts.

BUTTONS

BUTTON QUEEN
19 Marylebone Lane, W1 (Tube: Bond St.).

You have to go back a little farther than the tourist mainstream to find this shop, but it's convenient enough for you to go for it—especially if you sew, knit, or collect. The small shop has everything in buttons, from old to new, hand-painted to Wedgwood. The **Wedgwood** set is rather pricey, but other prices do begin at about a quarter per button. If you are considering making a sweater or having one made from a designer kit, come by here to get the buttons.

The store is only 2 blocks from Oxford Street, so don't let the address throw you. Get there through Cecil Court, and you won't mind the walk.

CHILDREN'S CLOTHING

Please note that there is a recent trend for the midrange multiples to add on clothing lines for kids, or at least for little girls. Some of these have free-standing stores (**Jigsaw Junior**); others, such as **Monsoon,** just have a few racks someplace in the rear of the store. **Brora** cashmeres for kiddies are incredible, as are the prices (see store listing later in this chapter), and Paul Smith for children is worth a look.

CARAMEL
291 Brompton Rd., SW3 (Tube: S. Kensington).

What would the British economy have done if Madonna hadn't moved to town and/or married an Englishman? The mother of two, Madonna is always on the prowl for funky fashions and has turned many a minor resource into a landmark. Most of the things in this store are designed by the Greek owner, who was disheartened by kids who only wore frills or Gap togs. Her house collection is called Caramelbaby & Child. Madonna bought young Rocco a pair of cashmere trousers for just over $100. Oy.

LA CIGOGNA
6A Sloane St., SW1 (Tube: Knightsbridge).

I am utterly amazed that La Cigogna has survived. The store stands for everything the 1980s stood for: overdressed kids in expensive togs. This shop is loaded with all those wonderful Italian designer clothes and shoes that very few of us can possibly afford and that few hip children even want to wear. But if you have a special occasion or are able to splurge, this is the place. If you have a daughter, the gorgeous array of party dresses seems endless.

OILILY
10 Sloane St., SW1 (Tube: Knightsbridge).

Dutch designer line known for its bright colors and twisty-twirly prints that combine whimsy with sophistication.

PETITE BATEAU
106–108 King's Rd., SW3 (Tube: Sloane Sq.); 62 S. Molton St., W1 (Tube: Bond St.).

CIGARS

A woman is a woman, but a cigar is a smoke—everyone knows that. And everyone who knows it has known it for a very long time, far longer than the current trend toward events called "smokers," which are actually PR events created by hotels and/or cigar-selling stores to boost interest and sales. Not to worry, London has long been a leading cigar capital of the world. That is partly because Cuban cigars are not illegal in Britain. Because it is currently illegal to bring in or sell Cuban cigars in the United States, my reporting on this subject is going to be limited.

However, there are a few major cigar retailers in London, and you can discuss your needs specifically with them. I happen to like to hang out at **Davidoff** because the men who shop there are so handsome. But don't mind me. **Harrods** and **Selfridges** also sell cigars.

DAVIDOFF
35 St. James's St., SW1 (Tube: Green Park).

From Geneva, Davidoff has shops in all the major capitals. Its London shop is on the corner of St. James Street right near Jeremy Street, firmly entrenched in Man Territory. The atmosphere is not as forbiddingly formal as Dunhill.

DUNHILL
30 Duke St., SW1 (Tube: Piccadilly Circus).

Alfred Dunhill is more than a cigar shop, but it does have cigars, humidors, and smoking paraphernalia galore on the mezzanine, where the atmosphere is masculine and clubby. If you're looking for the perfect gift for the man who has everything, surely one of Viscount Linley's bespoke humidors will do the trick. (Non–royal watchers will note that David Linley is the son of Princess Margaret and a major force in new British design.)

JJ Fox
19 St. James's St., SW1 (Tube: Piccadilly Circus).

Old cigar hands may know this shop as Robert Lewis. JJ Fox is the newer name. Indeed, we are talking about a merger here, the joining of two of London's top cigar dealers, James J. Fox and Robert Lewis. Now then, if you think Dunhill is intimidating, you have not visited this clubby little nook, where men speak Cohiba in quiet tones.

The setup is simple: There's a smoking club on two floors, and the ground floor is devoted to sales. And yes, there's a cigar museum. This is the shop noted for its Churchill memorabilia—Winston Churchill opened his account here in 1900 and used it right up until a month before he died, 64 years later.

COMPACT DISCS & TAPES

The London retail music scene is an accurate reflection of the music recording business itself: What was once a vital, creative maelstrom has become ho-hum and predictable, with a few giant megabuck companies dominating. Independent companies survive, if at all, by specializing. The three heavyweights—HMV, Tower, and Virgin—have all the amenities and services you'd expect to find in a warehouse, but they do have a mammoth selection, literally something for every taste. Virgin and HMV stores open at 9:30am and stay open until at least 7pm. Tower is even more accessible—open from 9am to midnight.

Since specialty shops are often haunts for collectors, listings for record dealers and other independently owned new and used CD, tape, LP, and 78 shops appear in chapter 9, "Antiques, Used Books & Collectibles."

There are some illegal DVDs sold in flea markets and street markets. My favorite such shopping experience was in Brick Lane, where I asked the vendor how I could know his DVD would even work. He whipped out a tiny DVD player from under his shirt and volunteered to let me watch some of the show. *Reminder:* Buying pirated DVDs is against the law.

HMV

150 Oxford St., W1 (Tube: Oxford Circus); 363 Oxford St., W1 (Tube: Bond St. or Marble Arch); 18 Coventry St. (Trocadero), W1 (Tube: Piccadilly Circus).

TOWER RECORDS

1 Piccadilly Circus, W1 (Tube: Piccadilly Circus); 62–64 Kensington High St., W8 (Tube: High St. Kensington).

VIRGIN MEGASTORE

14–30 Oxford St., W1 (Tube: Oxford Circus); 100 Oxford St., W1 (Tube: Tottenham Court Rd.); 527 Oxford St., W1 (Tube: Marble Arch).

CRAFTS

BRIDGEWATER POTTERY CAFE

735 Fulham Rd., SW6 (Tube: Parsons Green); Bridgewater (sans cafe and perhaps more convenient), 81A Marylebone High St., W1 (Tube: Marylebone).

This is not really for tourists, but if you are traveling with your kids and it's pouring (welcome to London), you might want to know about this do-it-yourself pottery shop, like the ones in the U.S. where you paint your own ceramics. Of course, they then have to be fired, so you will have to either return or arrange shipping. They have shops in Milan, Stoke-on-Trent, and Edinburgh and are open 7 days a week. And yes, they do birthday parties.

CRAFTS COUNCIL

At V&A, Cromwell Rd., SW9 (Tube: S. Kensington); Gallery Shop, 44A Pentonville Rd., Islington, N1 (Tube: Angel).

When I go to Islington, it's always for the flea market; when I go to the gift shop in the V&A, I always make sure to go to the rear of the store, where the Crafts Council has several showcases. It also arranges special exhibits.

THE TRUST SHOP
King's Walk Shopping Mall, 122 King's Rd., SW3 (Tube: Sloane Sq.).

Located in perhaps the world's most boring mall—possibly rents here are low—this shop sells crafts made by those who have been put into business by Prince Charles via the Prince's Trust, a nonprofit organization.

DEPARTMENT STORES

American department stores are mostly patterned on British ones, so you will feel right at home in just about any department store in London. All are in big, old-fashioned buildings and offer the kind of social security that enables you to know you could live in them. Most department stores have several restaurants or tearooms (and they all have clean bathrooms, although Harrods makes you either pay to use the loo or show a sales slip to prove you have bought something).

During the Christmas shopping days, department stores are open later than usual, which may mean until 7pm. They are rarely open until 9pm. Other than at Christmastime, department stores have 1 night a week—either Wednesday or Thursday—during which they stay open until 7pm or possibly 8pm, and just maybe 9pm; but a store that stays open that late is more than likely to be some kind of alternative retailing source, not a traditional department store.

All department stores have export desks that will help you with VAT forms; all department stores allow you to collect your receipts over a period of time to qualify for the VAT. Some may charge £4 to £6 ($6.60–$9.90) for the administrative work they must do on their end. The minimum amount of money you must spend to qualify for a VAT refund varies dramatically from department store to department store.

When you go to the VAT desk in any given store, allow some time not only for getting your paperwork processed, but also for standing in line while others ahead of you are dealing with theirs. If you can move right through, the process will take about 10 minutes. Do have your passport on hand or know your number by heart.

Note that many of the stores have attempted to reinvent themselves in the last few years and may be quite different from the way you remember them. The biggest changes are at Debenhams, Liberty, and Selfridges.

BRITISH HOME STORES (BHS)
252 Oxford St., W1 (Tube: Bond St.).

This is a big department store geared toward young families on a budget; it's snazzier than Kmart. The casual clothes for weekends may be OK or even fine and they have clothes for working women as well. The kids' clothes are cute; the home-furnishings items are worth a look-see for real-people products. But wait, I have found disposable fashion here—hot-weather clothes, weekend clothes, things that you don't want to pay more than £10 ($17) for. So don't write it off. Just enter with care. The main store is on Oxford Street, but there are branches around London and the United Kingdom. I call it the poor man's M&S.

DEBENHAMS
334–338 Oxford St., W1 (Tube: Oxford Circus).

Of the few look-alike department stores on Oxford Street (there are three or so of them, all of which are virtually indistinguishable from one another), this one is the best and the most American, although in my heart of hearts I dream that they will call me and ask me to take over the store, and I will then turn it into Target.

Lowest level: men's; **ground floor:** cosmetics and accessories; *one:* lingerie, women's formal, and women's shoes; *two:* home furnishings; *three:* kids, toys, cafe, and toilets.

DICKINS & JONES
224 Regent St., W1 (Tube: Oxford Circus).

Totally renovated and invigorated in an attempt to be the Harvey Nicks of Regent Street. Dickins & Jones is the high-end House of Fraser entry. The store has just had a major face-lift and wants very much to be taken seriously by milady. It has an excellent ground-floor cosmetics department as well as new emphasis on home furnishings and decorative touches, although the higher you go in the store, the more the modernization falls apart.

The store specializes in big-name designers and snazzy clothes from the middle range of these designers—variations from Yves Saint-Laurent, not the Rive Gauche line; Mugler Pour Mugler, not Thierry Mugler couture. They have two hat departments. Newest addition: a Michel Roux tearoom.

Lower ground: men's and luggage; *ground floor:* accessories and cosmetics; *one:* designers; *two* and *three:* women's; *four:* home style, kids, powder room, and spa.

FENWICK
63 New Bond St., W1 (Tube: Bond St.).

I adore Fenwick (say *Fennick*). In fact, I almost count it as my favorite stop on Bond Street. I've shopped Fenwick top to bottom and am happy to say this is a great source for affordable designer bridge lines, cheap-junk fashion looks, and terrific hair accessories. It now has a branch of Carducci's in the basement for quick eats.

The store isn't as large as a full-size department store, so you can give it a quick once-over and not be exhausted.

Lower ground floor: men's; *ground floor:* cosmetics, handbags, accessories, hat shop, and designer goods; *one* and *two:* designer collections; *three:* weekend collections and toilets.

FORTNUM & MASON
181 Piccadilly, W1 (Tube: Piccadilly Circus).

Your visit to Fortnum & Mason actually begins before you enter the store—the clock outside is very, very famous, so stand back and take a look. Then go through the revolving doors into a food emporium of fun.

Like many of the old department stores, Fortnum & Mason began (in 1707) as a grocery store; its founder, William Fortnum, was a footman in the household of Queen Anne. He collected and traded the used candle ends from the palace and saved his funds until he could open his own shop. He persuaded Hugh Mason, who owned a small shop in St. James's Market, to become his partner, and thus began Fortnum & Mason.

The firm's great success during the empire's reign had to do with supplying goods not only in London, but also to British families overseas. In the Victorian era, Fortnum & Mason also became famous for its fine-quality preserved fruits, jellies, and hams. Its hampers are a must for a status Christmas gift or for the picnics that you must eat (in the car park, no less) when you attend Royal Ascot or any of the events of The Season. Order ahead.

If you are curious about the rest of the store, you should be. It is like walking onto a movie set—as if nothing has changed since before World War II. Except the styles, which are actually chic and very much more with-it than you can imagine. A real find.

Lower level: china, glass, and silver; ***ground floor:*** foodstuffs; ***one:*** ladies' fashions and perfume; ***two:*** bedroom and cosmetics; ***three:*** gentlemen; ***four:*** antiques and collectors.

HARRODS
Brompton Rd., Knightsbridge, SW1 (Tube: Knightsbridge).

If you are serious about spending time in Harrods, pick up its free *Store Guide* at any of the doors—there are detailed maps to all of the floors and even a two-page list of the customer services offered within the store, which really is a city unto itself.

I have my own love-hate thing with Harrods. I hate to send you here if you have limited time or if you think this is the best store in London, yet I love to shop here for a few brief shining moments every time I'm in London. And the **food halls?** I could just move in.

There is no question that this store is a landmark and that it offers one hell of a lot of merchandise. The china department and the food halls are what become legends most; the children's toy department is almost as good as **Hamley's.**

Before I even give you the scoop on what's inside, let's hope that you can indeed enter the store to see it for yourself. It has recently enlarged its list of no-nos for visitors and enforces a very strict dress code. I got a postcard from an angry reader who said she was denied entrance because of her backpack. Jeans that are torn—even fashionably so—are on the banned list.

The food halls, located on the ground floor, are internationally known, with 17 departments in all. The department store itself covers 4½ acres of land and has 15 acres of selling space. This is good to remember when your feet are telling you to stop, but you don't even feel that you've made a dent in the store.

Ground floor: food halls, perfume, cosmetics, fashion accessories, jewelry, stationery, and clocks; *lower ground:* men's, gifts, stationery, and theatre tickets; *one:* women's clothing and shoes; *two:* china, glass, books, records, and housewares; *three:* furniture; *four:* children's and toys; *five:* sporting goods, hair, and beauty.

Don't forget that Harrods prides itself on being a full-service department store. Therefore, on the lower level, you will find a complete travel agency, export department, London Tourist Board office, bank, and theater-ticket agency. There is a hair salon upstairs on five; it opens at 9am, even though the store opens at 10am.

Harvey Nichols

Knightsbridge (corner of Sloane St.), SW1 (Tube: Knightsbridge).

Although Knightsbridge's other department store is much smaller than **Harrods,** it makes up for size with quality. It concentrates its energy on the latest high fashions for men, women, and children. Harvey Nichols, frankly, is a *real* store—not a tourist trap trading on an old reputation. Its styles are always the latest, and most of the major design houses are represented; there are lots of American designers.

Before we go any further, you must now repeat after me: Harvey Nicks. That's what you call the store. Anything else will label you a foreigner immediately.

I have checked out the hat department of every department store in London, and this is the single best one. It's not huge, and it's not overly dramatic—it's simply solid. I also like the home-decor floor with its own **Nina Campbell** boutique; the fifth floor—named "The Fifth Floor"—has the new food hall and a hotshot restaurant called, get this, **The Fifth Floor.** There is also a place for coffee, a snack, sushi, or a quick lunch between the fancy eats and the food halls, also on the fifth floor.

Speaking of food, the noodle bar on the lower level is a must-do.

Lower level: men's and noodle bar; *one:* hats, cosmetics, and accessories; *two* and *three:* women's fashions; *four:* home furnishings; *five:* food hall and restaurants.

House of Fraser

318 Oxford St., W1 (Tube: Bond St.).

Just like the old Macy's or the large department store of your coming of age, Evans has a good selection of its own private-label items and many designer names in promotional sections of the store where these especially made clothes are sold. The ceilings are low, and the store is more dense, so it's not as glamorous as other stores. In fact, I am not at all sure how they stay in business. The basement-level shop named Therapy is for teens & 'tweens and is fun.

Ground floor: cosmetics, accessories; *one:* men's fashions; *two:* women's and lingerie; *three:* women's, bridal, and children's; *four:* silver and kitchen; *five:* furniture.

JOHN LEWIS
278 Oxford St., W1 (Tube: Bond St.).

John Lewis is one of the many department stores standing on Oxford Street. By the time you get there, your eyes are beginning to cross, and you have no solid idea of why there are so many look-alike department stores on Oxford Street. But this store is somewhat different—it's a real-people store with a stiff upper lip. While it has fashion, it's much more of a meat-and-potatoes store. And there is a small stroke of quirkiness that makes the store a delight.

I like the ground floor—a source for high-fashion Alice bands (hair bands) at very moderate prices: £4 to £5 ($6.60–$8.25). In their drugstore (far corner), I buy small, plastic, travel-size containers for all my goods and potions.

Warning: This store does not take credit cards or bank cards—only cash or its own store card.

Basement: china and glass; *ground:* pharmacy, accessories, and crafts; *one:* fashion fabrics and women's fashion; *two:* home and bed; *three:* furniture; *four:* children's (includes prams); *five:* garden center.

LIBERTY
210–220 Regent St., W1 (Tube: Oxford Circus).

Oh my! The front part of Liberty was closed for renovations and I missed them; then they re-opened and I still miss them. The store is almost new wave in its contemporary feel and I am not used to it at all. But that doesn't mean there's anything wrong—the front of the store just looks too much like Barney's in New York to me. Still, it is gorgeous.

I personally prefer the Tudor-style Liberty building in the rear, which has a fabulous old-fashioned, market spree, visual feast feel to it.

Note: Only the first floor wraps around to connect the two buildings.

Tudor Building (rear): *lower ground:* men's and Oriental; *ground:* accessories and gifts; *one:* women's; *two:* home; *three:* furniture. Regent Street (front): *lower ground:* men's; *ground:* cosmetics, fragrance, and beauty; *one:* women's shoes.

LILLYWHITES
Piccadilly Circus, W1 (Tube: Piccadilly Circus).

Lillywhites is a small department store for sporting goods. All brand names (of sportswear and equipment) are sold, including America's and Europe's finest. There aren't any bargains in this store, but the selection is enough to keep your head spinning at Olympic speed. There is also equipment and outfitting for sports that are not played in the United States, so you can get quite an education. Snooker, anyone?

Ground floor: track suits; *one:* shoes; *two:* gym; *three:* books, video, and ski; *four:* racket sports; *five:* darts, snooker, watersports, shooting, and riding.

MARKS & SPENCER
458 Oxford St., W1 (Tube: Bond St.).

What a difference a day makes—or a year or two. M&S is back from the dead and even has some style to sell, along with the bread-and-butter clothing items. Their food divisions have always been fabulous, but now the clothes and many beauty products are making news. There are some lines created by famous designers, some lines that are exclusives that are available for only a few weeks, and there are the old faithfuls too. I've come back to Marks because they carry large sizes and have fashion basics at fair prices—this does not mean cheap prices. I pay about $50 for a pair of jeans, which I find high.

The Marble Arch flagship is by far the best—best selection and best renovation.

Lower level: supermarket; *ground floor:* makeup, women's clothing, Limited Collection, and Autograph Collection; *one:* ladies' formal, lingerie, plus sizes, and coats; *two:* men's and cafe; *three:* home style, luggage, books, videos, CDs, and cafe.

PETER JONES
Sloane Sq., SW1 (Tube: Sloane Sq.).

Another makeover, another contemporary scene. I really like Peter Jones for the trimmings, fabrics, and bed linens. That may sound like a strange combination, but these three departments are all strung together and make a great half-hour stop before you tackle King's Road or after you've shopped Sloane Street. Note, while most of the renovation is over, some departments have been relocated to a nearby space called PJ2; there is a free shuttle bus. For the most part, PJ2 represents the larger home-style items such as furniture and may not be a tourist destination.

I stick to the ground floor mostly, which is changed but still enormously fun. The sheets (and duvet covers) come in colors we simply don't get at home—solid colors, but high-fashion solid colors with a range not seen in America. There must be five or six different shades of green alone. But wait: Every year I get a query or two asking where to get an old-fashioned English pram. Answer: third floor of Peter Jones.

Frankly, most of the store bores me, but the basement kitchen and tabletop could be worth a look-see. This is one of the department stores that is *not* open on Sundays; weekday and Saturday hours are 9:30am to 7pm.

Ground floor: sheets and bedding, fabrics, and bath; *basement:* china, bathroom accessories, kitchenware, and stationery; *one:* hats, hosiery, and fashion accessories; *two:* fashion, lingerie, and nightgowns; *three:* children's; *four:* menswear and travel; *five:* fashion fabrics, silver, and needlework; *six:* toilets and restaurant.

SELFRIDGES
400 Oxford St., W1 (Tube: Marble Arch or Bond St.).

Selfridges is surely the Avis Rent-a-Car of Britain: There's no question that they try harder. In the last few years, the store has all but reinvented itself and has worked hard to upgrade the image and the merchandise. Many now say it's the best department store in Britain.

The store has a branch of **Miss Selfridge,** the store for teens and 'tweens, and is most famous for its ground floor and enormous makeup department. Also within Selfridges is a new Louis Vuitton store and a separate Prada shop. It's all here. The store also has a good magazine selection on the ground floor and a small food department, so it's a convenient place to do some "real" shopping. There's also a pharmacy. In short, the store has everything.

Upstairs is a new shopping area called The West Village, which sells many U.S. brands. (This a big breakthrough in Britain but possibly not too interesting to an American tourist.)

Basement: housewares; *ground floor:* food halls (not as interesting as Harrods, but fine for picnic supplies), cosmetics, accessories, paper goods, magazines, young fashions, and Miss Selfridge; *one:* export bureau and men's clothing; *two:* women's clothing (designers); *three:* kids' clothing; *four:* sportswear.

Selfridges has three restaurants, four coffee shops, and a juice bar. At 3:30pm, a gong is rung, and teatime is on.

FOODSTUFFS

A trip to any supermarket is always fun. If you are returning to the United States from the United Kingdom, you need to know what you can and can't bring back legally. Most of the department stores have food halls: The most famous (and rightly so) are at **Harrods,** but **Harvey Nicks** has interesting choices, and **Selfridges** has expanded its market. Most **M&S**

stores also have a grocery store. Note that M&S carries only their brand of foodstuffs.

The main supermarket names often have stores—be they small ones—in areas where a tourist may be shopping. **Tesco Metro** has stores on Oxford Street and one in Covent Garden. There is a **Safeway** and a **Waitrose** on King's Road. Canary Wharf, which is out of town but has a big mall and shopping area, also has fabulous grocery stores. If you are a true supermarket devotee, you may want to go to the Tesco on Cromwell Road—you will need a car or taxi and an arranged pick-up.

M&S is opening 50 **Simply Food** stores in the next few years; the test store is open at 55 Tottenham Court Rd., W1 (Tube: Goodge St.). Watch this space.

In spring, summer, or early fall, I urge foodies to take time to explore **Borough Market,** which is a small but atmospheric food market with fresh farm produce, imports from France, wines, a fish restaurant (named **Fish**), and street foods galore. Open only on Friday and Saturday (Tube: London Bridge). This may bore your kids, but if you care about the colors of food and the energy of a marketplace, this is for you—note the rumble of the train as it goes by, the peeling of the church bells next door, and the free wine tastings. Chorizo sandwiches are worth the wait.

CHARBONNEL ET WALKER
1 The Royal Arcade, 28 Old Bond St., W1 (Tube: Green Park).

Chocolatier that also makes powdered chocolate in a fancy tin for hot chocolate; great gift to bring home. During The Season they make strawberries dipped in cream and chocolate.

FORTNUM & MASON
181 Piccadilly, W1 (Tube: Piccadilly Circus).

See p. 146.

O & CO.
Covent Garden Market, 26A, The Piazza, WC2 (Tube: Covent Garden); 114 Ebury St., SW1 (Tube: Sloane Sq.).

O & Co., also known as Oliviers & Co., is a purveyor of all things olive—from oils to soaps—and was created by the same French genius who brought us l'Occitane. The olive oils are fabulous and much less pricey in Europe than in the United States: some £15 ($25) here and $36 in the United States.

PAXTON & WHITFIELD
93 Jermyn St., SW1 (Tube: Piccadilly Circus).

Photo op of a small store, carries mostly cheese but other foodstuffs as well.

R TWINING & CO.
216 The Strand, WC2 (Tube: Charing Cross).

There is no name more famous around the world for their tea; they also try to stay on top of food trends with line extensions, such as iced tea, and so on. Fun to browse, good selection, great for gifts. On the other hand, the brand is widely available in the U.S., so look for the unusual items.

THORNTON'S
254 Regent St., W1 (Tube: Oxford Circus); Covent Garden; and many others.

This is a mass-market maker of chocolates and candy items. I spent years addicted to their toffee, which comes in many flavors (I prefer "original"). They will personalize chocolate with a name or message written in frosting.

WHITTARD
Carnaby St., W1 (Tube: Oxford Circus); 209 Kensington High St., W8 (Tube: Kensington High St.); and many others.

This is a large multiple that sells tea, but also teacups, mugs, and gift items. They have excellent graphic designs and could be a good source for gift items at a fair price.

MALLS

....

The British do malls well in terms of Pall Mall; but as for shopping malls, don't hold your breath. Locals are keen on the new **Duke of York Mall;** it bored me to tears. Still, if you insist— this mall is right on King's Road (Tube: Sloane Sq.) where the Duke of York's headquarters used to be.

MULTIPLES (BRITISH)

....

A few successful chain stores dominate British retail, but don't look now: With money and finances as screwy as they have been in the last year or two, some of the most popular high-street merchants are fighting to stay alive. Many are closing branch stores, although basically there's still one of these shops on every high street in every main shopping neighborhood in London.

There are so many of them that they call them, uh, multiples. In the British business press, these stores are referred to as "high-street multiples" because they are usually found on the high street of every town.

AUSTIN REED
103–113 Regent St., W1 (Tube: Piccadilly Circus).

A chain of stores selling men's and women's traditional (read: boring) British clothing from the big makers—this is the place to shop if the Brit look—in its most conservative incarnation— is your need. Branch stores tend to be in need of renovation. All the sturdy and steadfast British big names are sold through these stores; you can sometimes bump into something fashionable.

If you have been invited to partake in The Season or if you are going to a social or business function at which you must look British, this is an excellent resource—you can't go wrong. You will find clothing here that you will enjoy wearing and that will help you "fit in."

Some branches of Austin Reed open early in the morning for the business crowd running an errand or two on the way to the office.

DOROTHY PERKINS
311 Oxford St., W1 (Tube: Oxford Circus).

Petite clothes are sold in specialty parts of some of the major department stores, but this high-street multiple is devoted to the smaller sizes and sells clothes for the professional woman at low-to-moderate prices (for Britain, anyway). They've changed the range slightly to include some street fashions as well.

EAST
103 King's Rd., SW3 (Tube: Sloane Sq.).

Everyday looks that have a slightly exotic feel to them because they are made in India and have more than a few details in common with style from Kenzo. This is a lifestyle fashion store—dress-up, casual, and weekend wear at moderate prices.

FRENCH CONNECTION
249 Regent St., W1 (Tube: Oxford Circus).

I spent years thinking this was a French firm, so sophisticates beware—this line is not only British, but is also made by the same firm that owns designer Nicole Farhi. Furthermore, they have now opened a flagship store right on Regent Street, and I giggle with delight every time I think of their ad campaign that just said: FCUK. Go ahead, you figure it out.

The line specializes in wearable fashions that have a touch of trendy around the edges but are not over the top. Prices are meant to be midrange, but in the United Kingdom that means they start out high. Sale prices may be more impressive. The store carries men's and women's clothing.

JANE NORMAN
153 Oxford St., W1 (Tube: Bond St.); 262 Oxford St., W1 (Tube: Oxford Circus); and others.

Low-end hot stuff.

JIGSAW
21 Long Acre, Covent Garden, WC2 (Tube: Covent Garden); 65 Kensington High St., W8 (Tube: High St. Kensington); 449 The Strand, WC2 (Tube: Charing Cross); 124 Kings Rd., SW3 (Tube: Sloane Sq.); 31 Brompton Rd., SW3 (Tube: Knightsbridge).

Jigsaw is a fashion chain selling hip-but-wearable fashion for women; many of the designs have been inspired by the latest big-money Euro trends. The line is such that a lot of merchandise is on the cutting edge (which means good, frequent sales) and much of it is for women under 40. Prices are moderate, the stores are always high-tech chic, and there's always something to see and be impressed with—even if you are just sizing up the hot looks. This chain is just beginning to move into the international market. Don't leave Britain without checking out at least one of these stores. They also do a men's range as well as Jigsaw Juniors for preteen girls.

MISS SELFRIDGE
40 Duke St., W1 (Tube: Bond St.); multiple addresses around town.

I could go on at great length about this store. And really, you haven't shopped London until you've seen these clothes. There is a Miss Selfridge department in the main **Selfridges** store, but there are numerous free-standing Miss Selfridge stores all over London. Its specialty is the young, kicky look at inexpensive prices—this is a find for teens or those who want to dabble in a trendy look without spending too much money. Latest addition: a Miss Selfridge shop inside the **TopShop** (see below) at Oxford Circus.

MONSOON
67 S. Molton St., W1 (Tube: Bond St.); 5 James St., Covent Garden, WC2 (Tube: Covent Garden); multiple addresses around town.

A chain of low-to-moderate-priced women's fashions made in India in current styles but of fabrics inspired by the mother country (India) and therefore gauzy, colorful, sometimes ethnic (but not always), and very distinctive. The look is very popular in the 'tweens-through-20s set. The business is so gigantic, and so popular during hard times, that there are now spin-offs, such as a chain of small stores called **Accessorize** selling only accessories, and a small chain for dress-up clothes named, appropriately, **Twilight.**

PRINCIPLES
The Plaza, Oxford St., W1 (Tube: Oxford Circus); multiple addresses around town.

Hot, with-it fashions at low (for Britain) prices, with plenty of designer knockoffs and in-step accessories. Many of the stores look—from the outside—like Next; don't be confused because the looks inside are definitely different.

TOPSHOP
214 Oxford St., W1 (Tube: Oxford Circus).

Now then, there are small branch stores of TopShop around London, but I don't want you to go to them until you have "done" the mother ship because you won't understand what I am raving about.

TopShop is simply heaven for those who love the latest looks at the lowest prices—this is a supermarket of cheap clothes with styles for men and women, or boys and girls, if you will. For some dumb reason, the men's clothes are on the street level on Oxford Street, so you may not even be tempted to go inside. Mistake.

Go in, go down, and gawk. Every possible trend has been translated into two floors of women's cheapie fashions, and you will go nuts touching and feeling and shopping. Many big-name designers do specialty lines exclusively for TopShop. This is my new favorite store in London, and it is conveniently across the street from my other favorite store, **SuperDrug.**

Heeeeere's Jenny: The One-Stop Shop for All Things Hot

TopShop, a fashion mecca and the self-proclaimed "world's largest fashion store," is five floors of all the best and hip looks for teens and 'tweens of all ages. It seems like miles and miles (kilometers and kilometers?) of hot skirts, trendy tops, and chic accessories; virtually no end to the fashion possibilities. Check out the bottom floor for vintage clothes and the "Bazaar" section for ultra-hip, one-of-a-kind designs.

Need help finding the perfect jeans or even an entire wardrobe? Don't get your knickers in a bunch. At TopShop you can get paired with your own **fashion analyst,** a complimentary service for anyone who makes an appointment. After a consultation about your specific look, you can either join your analyst and search through the racks, or sit and relax with complimentary food and drink while your new look is being sought. Other perks include VIP dressing rooms and express checkout. All this celebrity treatment, with no obligation to buy, and it's *free*. To make an appointment, call ☎ 020/7323-0326 or visit **www.topshop.co.uk/styleadvisor.**

WHISTLES
Covent Garden, WC2 (Tube: Covent Garden).

An on-the-edge chain with high-fashion looks and prices that are too high for the young people who can wear these clothes. The prices are even too high for me, even though I may be a little old for some of this stuff. When droopy is in, they do droopy. When wrinkled is in, they do wrinkled. Very L.A. clothes that actually work in fashion circles in London.

MULTIPLES (INTERNATIONAL)

MANGO
106–112 Regent St., W1 (Tube: Piccadilly Circus); 8–12 Neal St., WC2 (Tube: Covent Garden).

Spanish-made, young, trendy clothes, somewhat competitive to TopShop. There are more than 500 shops the world over, so they must be doing something right.

NITYA
120 Regent St., W1 (Tube: Piccadilly Circus).

I love this brand because it's good for tall women with a little extra weight. Hmmm. Well, anyway, the clothes are luxe yet usually have elastic waistbands . . . or no waist. They have an ethnic feel to them, somewhat droopy and Indian (South Asia, not American Native), often with embroidery. Prices are moderate-to-high but not outrageous; many of the items can be hand washed and travel well. It's chic, it's timeless, it's not found in the U.S.

PETITE BATEAU
106–108 King's Rd., SW3 (Tube: Sloane Sq.); 62 South Molton St., W1 (Tube: Bond St.).

French T-shirt firm with clothes for children and adults.

ZARA
*114–118 Regent St., W1 (Tube: Piccadilly Circus); and
other locations.*

I think Zara is to London today what Benetton was once to the
world—headed for street domination. There is one everywhere
in London. There is a Zara in New York, but this brand is not
well known by Americans, so please let me introduce you.

Zara makes well-priced, chic, fashionable clothes for work
and weekend. Without being silly or cheap, it copycats the latest jacket shape or skirt silhouette or whatever fashion gim-
mick is cutting edge so that you can look on-the-minute,
fashion-wise, but not go broke along the way.

PAPER GOODS & FILOFAX

FILOFAX
21 Conduit St., W1 (Tube: Bond St.).

This is a free-standing Filofax boutique, not a stationery store
that sells the stuff. It's rather fancy, considering the neighborhood and the clientele, and is replete with pages, inserts, and
various notebooks in many sizes. Prices are still half of what
they are in the United States, and they have sales and close-
outs. I always have a ball here. Note that they begin to sell calendars for the upcoming year about 8 or 9 months before you
need them, so don't be shy, even if it's July.

PAPERCHASE
*213 Tottenham Court Rd., W1 (Tube: Goodge St.); 167
Fulham Rd., SW3 (Tube: Fulham Broadway); many stores
all over town.*

The "in" place for paper goods, Paperchase offers a wide
range of products—everything from greeting cards, stationery,
Filofax pages, and party items to a variety of materials for the
serious artist. I often buy my Christmas cards here; part of the
proceeds goes to charity.

SMYTHSON
44 New Bond St., W1 (Tube: Bond St.).

If you're looking for stationery fit for a queen, stop by this very elegant shop, which has been producing top-quality paper since the beginning of the century. If you buy your writing papers at Cartier in New York, or at any of America's finest paper shops, you'll see some old friends here in London. Aside from the selection of writing papers, there's a wide variety of leather-bound goods, including address books and notebooks, diaries, and lovely desktop accessories. This is an old-fashioned, blue-blooded, very regal kind of place, a bit expensive, but cheaper than in the United States for the same goods.

PLUS SIZES

Marks & Spencer is known for its wide range of sizes, including larger sizes. Remember to use a sizing chart, as U.K. sizes may seem like U.S. sizes, but they are not. (See the Size Conversion Chart on p. 290.)

ANN HARVEY
266 Oxford St., W1 (Tube: Oxford Circus).

Wide range of looks for weekend, office, and dress-up at moderate prices; it's a multiple.

EVANS
214 Oxford St., W1 (Tube: Oxford Circus).

Another multiple, the competition to Ann Harvey but with various lines for different "looks" and even a made-to-measure department.

MARINA RINALDI
39 Old Bond St., W1 (Tube: Bond St.).

Marina Rinaldi is a branch of the famous Italian design house Max Mara and offers the same style and quality in plus-size clothes. The sizes begin at what is an American 14, which is a 16 in U.K. sizes.

RESALE SHOPS

••

BERTIE GOLIGHTLY
48 Beauchamp Place, SW3 (Tube: Knightsbridge).

Small shop that looks like m'lady's walk-in closets with tons of designer clothes and racks of Chanel. Organized by size; some accessories.

DESIGNS
60 Rosslyn Hill, NW3 (Tube: Hampstead).

Closed on Sundays when much of the Hampstead retail scene is hopping, so decide early on if you want to get a look at some slightly used designer duds. Prices are basically one-third the original price.

THE DRESS BOX
8 Cheval Place, SW7 (Tube: Knightsbridge).

Yet another. In fact, this one was here way before Pandora relocated around the corner. It's a staple.

THE LOFT
35 Monmouth St., WC2 (Tube: Covent Garden).

Designer resale shops are the latest retail rage—they are popping up everywhere. This one carries men's clothing on the ground floor and women's in the basement, and tries to specialize in the big international designers. You have to be the right size to make out like a bandit (as they say), but I was knocked out with the choices for my 24-year-old son. Try the website: **www.the-loft.co.uk**. Note that hours are unusual. Regular weekdays it's 11am to 6pm; the store is open on Sundays 12:30 to 4:30pm.

PANDORA
16–22 Cheval Place, SW7 (Tube: Knightsbridge).

Around the corner from Harrods, grandmother of all dress agencies. Locals call this a dress agency, I call it heaven. I'm talking £30 ($50) for a YSL blouse, £23 ($38) for an Hermès scarf. Armani jackets go for a mere £120 ($200). (Well, it's mere to some people.) Used clothes are no more than 6 months old.

The store is fairly large; there is a dressing room in the back. It has a strange system with automatic markdowns, which is explained on handwritten signs with a color code.

There's a wide range of types of clothing and sizes, some handbags, and a few accessories. I paid £295 ($487) for a Chanel cashmere sweater with cloverleaf buttons, and think I got the steal of the century.

Hours are Monday through Saturday from 10am to 5pm. It takes plastic.

SHOES

I have listed only the local names for special, traditional, or unusual shoes. See "Big Names (International)," above, for addresses of stores such as Ferragamo and Prada.

BERTIES
Covent Garden, WC2 (Tube: Covent Garden).

A famous London shoe resource at the moderate-price level, Berties has shops all over London, as well as branches and department-store distribution in the United States. It is famous for high style at moderate prices.

Church's Shoes
163 New Bond St., W1 (Tube: Bond St.).

What did you come to London for, if not to buy Church's shoes for him? These are traditional wingtips and slip-ons at high prices; otherwise, enjoy this tiny shop with the typical "well-worn" English interior. Actually, there are branches in the United States; the prices in London are usually equal to U.S. prices—but, get this: The United States has outlet stores.

F. Pinet
47 New Bond St., W1 (Tube: Bond St.).

This store is rather a Bond Street institution and is the kind of store I pass constantly in my regular Mayfair shopping rounds. That means that you, too, will find yourself going right by. This is where I spend time musing at the stock in the windows and wondering if I can ever wear "that kind of shoe" and where I never shop. Locals count on this resource for special-occasion shoes—dress-up shoes; colored leather shoes; creative, inventive designs; catch-me, catch-me shoes; and so on. They do carry flats as well as heels, but I am always attracted to the high heels in green snakeskin. Not for the horse-and-rider set.

French Sole
6 Ellis St., SW1 (Tube: Sloane Sq.).

This is the maker of the famous ballerina flats worn by Julia Roberts and so on; made in solids and prints and glitter or with contrast toes; more than 100 varieties.

Gina
42 Sloane St., SW1 (Tube: Knightsbridge).

The designer is named Emma Hope, and she is considered the last word in vamps. The shoes are high-fashion, expensive, and sometimes innovative. I think this is a good store, but not the last word. Let me know what you think or what I'm missing here.

Designer Emma Hope has gone on to open her own shop, near Patrick Cox, at 12 Symons St., which is just down the street from Sloane Street.

HOBBS
Covent Garden, WC2 (Tube: Covent Garden).

An excellent shoe chain for well-made, sporty, and dressy shoes at the top end of the moderate price range, but not so over-the-top that you can't afford them. Always reliable for fashionable, but not overly chic, footwear. Also handbags.

JIMMY CHOO
20 Motcomb St., SW1 (Tube: Knightsbridge).

If you are bored by Manolo (is this possible?), you'll swoon for Choo. Mr. Choo has shops in New York, Los Angeles, and Las Vegas, and he now also has a couture line of shoes. Prices begin at £300 ($500).

LK BENNETT
31 Brook St., W1 (Tube: Bond St.); other locations.

A source that has really taken off in the last year or two, Bennett actually sells clothes and shoes but is famous for the shoes and the wild colors available. Prices are moderate considering how much style you get.

MANOLO BLAHNIK
49–51 Old Church St., SW3 (Tube: S. Kensington).

OK, so maybe the average reader can't pronounce his name or afford his shoes. But those truly in the know, know Blahnik.

Manolo is one of the leading designers of expensive, creative shoes with vamp for the vamps of the world. They do not come cheap (in either case). He has a few stores dotted here and there in the shopping capitals of the world. The London shop is run by his sister, which makes it a must-do if you have a foot fetish. *Note:* Prices in New York may be less.

NikeTown
236 Oxford St., W1 (Tube: Oxford Circus).

Just do it? Next door to TopShop.

Patrick Cox
129 Sloane St., SW3 (Tube: Knightsbridge).

Cox originally made waves in the international world of fashion with his pink (and orange) patent-leather loafers on lug soles. The **Wannabe** line is almost affordable at under £100 ($165).

Russell & Bromely
24–25 New Bond St., W1 (Tube: Bond St.).

If you are looking for your favorite European designer shoe, such as Bruno Magli, Walter Steiger, or Charles Jourdan, stop by this very fashionable shop. There are several locations throughout London, but this elegant store serves social London, for those who want one-stop shopping with lots of brand choice. For men and women.

SHOOTING & FISHING

Farlows
9 Pall Mall, SW1 (Tube: Piccadilly Circus).

Although the store is almost 200 years old, they have totally renovated and launched a three-floor modern shop that sells what they have always been famous for: fishing gear. Not only are there truly thousands of rods, but there is an entire department devoted to saltwater gear and even technological advancements in clothing. Fear not; it's not all fish—there is an equestrian department as well.

Hardy Brothers
61 Pall Mall, W1 (Tube: Green Park).

They made Queen Victoria's fishing rod. Need I say more?

HOLLAND & HOLLAND
31–33 Bruton St., W1 (Tube: Green Park or Oxford Circus).

For those who don't shoot on weekends and possibly don't know, Holland & Holland is a gun maker. We are not talking bang-bang-you're-dead guns, but sporting guns, presentation guns, and important collectibles with prices that can easily reach to £250,000 ($412,500). A new gun takes perhaps 1,000 man-hours to create (more than a Savile Row suit) and costs about £10,000 ($16,500). I am ashamed to say that I love a lot of its fashions, scarves, accessories, and style. It just has that thing they call true style.

JAMES PURDEY & SONS LTD.
57 S. Audley St., W1 (Tube: Green Park or Marble Arch).

Gun and rifle makers; three royal warrants. Keep their catalog on your coffee table merely for the fun of it. Take your kids, as if you were in a museum. Pretend you are going on safari with Clark Gable or going shooting with David (the Duke of Windsor). Don't miss it. This store is right behind The Dorchester hotel.

SWEATERS & SHAWLS

The perfect sweater requires three ingredients: chilly weather, homegrown wool, and long winter nights. Today's sweater's value is based on who made it and how. A hand-knit sweater is more valuable and will always cost more than a machine-knit sweater; sweaters made with synthetics have the least value, while those made with wool or cashmere (or any other natural fiber, such as cotton, silk, or linen) have far more value.

Cashmere sweaters are valued by the number of plies or strands in the yarn—one to four is common. The higher the number of plies, the heavier the sweater, and the more expensive it is. Cashmere sweaters are sold year-round in the many cashmere shops London is famous for.

Cashmere is very tricky to buy because the price is very much related to the quality of the yarn and the way in which it is combed and knitted. The cashmere all comes from Mongolia, but the best cashmere sweaters come from Scotland, the United Kingdom, and Italy—this is what you pay for.

The $99 cashmere sweater you can find at any U.S. discount store is not the same quality as the £149 ($246) cashmere sweater you buy on sale at N. Peal or at one of England's icon sweater dealers. Any cashmere that has been produced in Scotland will cost more than a cashmere from the Far East, and the difference between a £120 ($200) sweater and a £300 ($500) sweater is invariably the quality of the cashmere itself and the way it has been processed.

Although most of us have known about England's reputation for cashmeres and wools, many people have not realized that a **pashmina** craze has broken out across the pond. For those who aren't onto it yet, pashmina is a cashmere-like fiber that also comes from goat hair. It's incredibly fine and soft, and it dyes very well. Pashmina is made into mufflers and shawls. (It is legal, whereas *shatush,* a softer-than-cashmere goat's hair, is not.) Pashmina makes the softest shawl in the world and can be dyed in the yummiest colors. Although some fashionistas will tell you pashmina is over, a classic is a classic as I see it.

Modern Cashmere Sources

BELINDA ROBERTSON
4 W. Halkin St., SW1.

You really need to take a taxi to this one; it's in an enclave of Belgravia that is only for the rich and famous. Miss Belinda is Scottish and has a shop in Edinburgh and a factory in Hawick, and now is conquering London with her fashionable cashmeres. Good store for color and chic; excellent cashmere shells to wear under suits. The **RobertsonB** line is less expensive. Custom colors and items can be ordered from the factories in Scotland.

BRORA

81 Marylebone High St., W1 (Tube: Marylebone); 344 King's Rd., SW3 (Tube: Sloane Sq.); 66 Ledbury Grove, W11 (Tube: Notting Hill Gate).

The Ledbury Grove store is new, created to take advantage of one of the newer hip neighborhoods being reinvented for style mavens. Brora is a Scottish resource and was doing plaids and tartans way before the new Burberry hit the scene. Now it has a **Baby Brora** line as well as plenty of cashmeres worn by models, socialites, and rock stars.

ELDON CASHMERE

166 Portobello Rd., W11 (Tube: Ladbroke Grove).

This store is open only on weekends or by appointment (© 020/7792-2571) and is more toward the far end of Portobello Market. The prices are not low, but the styles are fun and there are good gift items like hats, gloves, and so on. It also has baby clothes in cashmere.

LORO PIANO

47 Sloane St., SW1 (Tube: Knightsbridge).

The London branch of the famed Italian cashmere source features home style (home furnishings) and loungewear. The little bedroom slippers are the country-house gift of choice.

LUCIEN PELLAT-FINET

9 Pont Place, SW3 (Tube: Sloane Sq.).

This French designer makes the most expensive cashmere sweaters in the world but does set trends, so some people pay these prices. We are talking about £600 ($1,000) for a twin set, but take a look.

N. PEAL

Burlington Arcade, W1 (Tube: Piccadilly Circus); 192 Piccadilly, W1 (Tube: Piccadilly Circus).

For the quality- and convenience-conscious, N. Peal offers quite a variety of wools and cashmeres in a multitude of colors and styles. It is top-of-the-line in the business, but frankly, I could faint from the prices. I have, however, found one of the best gifts in the world from this store—it makes its own cashmere wash, sort of a fancy version of Woolite, sold in a travel size or a larger size. Very clever!

N. Peal is in the Burlington Arcade, in several different shops; all look small, but they have underground levels. As other merchants in the arcade go out of business, Peal moves into their space as well, so don't worry about lack of stock. Then there's a whole other medium-size shop on Piccadilly, near Hatchards.

Peal is the kind of shop you swear you won't patronize because of the high prices, but then you go back after you've been to every discount resource in London. Although you can get traditional sweaters in any number of places and at a variety of prices, Peal is one of the few outlets that sells fashion merchandise made out of cashmere. Notice that its sweaters are entirely different from the look-alikes you see everywhere else. It does have twin sets, bodysuits (called a "body" in British), and blends of cashmere and silk or even just plain, old-fashioned wool. The color palette will leave you drooling. The quality puts cheap cashmere to shame. And N. Peal has pashmina.

PICKETT
Burlington Arcade, W1 (Tube: Piccadilly Circus or Green Park).

I must give these people a lot of credit for being flexible; this was once one of the best pashmina sources in London, and although it still has pashmina, it has changed the focus of the store so it doesn't appear to be out of it from a fashion standpoint. The store also sells chunky ethnic-styled jewelry in semiprecious stones, and leather goods. I bought a pair of teal leather gloves here that brings tears to my eyes—the gloves are *that* beautiful.

PORTOBELLO CHINA & WOOLLENS
89 Portobello Rd., W11 (Tube: Notting Hill Gate).

If you love crazy fun, this one's for you. This is Bargain Sweater City. Sweaters that elsewhere cost £60 ($100) are £45 ($75) here. Sweaters that cost £90 ($150) elsewhere cost £60 ($100) here.

There are seconds; some of the merchandise is big-name without labels, but the help will tell you what it is. It is worse than mobbed on Saturday, and you have to be the kind that likes this kind of stuff to endure it.

The service is top-notch. The last time I was there, they pulled out zillions of sweaters for me, searched for cashmere twin sets for me, and were most helpful and polite, considering I didn't buy a thing and the shop was jam-packed. Prices here are among the best in London—probably in all England.

There is not a big selection. But if you give up on a sweater, you can always buy a teapot. Sometimes, there are baby cashmeres—another new hot item for babies who need luxury from infancy on—and pashminas, too.

THE WHITE COMPANY
8 Symons St., SW3 (Tube: Sloane Sq.).

The White Company sells more than white stuff. And yes, this is where you buy a cashmere hot-water-bottle cover for £75 ($124). This may not be the bargain of the century, but it's a great gift for the person who has everything. *Note:* they have a terrific outlet store at Bicester Village (p. 288).

Traditional Cashmere Sources

BALLANTYNE
153 New Bond St., SW1 (Tube: Bond St.).

Traditional styles and some with a bit of fashion flair (usually in the texture of the knit itself rather than the style of the sweater), twin sets galore, and fabulous colors. No bargains.

PRINGLE
112 New Bond St., W1 (Tube: Bond St.).

Wowie—another makeover and a snazzy one at that. Yeah, this was the Armani Emporio store, but that has moved across the road, so don't freak. Pringle is in the game to knock your socks off and replace them with cashmere socks.

Pringle has been great for classics; now they've added fashion and even what they call "washable" cashmere. I don't mean hand-washable (that's how I've always done mine), but machine-washable. Sweaters cost about £120 ($200) and actually seem a relative bargain. Adds a whole new bit of fun to the scene and energy of New Bond Street.

WESTAWAY & WESTAWAY
62–65 Great Russell St., WC1 (Tube: Holborn); 92 Great Russell St., WC1 (Tube: Holborn).

Still ticking after all these years! If you can't stand wondering who has the cheapest sweaters/cashmeres and the best selection of good prices, take my word for it and head to Westaway & Westaway. It's located across the street from the British Museum, and you are guaranteed to find any sweater in any color and style you may desire.

There are two shops, both of which carry a large selection of knitted garments from Scotland and Ireland, as well as the classic cashmere and lamb's-wool favorites. There are slightly discounted Burberrys and Aquascutum items, kilts, shawls, and yard goods in one shop, and sweaters, sweaters, sweaters in the other shop.

In both shops, notice that there are rooms upstairs and downstairs as well as a back, back room that you may have trouble finding if you don't know it's there. Please note that men's sweaters cost less than women's. Also remember that the styles here are very traditional and all colors may not be available.

To order, call toll-free in the United States (© 800/345-3219); this phone rings in London, so do use GMT when you phone.

If you reach the office after hours, you can leave your order information after the recording.

Tartans & Tweeds

Americans have so mangled British English over the centuries that there is now some confusion as to the difference between a tartan and a plaid—a difference that will get you in deep water when you come to buy one or the other. A *tartan* is a pattern of fabric, with alternating colors in the warp and the weft in which the colors repeat themselves in a set order. A *plaid* is a piece of clothing worn as part of a Scottish dress uniform. In the United States, the term *plaid* has come to mean a pattern of alternating colors set in a sequence, but in Scotland a plaid is *not* a tartan. Or vice versa.

Tartans signify the great clans of the Highlands, each clan having its own special way of weaving its colors and stripes into a particular sequence, which no one else can copy. There is usually a battle tartan and a dress tartan for each family or clan. The men who fought for a certain clan all wore the same pattern, and certain areas of the Highlands became known for these patterns.

Now then, if you want to get all gussied up in proper Highland attire, you probably want to wear the right tartan. You may easily discover the right one, either by using a chart for your last name or by using a map and finding the village your family came from. In London and Edinburgh, retailers have these lists right on hand and will gladly help you. You can also choose one of the two tartans authorized by Queen Victoria to be worn by those who don't have Scottish ancestry. Of course, a lot of people just pick what they like best.

A *tweed* has nothing to do with a tartan, and the two are rarely worn together. Tweed fabric is named for the River Tweed and is a blend of various colors of wool so that a pattern emerges. Many tweeds are named for the places that created them, such as the Harris tweed. Tweeds are often nubby with a rough hand. They are 100% wool and can be bought by the meter or as ready-made garments. Men's tweed jackets can sometimes be much less expensive in the United Kingdom than in the United States.

Tweed fabric bought off the bolt will be considerably cheaper—expect a 50% savings. If you're really into saving money, you'll buy the fabric in Scotland and then take it to Hong Kong to have the tailoring done there. Even if you're not Hong Kong–bound this year, you may think about the plan. The best thing about tweeds is that they never go out of style. Hang on to the fabric, get a classic suit made, and it will last 20 years—or longer.

TEENS & 'TWEENS

There are several acceptable teen looks these days, and London has them all, from vintage clothes to designer catwalk copies. Don't forget Mango and Zara, Spanish chains (see "Multiples [International]," earlier in this chapter). Don't forget "Vintage" and "Trendy," later in this chapter. There are entire streets, even neighborhoods, where the retail scene is geared to this age group. See reports for the under-25 crowd from Ethan Sunshine (p. 185) and my editorial assistant Jenny McCormick (p. 159).

DIESEL
Carnaby St., W1 (Tube: Oxford Circus).

There are a few Diesel shops in London, and the jeans are also carried in the big department stores. But this is where I send you for several reasons; like man, you have to do Carnaby Street, anyway. There's also a Miss Sixty (see below) right nearby.

Diesel is an Italian line, known for its jeans, but with a full line of casual fashions for guys and gals.

Earl Jeans
40 Ledbury Rd., W11 (Tube: Notting Hill Gate).

This is a brand, one of the famous-for-fit brands that the kids adore—this is their first free-standing store . . . or go to their own outlet store at Bicester Village.

Hennes & Mauritz (H&M)
261–271 Regent St., W1 (Tube: Oxford Circus); and other locations.

You are probably very embarrassed for me, but the truth is, I love this store and make it a regular place to check out, even if I don't buy anything. The store specializes in teen clothes and hot trends and cheap junk; and yes, I buy for me, so there. At least, I buy when I can find something that fits. They have copies of many of the latest looks to pop down the catwalk. All the young things shop here. I looooove it.

Even if you buy nothing, you've got to wander around listening to the young girls talking to each other about the clothes and their lives. Many of these sweet young things are American.

Note: I am faithful to the Oxford Circus main store, but there are tons of new branches around town, with several on Oxford Street closer to the Marble Arch end.

Miss Sixty
32 Great Marlborough St., W1 (Tube: Oxford Circus); and other locations.

Believe it or not, Miss Sixty is also an Italian brand, famous for its jeans and hot fashions, all of which are trend oriented and priced to fly out of stores, especially on the cute tushies of teenage girls. This is the new flagship for London; there's menswear and a sportswear line as well.

TopShop
214 Oxford St., W11 (Tube: Oxford Circus).

I've already listed this chain under multiples (p. 158), but since it's basically across the street from H&M and is teen heaven, I must remind you that it's here. Don't miss it!

Uniqlo
163–169 Brompton Rd., SW3 (Tube: S. Kensington); 88–90 Regent St., W1 (Tube: Piccadilly Circus).

This is a Japanese chain, inspired by Gap, that had intentions of taking the world by storm. World domination has not followed; some stores have closed. But there is a new one on Regent, although I do not know why. The prices are low, low, low. It's a lifestyle store with clothing for men, women, and children and unisex dressing rooms. Not long on style but good for basics.

TOYS & KID STUFF

The Disney Store
140 Regent St., W1 (Tube: Oxford Circus or Piccadilly Circus).

Give me a break.

Hamley's
200 Regent St., W1 (Tube: Oxford Circus).

Whether you have children or not, Hamley's deserves attention. And if you're looking for that unusual toy not readily available in the United States, Hamley's is a must. The gift shop on the street level is the best (and easiest) place I know of to buy gifts for all your friends and neighbors.

If your child collects dolls, you will have a tough time making a final decision. There's also a huge array of Britains, the small metal **British Regiment Guard** soldiers, for all the collectors in your family. Hamley's also sells puzzles and brain teasers; these can be good gifts for older children or adults and nice little travel rewards for train journeys or transatlantic flights.

If you are beginning to feel dizzy, you will be relieved to find a snack bar in the basement. Prices will not make you dizzy—although American toys are more expensive here— but **Corgi** toys are a bargain.

If you are wondering how you will get your packages home, Hamley's will ship them to your door. The paperwork takes about 20 minutes but is well worth the time. Make sure, of course, that you are sending home an unsolicited gift valued at less than $50. Otherwise, you will pay duty.

Even if you don't have children, don't know any children, or don't even like children, if you are interested in retail, go out of your way to visit this London masterpiece theater.

There is a tiny branch of Hamley's at Unit 3 of Covent Garden; it's so small that it just seems to be a zoo of stuffed animals. There's also a branch of Hamley's at LHR. You deserve the mother store.

HARRODS
Brompton Rd., Knightsbridge, SW1 (Tube: Knightsbridge).

Fabulous toy department; possibly as good as **Hamley's**. There's a sample of every toy imaginable, and the kids can play, ride, climb, bite, or torture the toys and each other. Toy department is on the fourth floor.

TROTTERS
34 King's Rd., SW3 (Tube: Sloane Sq.).

Trotters is a children's shop with a great formula and a lot of energy. It has toys, clothes, and a play area—all of it so cute that you'll find it impossible to resist. The shopping bag, with the big fat pig, is one of the best bags in London. There's another pig outside, to mark the store.

TRENDY

You will find plenty of trendy-like stores listed in the "Teens & 'Tweens" section of this chapter (p. 175), but those sources tend to have copies of the latest styles at low prices. For truly trendsetting sources, read on. Note that the original is usually expensive. But if you have to be the first in your block to own it, step this way. The look very often is a version of rock-star chic or rich hippie; forget the pearls.

CATH KIDSON
8 Clarendon Cross, NW11 (Tube: Holland Park).

Kidson is a fabric designer, but her small store sells clothes, accessories, and home-design items made from her fabrics. Some of her inspiration comes from American textiles from the 1930s through the '60s, but the prints are refreshing and especially fun when made into travel bags or totes. This store is part of the ritual walk from Portobello Road Market to The Cross (see below).

THE CROSS
141 Portland Rd., NW11 (Tube: Holland Park).

The Cross has a religious following, although the name actually comes from the fact that the store is located at the crossing of Portland Road and a street named Clarendon Cross. It's a small store, filled with one-off (one of a kind) designs made by the city's up-and-coming designers and bought up by regulars, who include magazine editors and movie stars. Prices are high, but that's part of the cachet.

MATCHES
60–64 Ledbury Rd., W11 (Tube: Notting Hill Gate).

Matches has eight stores in its small chain, but this one, on one of London's most famous streets for trendsetters, is the one you want to see. One of the owners, a former buyer for Harvey Nicks, prides herself on finding the goods before anyone else. It helps to be thin, but the clothes are worthy of a stare because they are so light and fresh and inspirational in terms of creativity and color.

SOMETHING
1–3 Chepstow Rd., W2 (take a taxi).

A small, cult find with big designer names, a chichi crowd, and an insider's reputation alluding that the store is the London version of Milan's best store, Corso Como 10. The clothes are from designers but aren't the ordinary names and are, therefore, hard to find elsewhere. The design space was created by the same man who did Madonna's house. Besides clothes, there are furnishings, CDs, and books.

THE WALL
1 Denbeigh Rd., W11 (Tube: Notting Hill Gate).

I am quite sure that the team at The Wall resents that I have placed them in the "Trendy" section of this book—I simply didn't know where else to put them in order to get your attention. They are perhaps the antithesis of trendy; they are classic in a non-fashiony, feel-good manner. These clothes are for fans of the American designer Eileen Fisher or those who like droop and drape and easy-to-wear, go-everywhere style. Prices are higher than I like and more than Eileen Fisher, but the clothes are timeless. Not for the under-35 crowd, perhaps, but a wonderful resource.

WILLMA
339 Portobello Rd., W10 (Tube: Ladbroke Grove).

This is not really part of the Portobello Road Market and is located close to the Golborne Road end of the stores—it's possibly best on a non-market day (anything but Sat) so that you can enjoy the creativity of the mix without being mobbed.

UNDERWEAR

....

AGENT PROVOCATEUR
*16 Pont St., SW1 (Tube: Knightsbridge); 6 Broadwick St.,
W1 (Tube: Piccadilly Circus).*

It's times like this when I hate my nature, my urge to tell you
that I just don't get it about this brand—it's expensive and not
worth the hype. Nonetheless, everyone else adores it, finds it
cutting edge, sexy, and oh-so-naughty. Beats me.

MARKS & SPENCER
458 Oxford St., W1 (Tube: Bond St.).

M&S has long been famous for their undergarments, created
with the St. Michael label. They have everything from plain
Jane to ooh-la-la. Prices are not low but quality is high.

VINTAGE

....

Don't get the subject head "Vintage" mixed up with the one
below it, which has to do with wine—now we're talking about
clothes, as in old clothes that never die and certainly won't be
forgotten. London has always had a large market for used, gen-
tly worn, and vintage clothing—partly because of the variety
of street looks and partly because prices are so dear that many
women prefer resale shops (see "Resale Shops," p. 163). Also
note that a few department stores, including **Selfridges,** have
vintage clothes departments.

Almost all the markets have vintage clothing dealers, including Portobello, Shepherd's Bush, Camden Passage, and Camden
Lock. There are also many charity shops in London where you
may do well, although these days they are selling old Voyage
sweaters for £200 ($330) and calling it vintage.

ANNIE'S
10 Camden Passage, N1 (Tube: Angel).

Good fun, lots to look at in a cramped shop, but no giveaway deals, and pricier than any teenager would want. A well-known source for big-name designers who have found their inspiration here.

CENCI
31 Monmouth St., WC2 (Tube: Covent Garden).

On an otherwise unassuming side street coming away from Covent Garden, this store has a wonderful rumble of jumble and fair enough prices. It's still a bit funky and very hit-or-miss, but you can get lucky.

HOXTON BOUTIQUE
2 Hoxton Sq., N1 (Tube: Liverpool St. Station).

Vintage sunglasses!

SHEILA COOK
283 Westbourne Grove, W11 (Tube: Notting Hill Gate).

Cook has moved several times, so don't be confused; this is the latest address. This new shop is right smack in the middle of the Portobello Road Market, just on the corner. Her vintage clothing has always been exceptional, which every movie company in the area knows. Prices tend to be a little high, but I have bought some items I thought were well priced.

STEINBERG & TOLKIEN
193 King's Rd., SW3 (Tube: Sloane Sq.).

Perhaps the best vintage clothing store in London and maybe one of the best in the world, this store is owned by an American, who is very friendly and always happy to chat. Every micro-centimeter of this two-level shop is crammed with stuff. The prices are not low, but the quality and selection more than make up for that. Note that there is no easy Tube stop; you can walk from Sloane Square or take a bus on King's Road.

VENT
178A Westbourne Grove, W11 (Tube: Notting Hill Gate).

This store is very, very small; it is hardly ever open (weekends are the best bet, but not too early in the morning) and is often crammed with Japanese tourists who arrive by the busload. I don't get it, myself, but others come to worship here. The store is small, the selection is small, and it's OK, but not knockout (unlike Virginia, below) to me.

VIRGINIA
98 Portland Rd., W11 (Tube: Holland Park).

Virginia was a movie star; her small shop looks like a movie star's dressing room or boudoir circa 1932. The store is in the trend-niche real estate right around the corner from The Cross and not too far from Portobello Road, so it's handy and is often visited by models and celebs.

WINE & WHISKY
....

Don't look now, but the vast majority of Brits buy their wine at the supermarket—Brits are extremely knowledgeable about wine and spend a lot of time researching labels from around the world, not just nearby France. The big supermarket chains are so powerful that they have private-label bottles from the best vineyards.

There are scads of articles about wine in all the newspapers and magazines, if you are looking for help in unknown territory. Also note that London auction houses do a big business in wines; they even now have En Primeur auctions whereby you buy the wine the year it is bottled (at an attractive price), and it is laid down until it's ready to be enjoyed. For more information, call Christie's at © **020/7389-2745.**

BERRY BROTHERS & RUDD
3 St. James St., SW1 (Tube: Piccadilly Circus or Green Park).

Most people just call this Berry Brothers; it is the single most famous wine shop in London with a branch at LHR Terminal 4. This is also the oldest wine shop in London, famous for its whisky brands as well as its wine selection.

CADENHEAD'S COVENT GARDEN WHISKY SHOP
3 Russell St., WC2 (Tube: Covent Garden).

I can't tell you that I completely understood everything that was explained to me while I was here; I can tell you that I stayed for an hour and had a ball. It seems that Cadenhead's makes the barrels that whisky is aged in, and they have their own stock of whisky, which they have continued to age beyond what the distiller chose to do with his liquid gold. Review an enormous blackboard menu of what they've got in kegs; then order up a bottle. There is some tasting allowed. Expect to pay £36 to £60 ($60–$100) for a bottle of supreme whisky, but we are talking very special and unique. This is boy territory or the place to buy a great gift for a man who appreciates fine whisky.

ODDBINS
11 Curzon St., W1 (Tube: Green Park); 4 Great Portland St., W1 (Tube: Oxford Circus); multiple addresses around town.

Oddbins is a multiple, one of the most popular liquor chains in the United Kingdom. It publishes its own tabloid newspaper with information that will help you with selections. I've bought a lot of specialty champagnes from here. Good prices, good selection. Worth visiting even if you just want to learn and aren't ready to buy.

ROBERSON
348 Kensington High St., W14 (Tube: High St. Kensington).

A young and new wine shop devoted to the British tradition of enjoying wines from all over the world, with a wine list bound like a book and selections from everywhere in the world, even Lebanon. You can also visit them online at **www.roberson.co.uk**.

The Vintage House
42 Old Compton St., W1 (Tube: Piccadilly Circus).

This is right in the heart of the theater district, so it's very convenient—the specialty is malt whiskies with more than 500 brands in stock.

The Sunshine Report:
An Excellent Vintage Year

While the local **Urban Outfitters** (4 Kensington High St., W11; Tube of same name) has a used-clothing section (**Urban Renewals**), it is far from your best bet for vintage clothing. It's fun if you're already there, but you'll do better to simply walk toward Notting Hill Gate, a few blocks away.

You needn't wait for the market day. Any day of the week, you can check out Pembridge Road's string of **Retro** shops, aptly named Retro Home, Retro Man, and Retro Woman (30–34 Pembridge Rd., NW11; Tube: Notting Hill Gate). The men's store has an enormous diversity of discount designer denim (try saying that 10 times fast . . .). They feature a large selection of denim pants and jackets (the Tennessee Tuxedo) with huge names to match: Evisu, G-Star, Edwin, Paul Smith, Helmut Lang, BDG (Urban Outfitters), Armani Jeans, and Levi's Engineered to name a few.

All are expensive, but there are serious bargains to be found if you are willing to be an unrelenting tag-checker. Items that haven't sold are marked down until they do, and since most people aren't willing to shell out £100 ($165) for a pair of pants that have been on someone else's bum, the prices do fall. Most jeans were under £70 ($116), but I saw some Evisu for £40 ($66), almost four times cheaper than regular retail . . . just be sure to scrub 'em good when you get home.

The best bargains, though, are to be found at Saturday's **Portobello Road Market.** Along the way you will see some great vintage shops, but the real deals are with outdoor vendors. In this case, you lose the option of the fitting room (unless you're willing to climb into the back of a truck . . .), so know your sizes well (check the Size Conversion Chart on p. 290).

The more popular items, as in the States, are old track jackets, ironic T-shirts, jeans, and worn hats. Most track jackets are above £25 ($41), and many T-shirts, strangely enough, are imported from America . . . so stick to Goodwill and the Salvation Army for those. The biggest bargains, once again, were the jeans.

I found one vendor with Levi's, Diesel, G-Star, Gap, and Divided (H&M) for £10 ($17)! In the case of Diesel and G-Star, that's ten times cheaper than retail.

Chapter Seven

....

LONDON BEAUTY

A BEVY OF BEAUTY BUYS

London is working its way to becoming the beauty capital of Europe, the international queen of drugstores/chemist shops. Maybe this is historically related to Vidal Sassoon and Mary Quant, who got there first, or is simply a sign of the times. Maybe no one can afford to shop anywhere more expensive than **Boots** or **SuperDrug,** so all the fun stuff is being launched at those stores.

Believe it or not, there are a dozen different designer hair-care brands on the shelves at Boots. I use mostly **Michaeljohn** products—the **Tea Tree** shampoo (and conditioner) actually tingles your scalp and makes you want to do the cha-cha. You can also find clay shampoo, which works on the theory that clay grabs the dirt and chemicals in your hair, absorbs them, and washes them down the drain when you rinse.

Yet there are scads of other brands and products for every need, in an ever-changing parade of beauty goods. There are products for colored hair (all colors) and greasy hair; products for the handbag and in travel size; and other products that claim to do everything but sing and dance. There's a huge revolution going on, and it's time to redo your look and get with the new trends, baby.

187

It's a virtual beauty war out there, and shoppers will find that their trip to London is the perfect time to pick up new merchandise, find trends, get spa treatments, or fix up bad hair days forever. Even though I live in Paris, I go to London regularly for my hair color. (Thank you for saving me, Debbie.) In fact, now my son Aaron goes to Michaeljohn in London and in Beverly Hills (p. 202).

Boots has gone for beauty in such a big way that its **Well-Being Centre** on Kensington High Street is one of the most exciting retail adventures in the United Kingdom, and it's looking to open more such concept stores. **Sephora,** the French beauty supermarket, will be open in several London locations by the time you read this; as we go to press, they are just warming up.

A few years ago **The Dorchester** was considered almost over the top when it opened a spa; now, every luxury hotel in London has a spa, and there is much competition among them for the latest in treatments and philosophies. There are also day spas that have nothing to do with hotels, as well as brands of treatments in drugstores that are branded by these day spas.

Part of the fun of buying cosmetics in London used to be snapping up the **Bourjois** brand, partly because it wasn't available in the United States (it is now, through Sephora stores) and partly for the giggle that comes with the knowledge that Bourjois makeup is made in the same factories as **Chanel** makeup. Now Bourjois is considered old chapeau, while a handful of cult makeup studios have opened their doors, and **Self-ridges,** the department store, has rebuilt its ground-floor makeup department as the largest in Europe. Teens begin teething on names such as **Mr. Mascara, Pixi, Ruby & Millie,** and more.

Can all these brands thrive? I doubt it. But who would have imagined that **Mary Quant** would not only still be in business, but going strong?

Sunday Beauty Shopping

As you know, most major department stores are open Sundays from noon to 5pm, and some open at 11am, if you need a beauty fix. Some Boots stores are also open. **Bliss Chemist** (5–6 Marble Arch, W1) is also open Sundays; it's open until midnight every night of the week, as well.

Tesco Metro stores (there are a few in downtown London) no longer carry its makeup or too much else in terms of beauty aids, but regular **Tesco** stores have tons of products. Some are open on Sundays.

UNSUNG HEROES

Finding brands you have never heard of that turn out to be great discoveries is one of the reasons we travel and shop. Here's a list of brands I have tested that are either exclusive to the U.K. or hard to find in the U.S. **Selfridges** has the largest beauty department in Europe. For a list of British hair-care brands, see p. 205.

Some American and/or Canadian lines have free-standing stores in London; these brands can be bought for less money in department stores in the U.S. or online if you do not have hometown access to names like **MAC** or **Kiehl's,** and so on.

ANGELA FLANDERS
Therapeutic pillow spray for 20 bucks. What can I say? The brand is sold in many department stores or at Angela's own store (96 Columbia Rd., E2; Tube: Liverpool St.), which is part of the snazzy "new" East End. This store is open only on Sundays, 9:30am until 2pm, in keeping with the Sunday-only nature of the Columbia Road Flower Market (p 113).

AUTOGRAPH
Makeup line with some treatment products created for Marks & Spencer and sold only in their stores. There's another M&S beauty line called Mein, which to me is such a terrible name that I refuse to test it.

DR. HAUSCHKA
This is a German brand that is found in the U.S., but not easily. It's a very large range of mostly treatments, all made from natural ingredients. The rose products are the most famous; many supermodels swear by this line. I use the rose oil on my cuticles.

ERNO LAZLO
He's baaaack. Well, actually, he's dead, but Penhaligon's bought this skin-care line and it now has a cult following. You can even buy some of the line at discount prices in the Penhaligon's outlet store in Bicester Village.

ORIGINAL SOURCE
This is an Australian brand; they need a distributor in the U.S. It's a low-end brand available in drugstores and grocery stores; the most expensive item costs £6 ($9.90). What I hate about the line is that it is rarely stocked by the brand, so various pieces of the collection are in different parts of a store. The best selection I have found is at the **Tesco** on Cromwell Road. Some **Boots** carry this brand; some don't. The line itself is bath oriented—my favorite is still Tea Tree & Mind, although various scents come in and out of fashion. The Lemon & Honey liquid soap is also a winner. *Note:* Price on the same item varies enormously. I have found the same item for £2 ($3.30), £2.30 ($3.80), and £2.50 ($4.10). Boots is the most expensive on this brand, but you are still talking under $4.

RUBY & MILLIE
Color cosmetics that are now getting mainstreamed—in the U.K., at least.

ST. TROPEZ

Despite the French name, this is a brand from Nottingham and it's a fake tan system, sold in three parts. The whole set costs well over £60 ($100), but you can often buy just Step 3, the tanning gel, for about £21 ($35). That may strike you as outrageous, but wait! I've tested this product and it is simply great, worth the money. I have been testing fake tans since they were invented—I have been through orange, streaks, and even beauty salon rip-offs. This is the first product I have found that actually gives you a natural tan and is easy to use. *Note:* Steps 1 and 2 are exfoliating and moisturizing processes that you can do on your own; Step 3 is the gel itself.

PHILOSOPHIES & GIMMICKS

And speaking of spray-on misting, there are several lines that offer pillow spray these days. Boots has a complete range of Sleep products, including a pillow spray.

One of my favorite new beauty lines is the **Feng Shui** line of bath products made (and sold exclusively) by **Tesco**. In short, aromatherapy is old news, Zen is hard to package, and spas are popping up all over the place. Holistics are gaining as a notion, meaning that beauty products and treatments created with vitamins, minerals, or proven cures are hard to resist. **Spraycology** is a line of treatments that you spray onto your skin so the treatment is absorbed. London has 'em all.

AROMATHERAPY

Aromatherapy began its international push from London years ago. It has been popularized in the United States and breathes on. A recent scientific study, reported on the front page of most British newspapers, revealed that aromatherapy works for those who *think* it works.

Shoppers please note: There is a difference between American aromatherapy and British. Although the effectiveness of both may be in the mind of the beholder, the British product usually has more juice in it.

The philosophical essence of aromatherapy is that different smells affect your mood and your body in different ways. It posits that you can manipulate your feelings and your health by surrounding yourself with certain types of fragrances. This has become such a big business that just about every manufacturer in the world, let alone Britain, has jumped on the bandwagon. You'll have no trouble walking into **Boots, SuperDrug,** and **Tesco** and finding a score of different types of aromatherapy products and treatments.

Even airlines offer samples of aromatherapy products that are designed to fight jet lag; some of the Hilton hotels have jet-lag treatments for their guests with aromatherapy massages; most of the new spa centers have some form of aromatherapy.

For an overview of available products, regardless of the brand, check out any large department store—especially **M&S,** now that they carry **Daniele Ryman**'s line—and any large **Boots.** American brands, such as Origins and Crabtree & Evelyn, cost less in the United States.

CULPEPER THE HERBALIST
21 Bruton St. (Berkeley Sq.), W1 (Tube: Green Park);
Covent Garden, WC3 (Tube: Covent Garden).

This small source for oils, soaps, potpourri, and even cooking items is a British multiple, with two stores in London's main shopping areas. You are likely to at least pass by the one in Covent Garden. The store has an old-fashioned and charming feel to it; the oils are of excellent quality. Its best product is the aromatherapy fan.

JO MALONE
150 Sloane St., SW1 (Tube: Knightsbridge).

Although I have been a huge fan of Jo Malone's products for years, and watched her grow from a tiny resource on Walton Street to become part of the LVMH empire with a glorious store in New York, I am astounded at the prices now.

That said, the chain is an absolute must-do, and the Sloane Street flagship is probably the best bet. Those on a budget may feel shy. On the other hand, if you are looking for the perfect gift for the person who has everything, this could be it.

I gave a bottle of Jo Malone's to a woman who offered a weak "thank you" to me; she obviously had no idea that I had spent the moon for her or that this item is the cult must-have of the United Kingdom. The Mandarin Oriental Hyde Park Hotel uses Jo Malone bathroom amenities—it may be cheaper to book there, take the amenities each day, and give them as gifts.

LUSH
123 King's Rd., SW3 (Tube: Sloane Sq.); 11 The Piazza, Covent Garden, WC2 (Tube: Covent Garden); 96 Kensington High St., W8 (Tube: High St. Kensington); 40 Carnaby St., W1V (Tube: Oxford Circus).

I'm not sure if it's proper to classify Lush as aromatherapy— maybe it's just bed, bath, and beyond. Quite beyond, my dears, quite, quite. Even all these years later, I am still amazed and amused.

If you tend toward asthma, you may find that you cannot even enter a Lush store, as the scent is heady. Several of the Lush products have a strong essence that affects their use, but then again, this is really a bath and beauty source. Like all aromatherapy, it's in the mind. Still, breathe deeply, think of your gift-giving list, cope, and smile. And buy the Red Rooster soap, if nothing else.

Lush is the most original and innovative store I've seen in years; they are growing like crazy and are destined to shortly be famous throughout the world (already open in Florence, Milan, and Venice). The store is set up like a deli; many of the products you buy from old-fashioned blocks, chunks, cakes, or loaves, which are carved to your desired size and then weighed to be priced and wrapped in plain paper. Other items have fabulous packaging, but if you compare prices, you'll note that you are paying a very steep price for the fancy packaging.

I cannot tell you that every product they make is the best in the world; I have tested many of their things and am smitten with many of these (I cannot live without Red Rooster soap), but some of the products are average. The bath bombs are a fabulous novelty and a great gift for someone who has seen it all, but they fizzle, so to speak, once dropped in the tub and the aroma doesn't last that long. Never mind; it's still very clever. The black-bread face mask is the best mask I've ever used.

There are prepackaged gift packs in the under-£10 ($17) price range. Expect to wait in line during the Christmas season. There are also a zillion Lush knockoff stores and products in London these days, if you like the gimmick but don't want to spring for the real thing.

NEAL'S YARD REMEDIES
15 Neal's Yard, Covent Garden, WC2 (Tube: Covent Garden); Chelsea Farmer's Market, Sydney St., SW3 (Tube: Sloane Sq.); 9 Elgin Crescent, W11 (Tube: Notting Hill Gate).

This well-known brand has become an icon in its cobalt-blue jars, although they also have products in tubes and other means of conveyance. They have excellent literature and do-it-yourself materials for using aromatherapy and essential oils and treatments and cures, as well as many natural products. Plus, there's a library. There are cosmetics and toiletries, homeopathic cures, body-care products, shampoos, bath goods, soaps, and more. They do have international mail order should you run out, although the line is sold in the United States at a number of stores.

BATH & BEAUTY

Also see "Aromatherapy" (above) and "Cosmetics & Makeup" (below); for heaven's sake, don't miss **Lush** or **Jo Malone.**

THE BODY SHOP
Covent Garden, WC2 (Tube: Covent Garden); 374 Oxford St. (Tube: Bond St.).

No trip to London is complete for me without a raid on at least one branch of The Body Shop, but nowadays I wait for the one at Heathrow's Terminal 4, where prices are slightly better. Some of the stores have a "well-being centre." (That's Brit-speak for spa treatments.)

The brand has not been doing so well financially and is not as famous as it was when it first made retail history for creating fair-trade items and green retail. Nonetheless, it's still fun. Shops are easily recognizable by their dark-green exteriors. Inside is a world of environmentally and politically correct soaps, scents, and other beauty products; some aromatherapy products; and a full line of men's and baby products.

Everything comes in small travel sizes for sampling purposes; I think the best fun in the world is to buy tons of these little jars and bottles for my own travel kit, for stocking stuffers for Christmas, or for making up gift baskets.

There is a branch of The Body Shop in every trading area of London, so don't think this is the only time you can stock up. I frequent the one on Oxford Street (across from the Tesco Metro). Product prices have gone up, so savings are now about 20% over U.S. prices.

BOOTS THE CHEMIST
Piccadilly Circus, W1 (Tube: Piccadilly Circus); and other locations.

In the Queen's English, Boots is a chemist. To Americans, Boots is a drugstore. To me, it's a way of life. No day in London is complete without a dose of Boots. Please remember my motto: *Not all Boots are created equal.* This means never pass a Boots without going in for a half hour.

The best thing about Boots is that it has a huge selection of health and beauty aids, usually at reasonable prices. Its house lines offer choices in many pharmaceuticals and beauty products.

And speaking of beauty products, see the separate listing below for Boots Well-Being Centre.

There is always a pharmacy, sometimes an optical shop, and always a selection of small appliances, such as hair dryers, should you discover that your French model will not work in England. (It won't—different plugs.) You can buy pantyhose here, film, some costume jewelry, and just about any brand of makeup or perfume.

Boots sells the **Bourjois** line of makeup from France and has its own line of ecologically sound bath and beauty products that imitate what's sold at The Body Shop. I buy its cucumber face scrub. It also has its own brand of Chanel-inspired (and packaged) makeup and beauty products, **No. 7** (it's a joke—like Chanel No. 5, get it?), which is the single best-selling cosmetics line in the United Kingdom. The eyeliner pencils are better than Chanel's.

Boots also has a makeup line for teenagers, No. 17, which is less expensive than No. 7.

One of the products you might want to check out at Boots is **Imedeen,** a vitamin supplement meant to change your skin and form a skin-defense system from within, which will help prevent premature aging. It's quite pricey, and I can't begin to tell you if it works or not, but a lot of young women are trying it. They say that after 3 months of use, you will see a difference. You may also be broke.

There is a Boots in almost every city in England and Scotland, most often located on the high street. In London, there's a store in every major trading area. Some are open Sunday, and some are not. The newer stores are better than the older ones. There's a great store in Canary Wharf; the Green Park store is awfully good.

BOOTS WELL-BEING CENTRE
128 Kensington High St., W8 (Tube: High St. Kensington).

Be still my heart, I am in love. If you are looking at this Boots from the street, it looks small and average, and you will think

I am nuts—so trust me on this. If you enter from the Tube, you will get a better idea of size and selection but not the total scope.

Sooooo, in this new life, Boots sells more upscale brands of makeup and fragrance as well as zillions of hair-care lines and all bath products big and small, great and tall. Upstairs, there's a spa, Chinese herbal treatment center, manicure station, and much more. Just drop me off here and pick me up on the way to the airport.

CRABTREE & EVELYN
6 Kensington Church St., W8 (Tube: High St. Kensington).

It's American. It's American. It's American. Now then, if you are remembering their iconic look of old-fashioned English, you might not be into their new concept, which is *moderne.* Most of the U.K. stores have stayed classical, which is confusing.

SUPERDRUG
197–213 Oxford St., W1 (Tube: Oxford Circus).

SuperDrug is a multiple with branches all over town. Not each branch is as fabulous as its sister, so I pop into as many as I can find; the Oxford Street store is my regular. It is often my first stop in London, and then I walk to Regent Street from there.

With a hair salon in the rear and a pharmacy and drugstore, this is a younger, hipper version of Boots, and may be a few pence less expensive than Boots. I have often found brands to test here that later came to Boots, but that was before Boots started its Well-Being Centres. Still, it's worth a look and a few minutes of browse time—plus, it opens at 8am, if you have jet lag and happen to be up early and want a treat.

COSMETICS & MAKEUP

I also discuss this subject in the bath and beauty section above; there's a lot of overlap, as **The Body Shop** also has a makeup line and so on. Also, **Boots the Chemist** sells two very important lines: **Bourjois,** the French dime-store brand made in the same factories as Chanel, and **No. 7,** the house brand, which I like very much. Their new makeup for teens is **No. 17.**

Also note that British women have traditionally bought most of their cosmetics and makeup in the major department stores. **Dickins & Jones** (224 Regent St., W1) has redone its street-level makeup department to carry more brands (even cult brands, such as **Makeup Forever** from Paris) and has one of the best selections in the city; Harrods is an old staple. The biggest news in terms of department stores is the new beauty area at **Selfridges** (400 Oxford St., W1), now the single largest piece of beauty real estate in all of Europe.

While we're on the subject of the big department stores, **Liberty** (220 Regent St., W1) has an OK makeup department, but I adore its house brand of soaps (grapefruit and jojoba) and bath items.

Several of the lifestyle stores have branched into makeup, aromatherapy, and bath goop, including **TopShop, Miss Selfridge, Next, French Connection** (which is a British firm, not a French one), **Principles,** and **Warehouse.** Famous-name stores that also sell makeup include **Mary Quant,** while beauty salons have gone into spa treatments, aromatherapy, and makeup colors—**Molton Brown** is a good example here.

SpaceNK, with a few branches around town, sells hard-to-find brands and has been so influential that it has branches all over the United Kingdom and is being copied in some Euro cities. Many of the brands are American, so you don't want to load up on those while in the U.K.

The problem with makeup in Britain is usually price—so look for less-expensive brands or items you can't find in the United States. The hottest local brand is **Ruby & Millie,** which is sold in most Boots stores. **MAC** is more expensive in the United Kingdom, as are most U.S. or Canadian brands.

English Brands

MOLTON BROWN
58 S. Molton St., W1 (Tube: Bond St.).

Famous hairdresser and maker of Molton Browners (hair twists), the salon has a product range that is so successful, it's sold at Harrods and all over the world. They have bath and spa items, aromatherapy, a men's line, and makeup. I had a ball at their outlet store in Bicester Village (p. 288).

PIXI
22A Foubert's Place, W1 (Tube: Oxford St.).

Located right off of Carnaby Street, this itty-bitty shop sells a makeup brand created by a team of Scandinavian girls. They also do facials and massages and let you play with the makeup all day. Prices begin at £10 ($17).

SCREENFACE
24 Powis Terrace, W11 (Tube: Notting Hill Gate).

Stage makeup resource often used by celebs or their makeup artists.

SPACENK
(Thomas Neal's) 37 Earlham St., WC2 (Tube: Covent Garden); 45 Brook St., W1 (Tube: Bond St.).

SpaceNK specializes in cult brands, which is great, but many of them (Nars, for example) are American. Doesn't sound American, but it is—and priced accordingly. We don't buy American in London, do we? Shu Uemura is a Japanese brand carried to some small extent in the United States, but it's also sold here, which is a great place to play with all the colors. There are many brands you haven't heard of or played with; spend a few hours and have a ball. There's enough selection that you can buy British and come out with many unique products.

International Big Names

Department stores fight to carry the big international brands, some of which have exclusive relationships with specific department stores. These brands have free-standing stores; all are also available in the United States. Note that the French makeup department store **Sephora** does not have any stores in London proper—there's one in the 'burbs at the Brent Cross Shopping Centre.

AVEDA
10 Marylebone High St., W1 (Tube: Marylebone).

KIEHL'S
29 Monmouth St., WC2 (Tube: Leicester Sq.).

L'OCCITANE
237 Regent St., W1 (Tube: Piccadilly Circus).

MAC
109 King's Rd., SW3 (Tube: Sloane Sq.).

SHU UEMURA
Thomas Neal Centre, Neal St., WC2 (Tube: Covent Garden).

BEAUTY STROLL

If you just want to see a lot of famous brands in beauty and cosmetics in a short period of time, take a little walk along South Molton Street (Tube: Bond St.) and find these brands. Note that Brook Street runs perpendicular to South Molton Street when Molton dead-ends.

FACE STOCKHOLM
55 S. Molton St.

JO MALONE
23 Brook St.

MAKEUP FOREVER
51 S. Molton St.

MOLTON BROWN
40 S. Molton St.

HAIR

Who knew that in a country where it rains so often, so many hairstylists would become stars? There's so much going on in this section that I have broken it down into two parts: stylists and products. Better-known salons are invariably located in the Covent Garden area or the West End. There are hair salons in all the major department stores and hotels; neighborhoods all have their share of local hairdressers.

As for products, the choices are absolutely astounding. Some lines have unique products you may have never heard of; others simply offer packaging gimmicks.

Stylists

CHARLES WORTHINGTON
34 Great Queen St., WC2 (Tube: Covent Garden).

Worthington is sort of an older-generation name; he has the salon in The Dorchester and is another one who was puttering along at an average pace until he went to America and became famous. Prices are affordable, and the Covent Garden salon is very hip and worth going to, if only to be part of the scene and to hang out at the juice bar and eavesdrop on Bridget Jones. Wash, cut, and dry: about £45 ($74).

DANIEL GALVIN
42–44 George St., W1 (Tube: Baker St.).

Galvin is one of several hairdressers who rode the Princess Diana tresses to fame and fortune. He is known in the fashion magazines for his Midas touch with color.

JO HANFORD
30 Mount St., W1 (Tube: Marble Arch or Bond St.).

Known as the best hair-color artist in London, Hanford has a salon near The Dorchester but also sells hair-color products in Boots stores.

JOHN FRIEDA
75 New Cavendish St., W1 (Tube: Great Portland).

Although John Frieda is indeed a British hairstylist, he made his name and his fortune in the United States. He's known for his products, not for his salon, and most who come to the salon do so because they like the products, including one collection designed for straightening curly hair. Cut and dry is about £60 ($100).

MICHAELJOHN
25 Albemarle, W1 (Tube: Green Park).

I have been friends with the John (and also the Michael) of Michaeljohn for more than 20 years; I did their *People* magazine story when they first opened in Beverly Hills. Now, John's daughter Kate, whom I've known since she was 6, does my hair in London when she's free—otherwise, it's Pierre. Talk about connected.

To be honest, I hadn't taken the time to have my hair done in London for several years, mostly because my hair was short for a while and I could do it myself. Now that my hair has grown out, and I had been spending many a bad hair day on the road, I popped in again. After hugs and hellos, I was sailing out the door and bumped into a woman, a stranger, who reminded me of why I had come to Michaeljohn in the first place and why I have returned—she was the image of everything I wanted to be. Although she was about my age, she had a timeless classical style to her and a quick smile that made me feel at home and comfortable with who she was and who I am.

So now I'm back to tuning up when I come to town, especially having my color done (book Debbie—she's a wizard), as it had become a big mess after a year of experimentation in France. Spa services are available downstairs and at a range of spas located in country-house hotels outside of London.

Although they are one of the royal hairdressers, there is nothing stuck-up about the salon. Wash, cut, and blow dry: about £60 ($100). Oh yes, try their products also (p. 206).

The Sunshine Report: Ethan's Fabulous Makeover Adventure

When I was 17 and in a popular high-school band, all the members decided to grow their hair out to be more "rock 'n' roll." So for 3 years I stopped cutting my usually short-short hair and let it grow to beyond my shoulders. But over the course of 3 years, something occurred to me; I realized that to have long hair without it looking frizzy and gross, you have to condition it . . . and there is absolutely nothing "rock 'n' roll" about having to buy Pantene Pro-V. That's where **Michaeljohn** comes in.

While in London I visited their salon and had a consultation with the artistic director, Tim Traverso, and the technical director, Clare Lodge. I explained to them that I hadn't had a proper haircut in 5 years, and that I wanted something that could look nice (if I wanted it to) or look kind of crazy (if I wanted that). They suggested two shades of blonde highlights and a textured, spiky cut. I had my hair dyed, washed, and then cut. It was great. Everybody was super-friendly and talkative, and in the end I was really happy.

My hair looked short and clean, but not dorky. The best part was that Tim explained to me how to make it look that way on my own, since if you don't use the right hair stuff it will just look stupid and poofy. I strongly recommend Michaeljohn to anyone looking to start over image-wise and treat themselves to something truly fantastic.

NICKY CLARKE
130 Mount St., W1 (Tube: Bond St.).

I believe Nicky Clarke became famous as the hairdresser to Sarah Ferguson when she became the Duchess of York. He's been doing models and editorial pages for years and also has a full range of products. They say the wait list for a cut from Mr. Clarke himself is 6 months; his cut: £300 ($495). My girl-friend Ruth has the Nicky Clarke secret of London: She goes to his brother, who has his own salon in the Marylebone area.

TONI & GUY
8 Marylebone High St., W1 (Tube: Marylebone).

Toni & Guy began as sort of a hip, funky, slightly punk, and a little bit outrageous fashion source, truly on the cutting edge. They've worked hard to keep a touch of the outlaw in their style while becoming so mainstream as to have many salons and begin an international empire. Prices are much more moderate than the other big names. Wash, cut, and dry for about £40 ($66).

TREVOR SORBIE
27 Floral St., WC2 (Tube: Covent Garden).

Another name made famous in the Diana years; he hails from a background with Vidal Sassoon but is best known for being on the floor himself and being available to real people. A cut with him costs a mere £90 ($149), which is a steal by star-snipper prices in New York and London.

VIDAL SASSOON
45A Monmouth St., WC2 (Tube: Covent Garden).

Vidal Sassoon was the first celebrity hairstylist and is possibly still the most famous name in hair in the world. Although he rarely does hair personally, and lives mostly in California, the beat goes on. He has not only an important salon, but a training school where you can get a bargain haircut: Vidal Sassoon School, 56 Davies Mews, W1 (Tube: Bond St.); © 020/7318-5205; open Monday through Friday from 10am to 3pm. Prices at the school begin at about £10 ($17); in the regular salon, you will pay £45 ($74).

Products

These products are usually sold at the salons themselves, but can also be found at most chemist shops. The big **Boots** (Kensington High St.) has the best selection of brands. Not all Boots stores carry all brands.

CHARLES WORTHINGTON TAKE AWAYS
This is a genius concept of marketing and packaging: a complete line of travel-size hair care products that fit in the handbag or travel kit. Each product comes in a different shade of pastel package, with 2.5 ounces (75ml) of product in it. Each unit costs about £1.50 ($2.50). I bought a selection of them as a gift—great for the person who has everything, who likes to try new products, or who travels a lot.

JOHN FRIEDA
Although British born, Frieda actually made his name and his product line in the United States before taking on the United Kingdom. Now, he has a large product line, including many products for curly hair, as well as concept products. There is a separate line for blondes. This summer, a new line for the beach was introduced. The products are almost fashion accessories.

MICHAELJOHN

I use this line, officially called **Salonspa,** because it's good—and because I am addicted to the scent. I buy it at Boots, although all Boots stores do not carry the line or have the full range.

I use **Mighty Mousse** (cute, huh?) and **Root Lift** the most, aside from the shampoo and conditioner. They are packaged in plastic, which makes them safe to pack. Prices range from £1.50 to £6 ($2.50–$9.90).

NICKY CLARKE

What attracted me to the Nicky Clarke toys was the **Colour Therapy** line; I've had a lot of fun using a copper goop called a polisher and texturizer. There is a huge range of products, some for specific shades of colored hair and some for normal hair, whatever that is.

NAILS & MANICURES

Manicures are very expensive in London (like everything else), but if you are used to American manicures, at least you have a shot at getting what you're used to or the kind of repairs you need. Many spas and most hair salons have manicurists; there is a manicurist at the **Boots Well-Being Centre** on Kensington High Street.

AMAZING NAILS
21 S. Molton St., W1 (Tube: Bond St.).

This is what it's come to on South Molton: The once-fanciest retail street in London now has nail salons. These people really are amazing, though not as keen for your business as Nails Inc. (see below), with hours at a civilized Monday through Saturday from 10am to 5:30pm.

HEATHER MISCAMBLE
© 07887/544-971.

I do not know Ms. Miscamble; I found her and her phone number in an article about supermodel Naomi Campbell, who swears by this woman. The manicurist comes to you, which should make life easier.

NAILS INC.
41 S. Molton St., W1 (Tube: Bond St.).

Like I said, there goes the neighborhood—although this is quite a chic nail salon. Note that the hours are most helpful: Monday through Friday from 8am to 8pm, Saturday from 10am to 7pm.

NYNC
17 S. Molton St., W1 (Tube: Bond St.).

This one is a chain, a very successful one, with salons all over town and products for sale in department stores and drugstores. At least the prices are reasonable: Manicures cost less than £14 ($23). The brand may just conquer Europe.

PERFUMES & TOILETRIES

CZECH & SPEAKE
39C Jermyn St., SW1 (Tube: Piccadilly Circus).

Trendy Italian and old-fashioned English in the same breath, this bath shop specializes in brushes and bath-time accessories, as well as its own brand of fragrances, which have somewhat seeped into the cult of better-known, little-known brands. The shop is all gray, black, and brass; the packaging is very special in a high-tech/traditional manner. One of the most interesting shops in London, with a product line that not too many Americans know about. The ideal gift for the person who has everything.

D. R. HARRIS & CO.
29 St. James's St., SW1 (Tube: Piccadilly Circus or Green Park).

This is one of my best secret London finds, although I sort of owe it to a Jilly Cooper novel. This old-fashioned apothecary sells its own lines of goods; **Skin Food** is the cream that I learned about in the novel. There are also men's colognes and shave products, quill toothpicks, and almond-oil moisturizers.

J. FLORIS LTD.
89 Jermyn St., SW1 (Tube: Piccadilly Circus).

London has two leading local perfumers; Floris is one of them. Special floral perfumes include Roses, Lilies, Lavender, and on and on. They are so classically English. The firm was begun in 1730 and kind of looks and feels like it: true Brit style and old-fashioned vibes. Even the packaging is fabulous. Royal warrant. Several hotels use Floris for their amenities; the ones at The Dorchester are specially made by Floris and include a lemon-curd shower cream that I can't get enough of.

JAMES BODENHAM & CO.
88 Jermyn St., SW1 (Tube: Green Park).

Related to the Floris family by marriage, James Bodenham is a Victorian kind of shop with gift items, as well as potpourri and smell-good items and fragrances. There are many food items (jams and spices, as well as teas), but it's the apothecary nature of the store that makes it so much fun.

MILLER HARRIS
14 Needham Rd., W11 (Tube: Notting Hill Gate).

Book 6 months ahead for a private consultation to create your own scent. © 020/7221-1545.

PARFUMS DE NICOLAI
101A Fulham Rd., SW3 (Tube: S. Kensington).

Tiny French brand created by a member of the Guerlain family.

PENHALIGON'S
41 Wellington St., WC2 (Tube: Covent Garden); 110A New Bond St., W1 (Tube: Bond St.); Burlington Arcade, W1 (Tube: Piccadilly Circus).

The other leading perfumer, alongside Floris. Except they are much more than Floris and they have really widened the range and their image in the last 5 years. Now they make great little leather goods.

Although well known for its toilet water and soap that men adore, Penhaligon's also holds a royal warrant. Their products are produced according to the original formulas of William Penhaligon, who began his business as a barbershop in 1841. It's very "olde England" in here and fun to sniff around. Kids seem to like it, too.

They also do exclusive hotel amenities and have re-launched the **Erno Lazlo** brand of skincare. For a whole lot of fun, check out the outlet store at Bicester Village.

SPAS

Spas have become the jewel in the crown of many a luxury hotel, beauty center, and airport. Virgin Atlantic has incredible spas in both Heathrow and Gatwick airports; British Airways recently installed a Molton Brown Travel Spa in its Terminal 4 lounge for business- and first-class passengers, who actually get the treatments for free.

For the poor man's spa, see **Boots Well-Being Centre**, earlier in this chapter.

BERKELEY HEALTH CLUB & SPA
Berkeley Hotel, Wilton Place, SW1 (Tube: Knightsbridge).

Hotel guests are automatic members of the health club; nonguests can buy a 1-day membership, which includes use of the pool and gawking at the rollback roof. The spa portion uses products from **Christian Dior.** Treatments are either a la carte or by the package and begin at £30 ($50); there is a Retail Therapy package, thank God. ℭ 020/7201-1699.

CLARIDGE'S SPA/OLYMPUS HEALTH & FITNESS SUITE
Brook St., W1 (Tube: Bond St.).

Claridge's is one of the few luxury hotels that allows nonguests to book into its spa. The spa is small, and the rich and famous guests want their privacy, so it's a good match. The spa products are from **Anne Seminon** in Paris, a cult brand for those who know. Since I use this brand and adore its treatments, I booked with Ewa Berkmann from the Paris spa, who gave me a facial and foot treatment. I'm going back for the jet-lag treatment. The treatment was so fabulous that I came away sighing, "This is better than sex." Indeed, Ewa gives a better treatment here than in Paris.

The staff is very discreet and will not name names, but it's known that certain celebs come to town specifically for treatments or workouts with various spa heroes, who travel the jet-set circuit in order to pamper those who need it most. ℭ 020/7499-2210.

ELEMIS DAY SPA
23 Lancashire Court, W1 (Tube: Bond St.).

I became addicted to Elemis spa products long before this spa opened; they have been used onboard the *QE2* and are also sold at SpaceNK, where I loaded up on many bath products. Now, you can wallow in the products and be smoothed out of stress or jet lag or cellulite or whatever; treatment packages begin at £105 ($173). About the address: This is just off New Bond Street. ℭ 020/7499-4995.

SPA AT MANDARIN ORIENTAL
66 Knightsbridge, SW1 (Tube: Knightsbridge).

The addition of the spa to this hotel is part of the remake of the hotel and the enrichment program to keep it in tune with the luxuries of the Mandarin Oriental brand. The spa is large, has many therapies, and is best known for its stone therapy. © 020/7838-9888.

Chapter Eight

....

HOME FURNISHINGS & DESIGN RESOURCES

THE NEW LOOK

If you think British home style is all cabbage roses and dark wood, you can think twice and get a look at the Tate Modern . . . or even the renovations at Liberty, the department store. Contemporary styles have become popular; the Continental-Zen style has arrived, epitomized by the Giorgio Armani home-furnishings store on Bond Street.

Even the traditional British makers divide themselves into several schools of thought; from the cozy chic of **Nina Campbell,** who epitomizes the new version of old-fashioned English style; to **Tricia Guild,** who blazes forward with crafts and hot colors and lots of wow; to **Terence Conran,** who stands for a very clean, graphic, simple sort of cross culture—very chic, but at a price. **David Linley**'s craft-luxe takes a classic place in local design—his store is now huge and business is booming. He's possibly the only royal who has found a calling early in life and thrived in it.

ENGLISH DECOR

Ralph Lauren has proved quite handsomely (and expensively) that Americans want the old English, shabby-chic, hounds-and-horses, cabbage-roses-and-faded-fringes look of yesterday.

After all, the real thing has taken generations to develop. However, fear not. You can actually wander throughout certain areas of London and see showroom after showroom, each with a different—but totally acceptable—version of "The Look."

It's been said that the British national character is one that resists change and has tremendous respect for tradition. So it is with English decorating: The themes show a slow transition as generation after generation adds only a small mark to the whole look, but when you look at the whole—there is a lot of choice.

Professional Sources

For those of you who prefer to go to the trade sources, here are a few rules you ought to be aware of when buying in London:

- Have plenty of business cards on hand—if you are working as a member of the trade, introduce yourself when you enter a shop; ask upfront what trade discount or courtesies are offered.
- It is proper etiquette for dealers to identify themselves; they usually give themselves away by their knowledge anyway, but go ahead, tell 'em who you are. If you've brought along an expert for a second opinion, don't be shy. Introduce.
- British decorating and design houses are not in the business of reducing prices unless you are an established client with an open account. Be prepared to show that you are indeed a professional, that you have a credit rating, and so on. It's best to have at least three references from big U.S. firms where you hold open accounts. It's not a bad idea to have U.S. showrooms write, call, or fax ahead to a London showroom before you arrive.
- Very often, English design firms will not take personal orders from out-of-towners. This is especially true if the firm has an agency in the country where you wish the goods to

be shipped. They will not compete with their own overseas agents.

- Unlike U.S. design firms, British design firms will sell goods directly from their London showrooms to anyone. You don't even need to pretend you are a member of the trade. (If you are a member of the trade, however, there's a 10% discount; be prepared to show resale number and business card.)
- Be prepared to handle your own shipping.

In flea markets and at fairs:

- When shopping in a market, such as **Bermondsey,** or on **Portobello Road,** expect to bargain. If you pay the price as marked, you will be overpaying. In this kind of circumstance, having a knowledgeable local at your side can be beneficial. As a member of "the trade," you are expected to know the proper value and negotiate accordingly. At least know the U.S. price for a similar item. "Can you do better?" is all you need to say.

    Note: Bermondsey is a very tricky market because dealers come early and are known to each other. At 10am, you won't convince anyone that you are a dealer.

- Deal with cash when possible. Often, a store will offer a discount for cash transactions because then they do not have to deal with credit card fees. In the markets, only cash is accepted. Many stalls will not even take traveler's checks. If the store does not offer a discount for cash, ask to see the owner and make your point.

While you're there:

- When you're in the fabric house, ask if there are any close-out bins. Quite often, fabrics are discontinued or half rolls are sold, and the showroom cannot sell the leftover pieces. There just might be some wonderful leftovers that are perfect for your home or for a piece of furniture you hadn't thought of re-covering.

- If you are buying fabrics that need trimmings to match, buy them at the same time and with the fabrics in hand. The English trimmings (fringes, ropes, tassels, and so on) are designed and colored to match the fabrics. Do note that, in Brit-speak, the word *fringe* refers to the bangs of a hairstyle. Use the word *trim*. These trimmings are not cheap, but they can be much, much less in England than in the United States. Also, the London selection is superior to what you'll find in the United States.

- When buying wallpaper, ask about the life expectancy of the paper. Once again, printing processes differ, and the wallpaper you are dying for could, in fact, be printed on a paper that is not as sturdy as your needs. Many of the **Laura Ashley** papers are wonderful, but have a life expectancy of only 4 to 5 years. Some are not coated, and they absorb dirt at a rapid rate. These are considerations that every designer worries about when doing a design job. Since you will be doing it yourself, you must be aware! There are Laura Ashley vinyl wallpapers, but there are two types: British vinyl and American-made vinyl from a different company. Not all patterns are made by both houses.

Basic Sources

Several of the department stores have reinvented themselves in the last year to beef up their home-decor departments; all are good sources of ideas and items you might not find at home. **Liberty** has a new bed department, while **Dickins & Jones** has totally redone home furnishings. **Peter Jones** has long been one of my regular haunts; see the department-store section (p. 151) for details and addresses.

The big names of European design all have shops in London; the question is whether you have such a shop near where you live in America or whether the VAT refund will make the price better.

Other tips:

- If you are planning to buy a lot of furniture, make arrangements with a shipper before you start your spree (see "Shipping," later in this chapter). Very often, the fabric houses will ship for you, but the furniture dealers prefer that you make your own arrangements. If you are buying antiques valued at over £2,000 ($3,300), you will need to have an export license from the British Customs offices. A good shipper will also help arrange this for you. It is easier to have all your goods arrive in one container than in dispersed shipments. Ask your shipper whether they will pick up from a variety of sources and whether there is any charge for this extra service. Be sure to get the best insurance possible on your goods. Don't save money on shipping. Shop the options, but buy the best.

- When buying at auction, be aware that you will be bidding against dealers who know their goods and what they are worth. Do a very careful inspection of the auction items the day before and check carefully for repairs and/or replacement of parts. The technology of furniture repair has made it possible to repair and/or replace damaged parts without the untrained eye being able to see the work. If you are not buying to collect but only to enjoy, this won't matter. However, if you are collecting Georgian antiques, every repair changes the value of the piece. If the dealers are not bidding, take their cue that something is wrong.

    If you want a piece badly enough, however, you can very often outbid the dealers. They need to resell the piece to make a profit and, therefore, need to stop well under the street value for that piece. This is where you will have the advantage. You can save money and get a valuable collectible, piece of furniture, work of art, or carpet while having the fun of beating the dealer.

- When buying period pieces, whether at auction, through a dealer, or at a stall, remember to get papers of authenticity. Any item 100 years old or older is free of U.S. Customs

Measure for Measure

English fabrics are sold by the meter or the yard. Ask.

Always verify the width of the fabrics (most American fabrics are 54 in. wide) and the size of the repeat, as both will affect the amount you need to purchase. If you are buying for a particular piece of furniture, take the measurements of the piece and a photo with you. Most fabric houses have trained staff who will help you determine how much fabric is necessary for your job. If there is any question, buy extra. Yes, you may be able to find the same fabric at home, but the dye lot will be completely different, and your two pieces will never match. You can use the extra for pillows if you don't end up needing it for your job.

Allow for the repeat. If you have no idea what I am talking about, you should reconsider your abilities as an interior designer.

Wallpaper rolls are very often double rolls, not single rolls. That is to say, one single British roll measures almost as long as two American-size rolls. Ask.

duties. However, you will be asked for proof of age by officials. They are on to tricks in this area, so don't try to pass off a new tea service (set) as antique. However, this is also a gray area in British law. If you buy a chair that is Georgian but has had some parts replaced, this would be considered a reasonable restoration and would be fine. But if more than half of the chair has been restored so that most of the parts are new, the law is not clear, and your chair may not be considered duty-free.

- Don't expect to be able to buy a national treasure. Important pieces must be approved for export by the country of origin before they are granted an export license. If you are bidding against a museum in an auction, it is quite possible that the work will be awarded to the museum even though you can outbid them. All countries are unwilling to let go of their finest works of art and furniture.

- If the work of art or piece of furniture is not wanted by the museum, be sure that the price you are paying is not more expensive (taking shipping, insurance, and so on into account) than it would be to buy a similar piece through a dealer in the United States.

Booking English Style

If you're as interested in English style and decor as I am, you'll have a ball with all the magazines the news agent can sell you. Go to several different news agents, because even the biggies in the train stations don't always have the full range.

British publishing has far more choices in the subjects of design, architecture, style, crafts, and reference for buying antiques. Alas, British book prices are also outrageously high. Make sure there is no American edition of a book you are planning to buy before you go hog-wild at your nearest **Hatchards** or **Dillon's.**

Also, note that if you buy price guides, prices will be in pounds sterling pegged to local values; many items are more (or less) valuable across the pond.

For an almost staggering selection of books on design—not just British—be sure to visit the **Design Centre of London** (28 Haymarket, SW1; Tube: Piccadilly Circus), which has a huge bookselling space divided into many categories of the arts, including architecture.

Design on Sale

Not only do showrooms have sales, but there are also big social sale events held once or twice a year—usually to raise funds for charity—where designer furnishings are sold off. The Grand Sale is an annual event sponsored by *House & Garden* and held in a huge hall for maximum fun; it's usually in the fall—ask your hotel concierge or watch for ads in the magazine's pages.

Also pick up brochures in design showrooms; frequently, they announce sale events. Last time I was shopping at **Designer's**

Guild, they were handing out flyers about their next warehouse sale! There are also ads in the newspapers about such special sales and clearances.

Design Shows

Chelsea Design Week This is an event for the trade: It includes complimentary chauffeur-driven cars to whisk you to various participating showrooms, where they lay it on thick. Only the big names play. One day is open to the public. The event is usually in March; write Chelsea Design Week, The Basement, 4 Charlwood Place, London SW1V 2LU.

Decorex Almost 20 years old and still ticking, a popular show for the trade and for pros, although you can possibly wangle a way in. Call ✆ 020/7833-3374.

100% Design Another trade show, but wait—the public is invited on the last day! It's usually in the fall; ✆ 020/8849-6211.

Chelsea Crafts Fair Annual event, usually in the fall, open to the public and featuring more than 200 artisans. Call ✆ 020/7278-7700.

Auctions

The designer's best secret is the London auction, where more and more people are hoping to get a deal. Because prices are set at auctions and then determined for similar items throughout the art and furniture world, you may not find a bargain at all. Naturally, the London auction scene is the big time, whereas country auctions are easier to deal with and may offer better prices. I must admit, with a warning, that we went to a country auction and found that the furniture was desirable and well-priced, but the cost of shipping it back to the United States did not justify buying anything.

Nevertheless, auctions are a tremendous amount of fun and should be considered for pure entertainment's sake. In London, however, there are certain auctions that are quite serious and important and, while fun, are taken without much of a sense of humor. If you attend a big auction at a prestigious house, ask around about proper wardrobe. Women should plan on simple suits or silks for day. Evening auctions can be black-tie events—they are seldom white-tie. Viewings are almost always during the day, as are the majority of auctions. Proper business clothes are essential, even if one isn't bidding.

Like all major cities, London has an auction season: October through May. Country auctions are often held in the summer, but fancy auctions are held only at auction houses in the city during the season. Occasionally auctions are closed to the public (such as the fur auctions in St. Petersburg, Russia, where pelts are sold to furriers in lots), but usually, you can be admitted to an auction by catalog or for free. Weekly auction programs are published in the *Times* on Tuesday and in the *Daily Telegraph* on Monday. Some houses sell certain types of works on specific days of the week, such as china on Monday and European oil paintings on Friday. In season, there will be about 100 auctions a month in London alone.

Various auctions have various functions in their respective fields; often, it is to set the prices for the rest of the world. On the other hand, you shouldn't be intimidated. You may indeed get a real "steal," or you may be shopping in a country where the market price for an item you're interested in is considerably less than in the United States.

Please note that there is no VAT on antiques.

Do be wary of fakes at auctions, particularly from the less-famous houses. If you buy an item because you love it, and if it doesn't matter to you whether it's real or not, that's one thing. But if you are buying for investment, name-dropping, or status-seeking purposes, use a house expert or, better yet, a private expert as a consultant. The better houses will not intentionally sell you a forgery or a fake; small-time auctioneers may not care what's in the lots, as long as they move them out. A house may even admit that they don't know if a piece is authentic. **Sotheby's** uses the full name of an artist in the catalog listing when they know the work is authentic, but only the initials of the artist if they have some doubt as to the provenance of the work.

The experts at the big auction houses are trained to not only know their stuff, but also to be informative and polite. If you want to bone up on a point of curiosity or just pick someone's brain, wander into a good auction house and speak to someone at the front desk. They may well give you information you never knew or turn you on to a free and expert opinion.

The most famous auction houses in London are **Sotheby's** and **Christie's,** but don't underestimate **Bonham's,** which has been around since 1793.

BONHAM'S KNIGHTSBRIDGE
Montpelier St., SW7 (Tube: Knightsbridge);
www.bonhams.com.

CHRISTIE'S
8 King St., St. James's, SW1 (Tube: Piccadilly Circus or
Green Park); 85 Old Brompton Rd., S. Kensington, SW7
(Tube: Earl's Court).

SOTHEBY'S
34–35 New Bond St., W1 (Tube: Bond St.).

There are also stamp and coin auctions. **Harmer's** (91 New Bond St., W1; Tube: Bond St.) is the leading stamp auction house; **Stanley Gibbons** (399 The Strand, WC2; Tube: Charing Cross), another famous house, has an auction about six times a year. Don't forget country auctions that you may find on a weekend outing, which usually are charming—but remember that if there was something truly important to sell, it would have gone to a big house in a major city to command a big price. So enjoy. At a country auction, expect to pay cash for your purchase. Be prepared to make your own shipping arrangements (p. 223).

When you shop at an auction of any kind, remember:

- The house is not responsible for the authenticity of the article.
- There is a house commission charged to the seller, but the buyer will have to pay taxes. Some houses also commission the buyer—ask, as this can raise the price of your item by another 10%. This is called "the buyer's premium." There's a recent trend, in order to reel in the big auctions, for the house to cut the commission but raise the premium. Know your terms and ask questions.
- You are entitled to know the price a similar item went for in previous years and the price the house expects the item to go for at the current auction. Often these prices are posted at the viewing or may be published in the catalog. The house's expectation of what something will go for at auction proves meaningless several times a year, but it is a beginning.
- Find out before you bid what currency you must pay in. International houses often accept many currencies, and you may do better with your dollar converting to one rather than another. This can pay off with a large purchase.
- If bidding is not in U.S. dollars, keep a calculator in your hand during the bidding to know what the prices are; remember to calculate at the current American Express rate of exchange rather than the bank rate. The bank rate will be more favorable than the one you will actually be paying, so don't cheat yourself by an inaccurate conversion.
- Expect to pay tax on the item when you call for it. Find out the tax ahead of time. VAT is not paid on antiques.
- The auction house may pack and ship your purchase for you, but it may be cheaper to do it yourself, or ask your hotel concierge to handle it for you.
- Make sure that the item you are about to buy is allowed to leave the country! Some countries won't let you out with what they consider to be items of national heritage. Conversely, make sure you can get it into the United States. You

will not be reimbursed if the government confiscates any of your property (normally because of fakes). If the item is an antique, get the papers that verify its age. According to Customs, an antique is any item 100 years old or more.

• Don't bid against Bill Gates.

SHIPPING

The good news: You've just found the most wonderful, gorgeous, fabulous, chic, and inexpensive sideboard. You've longed for one for years and know it will be the envy of all who see it.

The bad news: It certainly won't fit into your suitcase.

Whether the item is as cumbersome as a sideboard, as small as a few bottles of perfume, or as fragile as dinner plates, you can arrange to ship it home. All it takes is a little time and a little more money.

To make shipping pay, the item—with the additional cost of shipping, duty, and insurance (and Customs agent, if need be)—still should cost less than it would at home, or be so totally unavailable at home that any price makes it a worthwhile purchase. If it's truly unavailable at home (and isn't an antique or a one-of-a-kind art item), ask yourself why. There may be a good reason—such as it's illegal to bring such an item into the country! If you are indeed looking for a certain type of thing, be very familiar with American prices. If it's an item of furniture, even an antique, can a decorator get it for you with a 20% rather than a 40% markup? Have you checked out all the savings angles first?

Your Options

There are basically two types of shipping: surface and air. Air can be broken down two ways: unaccompanied baggage and regular airfreight.

Surface mail is the cheaper of the two. Surface mail may mean through the regular mail channels—a small package of perfume would be sent through parcel post—or it may require your filling an entire shipping container, or at least paying the price for use of an entire container. Many people make the mistake of assuming that only the weight of an item will matter in the shipping. Although weight matters, there may be a 500-pound difference per price bracket!

A piano may weigh more than two Queen Anne chairs, but they may cost the same to ship. Surface mail may take 3 months, but we've had delivery in 3 weeks. Allow 3 months to be safe, longer if so advised by the dealer.

If you are shipping books (antique or otherwise), note that there are special surface rates and no U.S. duties.

Generally speaking, rates are per cubic foot and include:

- Picking up the purchase
- Packing the goods (crating may be extra)
- Handling export documents
- Sea-freight charges
- Customs clearance on the U.S. end

If you want to save money, ask about "groupage" services. Your goods will be held until a shipping container is filled. The container will then go to the United States, to one of only four ports of entry (Los Angeles, New York, San Francisco, or New Orleans), where you can meet the container at the dock, be there when your items are unpacked, and pay the duties due. A full container is 1,100 cubic feet of space (or 8½ ft. by 8½ ft. by 20 in. long—or big enough for about 100 pieces of furniture) and will not be delivered to your door (no matter how much you smile). A container to New York will cost you £3,000 ($4,950), which includes wrapping, shipping, and London paperwork. U.S. collections and bills of lading usually add £100 ($165) to the bill. Insurance costs 1.5% of the total value of the goods.

Airfreight is several times more expensive than surface, but it has the assurance of quick delivery. You can airfreight small items up to 50 pounds (in weight, not price) through traditional business services such as DHL and FedEx. Or you can use freight services that will airfreight larger-size packages and even furniture.

If your purchase is so delicate and so important as to need to be flown, it may indeed need an international courier, which is a person who hand-carries the item for you. (This is often done with pieces of art or valuable papers.)

You can find a list of shippers and packers in the back of the annual *Guide to the Antique Shops in Britain,* published by Antiques Collectors Club. When you choose a shipper, ask for a "buying kit," which includes a complete set of paperwork.

Among the most famous names in the trade:

- **Davies Turner,** Overseas House, Stewarts Road, SW8 (© **020/7622-4393;** fax 020/7720-3897).
- **Featherston Shipping,** 24 Hampton House, 15–17 Ingate Place, SW8 (© **020/7720-0422;** fax 020/7720-6330).
- **Fentons,** Beachy Road, Old Ford, E3 (© **020/8533-2711;** fax 020/8985-6032).
- **Gander & White,** 21 Lillie Rd., SW6 (© **020/7381-0571;** fax 020/7381-5428).
- **Lockson Services Ltd.,** 29 Bloomfield St., E1 (© **020/ 7515-8600;** fax 020/7515-4043).

But Wait! An Even Better Bet

Here's one more source, which I actually discovered in France, and it may be your best bet yet because they have offices in New York and London and three different offices in France— in Paris, at the St. Ouen Flea Market, and in the South of France at the big flea-market city of Isle Sur La Sorgue:

Hedley's Humpers, Units 2, 3, and 4, 97 Victoria Rd., London, NW10 (© **020/8965-8733;** fax 020/8965-0249); New York office: 30 Thompson St., New York, NY 10013 (© **212/ 219-2877;** fax 212/219-2826).

I've found another service that might be helpful if you don't have enough for a container but need some help with your parcels. Stop by any British post office and investigate

Parcel Force, the parcel delivery branch of the U.K. Post Office. You can call them at ✆ 0800/44-22, which is a toll-free number in the United Kingdom.

Insurance

Insurance usually is sold by the package by your shipper. Don't assume that it's included in the price of delivery, because it isn't. There are several different types of insurance, with deductibles or all-risk (with no deductible), so you'll have to make a personal choice based on the value of what you are shipping. *Remember:* When figuring the value of the item for insurance purposes, include the price of the shipping.

If you bought a desk for £600 ($1,000) and it costs £300 ($500) to ship it home, the value for insurance purposes is £900 ($1,500). If you have the replacement-cost type of insurance, you should probably double the price, since that is approximately what it would cost you to replace the item in the United States.

THE DISH ON DISHES
....

The British are blessed with a crazy location in the sea of geography: They've got coal and they've got clay. As a result, they have a centuries-old tradition of producing bone china. You can visit the china factories in the countryside or you can visit all the china stores in London.

- Most china stores in London sell only first quality. The prices are usually 30% less than in the United States, but if the dollar is bad, that savings may shrink. During sales, especially in January, you may discover a 50% savings. During sales, some of the biggies (like **Harrods** and **Lawley's,** for example) do truck in seconds, which are so marked.
- The problem with really saving big on china comes with the shipping. China must be packed, crated, and insured, and—in some cases—you must pay duty on it (not if it comes home

in parcels worth under $50 and marked "Unsolicited Gift"). Even with VAT refunds, you will still raise the cost of your purchase appreciably. But that doesn't mean you shouldn't consider a big haul. It just means you need to mentally register the landed price, not the asking price.

- Prices on the same items are supposed to be the same in each retail outlet but may vary by as much as £2 ($3.30) per place setting. If a retailer is overstocked with a certain pattern, he may deal on the price of a large order.

- If you want to buy seconds, consider a trip to Stoke-on-Trent; if not, come to London for the January and June/July sales, or even order by telephone during a sale period.

- Silver, even silver plate, is getting more and more expensive each year, but is still a good bet when bought secondhand. Avoid the fancy stores and stick to street markets, such as **Bermondsey** or the famous **London Silver Vaults** (p. 229). By law, silver must be marked—look for marks or ask. To bring silver (or plate) into the United States tax-free, it must be more than 100 years old. Get a receipt that says so from the dealer at the time of purchase.

- England is also famous for its lead crystal, although the most famous brands come from Ireland or Scotland. You can buy crystal during the big sale periods when you buy china, or head for the factory-outlet stores, which usually feature the best prices on discontinued patterns. If you are filling in an existing pattern, you may want to buy at the airport either in London or Shannon.

RESOURCES: CHINA, CRYSTAL & SILVER

••

CHINACRAFT
98 The Strand, WC2 (Tube: Charing Cross).

Chinacraft has several stores in London and offers stock on all the biggies—Spode, Minton, Royal Crown Derby, Wedgwood, Aynsley, Coalport, and Royal Worcester. Quite a selection of crystal is available, including patterns from Waterford and Baccarat.

Oh, yes, and here's a little secret or two for you about Chinacraft: If you buy a lot (more than £300/$500), see if you can politely negotiate a discount. The salespeople are used to big spenders who will come in and order half a million pounds' worth of delectables, but you can buy less and still get a discount—if you are nice. Discounts vary on stock—if they have a lot of something they want to move out, they will discount it upfront. Anyone walking in may ask about a pattern, and they may tell you that they'll take 15% off on that pattern. On another pattern—perhaps one that is out of stock and has to be ordered—a discount would be impossible. It's all very flexible.

Please note that Chinacraft owns **Reject China Shop** (see below), and there's not a lot of difference between the two in terms of price; it's all a matter of marketing and showmanship. You can shop online with Chinacraft (**www.chinacraft.co.uk**) as well and even get U.K. prices before your trip so you can comparison-shop in the United States.

LAWLEY'S
154 Regent St., W1 (Tube: Piccadilly Circus).

I love Lawley's because of the contrast in styles: its blue carpets and velvet cases and department-store elegance during the year, and its plank tables of bins of seconds during the sale periods. The selection is vast and the sales are excellent.

The sales are advertised in the regular newspapers (such as the *Times,* not the *Sun*) and are called midwinter and midsummer sales. That means the January sale is in the second to third week in January; ditto the summer sale—it's in the middle of June. Don't assume that all London summer sales are in July.

During the sale period, you will get factory prices right there in downtown London, on Regent Street, no less.

Plate collectors' note: Lawley's caters to the collector set for all categories of china.

THE LONDON SILVER VAULTS
53–64 Chancery Lane, WC2 (Tube: Chancery Lane).

This takes a little getting to and may require a taxi, but if you love silver, I beg you to include the Silver Vaults on your shopping list. It's just great, good fun.

Originally founded in 1882 as a large safety-deposit box and now in the Holborn section of London, the Silver Vaults comprise 35 shops selling a variety of large and small items at all prices. Only one shop is at street level; the rest are underground. Expect to find everything from silver buckets to Fabergé jewelry.

MORRIS & CO.
387 The Arches, Geffrye St., E2 (Tube: Liverpool St.).

One of the hip new stores in the East End, Morris & Co. specializes in craft pottery. The store is open 7 days a week but hours vary with the season. Since it's in the East End, you might want to call before you head over (© **020/7739-8539**).

PORTOBELLO ROAD CHINA
85 & 89 Portobello Rd., W11 (Tube: Notting Hill Gate).

If you're the type who loves heaps of dishes—often at excellent prices—then you'll love this shop, a division of Portobello Road Cashmere Shop, a few doors away (at no. 160). The shop is just shelves and shelves of dishes with an especially keen eye toward blue and white and big names in English Potteries (such as Spode and so on). Open only Friday and Saturday, or by appointment (© **020/7792-2571**).

REJECT CHINA SHOP
1 Beauchamp Place, SW3 (Tube: Knightsbridge); Covent Garden, WC2 (Tube: Covent Garden).

OK, let's get this straight: There are no bargains here. Sometimes, there are seconds, which are priced lower than firsts, and, true, the Regent Street shop is a lot of fun, but these stores are marketed to imply that you are getting a bargain, when in fact, prices are the same as elsewhere. In fact, prices are the same as at Thomas Goode! Shocking, huh?

Still, the stores are convenient to the tourist trade and are stocked to make you think you've found rock-bottom prices. On Beauchamp Place, not far from the museums on Cromwell Road, there's a small store right on the corner.

The Covent Garden store is tiny and specializes in mass-market teapots with a few pieces of Portmeirion and some blue-and-white; all at the going bargain price you can find around town. No bargains, but the store is tiny and crowded and cute and definitely part of the fun of shopping Covent Garden.

There is also a large store on Regent Street; most of the action is downstairs.

RICHARD BRAMBLE COLLECTION
Studio: 56B Vauxhall Grove, SW8 (Tube: Vauxhall).

I discovered this man's work at **Borough Market,** and it is so stunning that I had to share. It is by far easier to view at the market than by making a special trip to the studio. Bramble paints food on white plates, but it is stunning and chic and is often used by the world's most famous chefs. In fact, there is even a cookbook called *The Star Chefs Cookbook* that features recipes from Michelin chefs and Bramble's dishes. Not cheap, but worth the scratch. It's open by appointment only (✆ 020/7587-1471; info@richardbramble.com).

THOMAS GOODE
19 S. Audley St., W1 (Tube: Green Park or Hyde Park Corner).

If you're looking for the ultimate shopping experience for your selection of china, glassware, silver, or exquisite accessory pieces, this elegant shop is a must. In fact, if you were looking to pick one simple, very London, very elegant shopping experience that epitomizes why you travel, why you have to shop in foreign cities, and what can be gained by educating your eye in the world's best cities, well, Thomas Goode just might be your choice. This is theater as well as shopping.

The store is almost the size of a city block and rambles through a variety of salons; don't miss any of them—including the far back where the antique knickknacks are sold, or the far side where there is now a tearoom (with very high prices). Also check out the bomb. Yes, the bomb. Don't bring your children (breakage!). Do bring your credit cards. And possibly your camera.

Goode carries all the top European brands of china (but no Wedgwood!) and crystal and has monogram services available on the premises. They have a number of innovative designs for tabletop and a lot of expensive doodads that you can also find at a plebeian place such as **Harrods,** but which are much more pleasing to the eye in the surroundings of Thomas Goode. The sales help is incredibly well bred and nice.

RESOURCES: ENGLISH MODERNE

Contemporary looks are frequently combined with old-fashioned architectural styles in London; the look has moved through the 1960s and come out the other end with clean lines and moderate prices.

THE CONRAN SHOP
81 Fulham Rd., SW3 (Tube: S. Kensington).

The Conran Shop should not be confused with the now-defunct Conran's in the United States. The rehabbed Michelin House with its Art Deco tiles and hoopla welcomes you first into a cafe, then into a store of mini-showrooms with modern Yuppie furniture. Go downstairs for a less stark and more moderately priced version of the first floor. Here's where you'll find the fun: baskets, gifts, dried flowers, china, toys, books, foodstuffs, coffees, luggage, umbrellas—everything.

Habitat
196 Tottenham Court Rd., W1 (Tube: Goodge St.); 206 King's Rd., SW3 (Tube: Sloane Sq.).

Habitat made British home-furnishings history, although not in the same way as Mr. Chippendale. After the spare Scandinavian look came the modern British look—an update of Scandinavian chic with a touch of high-tech. It was all begun by Terence Conran, who was later knighted for his contribution to the world. Habitat, although no longer owned by Sir Terence, is still a glorious place to shop, even if the look isn't the newest look and you can see a lot of this stuff in the United States.

Note that there is a difference between **Habitat** shops and **The Conran Shop** in Michelin House in London.

Heals
198 Tottenham Court Rd., WC3 (Tube: Tottenham Court Rd.); 234 King's Rd., WC2 (Tube: Sloane Sq.).

Heals is the mother of English modern design and the source of Terence Conran's inspiration. Heals is a furniture and lifestyle department store in the real-people part of London not far from Regent Street. (It takes some degree of purpose to get there.) It is expensive and offers similar looks to all modern housewares stores, but better quality and therefore higher prices. You'll find the squishy sofa of your dreams here (hardly a tourist item) and plenty of yummy bed and tabletop linen. Convenient to the store is a branch of practically everything else as well so that you can see the same looks established by Heals and then copied at Habitat and Pier 1 Imports. They have great sales.

The King's Road store is newish; it's across from Chelsea Town Hall.

Muji
26 Great Marlborough St., W1 (Tube: Oxford Circus).

Don't freak about this address—it's half a block off Regent Street, right behind Liberty. Also note that there's a branch of Muji in every trading area in London, so there are dozens of them.

OK, so Muji is a Japanese company and the subject is English moderne. But this firm has so much become part of the look that I'd be remiss to not include it. Actually, Muji is a lifestyle store, and the look works well with the simplicity of Conran's vision.

I shop here for the containers and travel-packing possibilities more than for home furnishings and decor. The look is lean and spare and simple in the best Japanese manner, but there are all sorts of gadgets and gimmicks.

RESOURCES: FABRICS & OBJETS D'ART

It's hard to separate the fabric, furniture, and collectible sources from one another. Most often, a fabric showroom will also carry a line of furniture, and a furniture dealer will have an exclusive line of fabrics. Many of the showrooms make individual items out of their fabrics—cosmetics bags, novelty gifts, and such.

ANNA FRENCH
343 King's Rd., SW3 (Tube: Sloane Sq.).

Although Anna French features a lot of lace and lacy looks, her design showroom offers a complete range of all the items necessary to the country-English postmodern look: marbleized wallpapers, faux finishes, swags of lace, and fabrics printed with big flowers that aren't cabbage roses. The look would coordinate well with many **Jane Churchill** or **Designer's Guild** choices; there's a lot of Arts and Crafts inspiration in current works. But more classical possibilities are also available. Open to the public.

CATH KIDSON
8 Clarendon Cross, W11 (Tube: Holland Park).

Kidson does her own prints, sort of 1950s style, and her work is bright, clever, and unusual for the United Kingdom because it offers a totally different take on retro. There are assorted items, such as travel kits, made out of her fabrics. But there are also wallpaper and fabric by the yard. There's a Kidson boutique in the lower level at Selfridges, if you want to get an idea before you head over there.

THE CLOTH SHOP
290 Portobello Rd., W11 (Tube: Ladbroke Grove).

It is, in fact, going from the sublime to the ridiculous to have listed some of the most famous names in English design and then plop you right over to Portobello Road—but I can't help myself. This shop is just as important in its own right, but it's very different from any other listing here—the shop sells old and used linens. Some are antiques; others have been dyed to fun, fashion colors. There are also fabrics off the bolt.

COLEFAX & FOWLER
110 Fulham Rd., SW3 (Tube: S. Kensington); 151 Sloane St., SW3 (Tube: Sloane Sq.).

The king of English chic is located, appropriately, near South Molton Street and Old Bond Street, home to all the best designers. Entering the Colefax & Fowler showrooms is like taking a step into an English country home. The building was built in 1766 by Sir Jeffrey Wyattville and is clearly being held together with chintz. Inside, the rooms are the size of small sitting rooms, the carpet is worn, and the furnishings are old. However, this is all part of the mystique. Upstairs houses the most magnificent collection of English chintzes ever to be desired by an Anglophile. Every year, its designers bring out a new collection of fabrics and wallpapers more beautiful than the previous year's—assuming you like the look, of course.

Anyone may browse and buy.

DESIGNER'S GUILD
267–271 and 277 King's Rd., SW3 (Tube: Sloane Sq.).

Tricia Guild has been going for a long time with her Designer's
Guild, one of the best-known sources in town for all the pieces
you need to put together a look. She has prospered because
she has been able to change that look and not grow stale. The
effect is stupendous. If you're tired of the old country-English
look, you'll revel in all this color and excitement. There are
two shops, a few doors apart. Don't miss either. Even if you
aren't going to buy so much as a meter of fabric, come in and
absorb all the trends. This is hot. Warehouse sales are advertised annually. Open to the public.

JANE CHURCHILL
151 Sloane St., SW1 (Tube: Sloane Sq.).

The line designed by Jane Churchill is English in feeling (it goes
with her last name), but international in scope. It's higher
in cost than **Laura Ashley,** but with a younger look than
Colefax & Fowler. The look is very packaged and is positioned
a few rungs up from Laura Ashley. The line and look have
expanded to various forms of cutie-pie; I find the dancing
veggies a bit much, but at least the woman is not vegetating.
Quite affordable and worth looking at.

Trade operates a separate business; the shops provide regular retail for the general public.

JOHN STEFANIDIS
253 Fulham Rd., SW3 (Tube: Fulham Broadway).

One of the big-time hotshots of British interiors, with his own
books and his own following, Stefanidis offers a more modern version of Colefax, without a look over the shoulder to
the English manor house: no big cabbage roses to blind you.
The small showroom offers two floors of things to look at,
including wallpaper, fabric, furniture, and some gift items.
We're talking about £35 ($58) for a roll of wallpaper—but an
English roll of wallpaper is double the size of an American one.

The shop is in a wonderful location near a string of other design showrooms and antiques shops; anyone may browse and buy.

Nicholas Haslam
12 Holbein Place, SW1 (Tube: Sloane Sq.).

To show you are "in," please refer to this man as "Nicky" and act like you know him and his famous touch: his handmade kilim shoes. The shop is on a small street that intersects Pimlico Road and Sloane Square. His showroom is a wonderful collection of every period and style, with preference to none. The truth is that Nicky Haslam is one of London's more sought-after designers, with a very versatile design ability. He will do both small and large jobs, but you must have an appointment to meet with him in person.

Nina Campbell
9 Walton St., SW3 (Tube: S. Kensington); 7 Milner St., SW3 (Tube: S. Kensington).

One of the most famous names in London design, Ms. Campbell became well known to Americans when she stepped in to rescue the Duke and Duchess of York from their American design team. Now she has two boutiques, one for antiques and one for stuff.

There is also a boutique in **Harvey Nichols** with more of the same merchandise. I bought a fabric-covered "bulletin board" (the most chic bulletin board ever created, I might add) for a wedding present—it was £35 ($58), but so sophisticated you could die for it.

Osborne & Little
304 King's Rd., SW3 (Tube: Sloane Sq.).

Along with Colefax & Fowler, Osborne & Little reigns as top of the line for The Look. The firm began as antiquarian booksellers, with a sideline of hand-printed wallpapers. However, when Sir Peter Osborne and his brother-in-law Anthony

Little won the Council of Industrial Design Award for their first wallpaper collection in 1968, they began a revolution in the interior-design and manufacturing business. Shortly after, the firm gave up the interior-design aspect of the business to concentrate on the design and production of fine English wallpapers and fabrics.

Osborne & Little designs are wonderful because they are always based in history but not limited by it. A charming English botanical print might be reinterpreted in bolder colors. A whole line of wallpapers reflects the paint effects of marbleizing and stippling found in old Italian villas. Because they are now machine-produced, the fabrics and wallpapers are even affordable. The showroom is quiet and dignified—just the kind of place where you might like to have high tea.

Anyone may browse and buy.

THOMAS DARE
341 King's Rd., SW3 (Tube: Sloane Sq.).

More flair of a different sort, very in and very with-it in a soft, cozy, comfy, slightly whimsical, lighthearted style. Popular with the Yuppies.

VESSEL
114 Kensington Park Rd., W11 (Tube: Notting Hill Gate).

This shop specializes in tabletop but is mostly a gallery for art glass.

WARNER & SONS LTD.
7–11 Noel St., W1 (Tube: Oxford Circus).

Benjamin Warner began the firm in 1870 as a silk-weaving company. As a matter of fact, Warner & Sons still uses the original silk-weaving Jacquard hand looms for some of its work. The archives document more than 30,000 fabrics by name of designer, year designed, and a sample of the fabric whenever possible. Warner will reproduce any of the designs in its

A Resource for Dogs

Don't miss **Stephanie Hoppen** (17 Walton St., SW3; Tube: S. Kensington). This small gallery has portraits of dogs that are divine; you can also commission a portrait of your family pet. Since it's on the sensational Walton Street, there's no excuse not to stop in, even if you are a cat person.

archives for a minimum order of 120 meters (394 ft.) per colorway. It will also custom-design a fabric for your job if a reproduction is not to your liking. Trade preferred.

RESOURCES: GARDEN DESIGN

COLUMBIA ROAD MARKET
Columbia Rd., E2 (no nearby Tube; bus 26, 48, or 55).

This is a Sunday-only event, and it's over by about 2pm. While there are flowers and plants and greens sold in flats in the street, there's also a big boutique scene—so this isn't a "just gardens" kind of thing.

THE CHELSEA GARDENER
125 Sydney St., King's Rd., SW3 (Tube: Sloane Sq.).

This source is actually right off King's Road, hence the unusual address; don't panic—it's right in the heart of things.

By all means, you must poke into this little enclave of green and park and retail and great stuff—most of the space is taken by The Chelsea Gardener, a nursery and garden shop, but there's a mini-mall of other stores here too, including a branch of **Thomas Neal's.**

The Chelsea Gardener is open 7 days a week. It has books on design products as well as plants.

RESOURCES: RIBBONS & TRIMS

....

J. T. MORGAN
Chepstow Corner (Shop 28), Chepstow Place, W2 (take a taxi).

This is near Ledbury Grove, the hot new area I've been raving about; there are many antiques shops nearby as well as home-furnishings sources. The store has zillions of buttons as well as trims for home and for costumes and dress-up.

TEMPTATION ALLEY
361 Portobello Rd., W10 (Tube: Notting Hill Gate).

More than 6,000 trims.

VV ROULEAUX
Atelier: 32 Old Burlington St., W1 (Tube: Piccadilly Circus or Green Park); Trade vaults: 6 Tun Yard, Peardon St., SW3 (take a taxi); Retail stores: 54 Sloane Sq. at Cliveden Place, SW1 (Tube: Sloane Sq.) and 6 Marylebone High St., W1 (Tube: Bond St. or Marylebone).

This store is convenient to Peter Jones and not far from its old location. But if you are a regular, do note that it has moved. Also note that the company has expanded and now has a few other stores; the one on Marylebone High Street is the best.

If you're doing a home-fabrics-and-trimmings spree and are a simple ribbon freak as I am, it's easy enough to get to one of their shops. The stores all have tons of ribbons and trims and swags and things that will make you swoon with their beauty and grace. There's also a large selection of fabric flowers in velvet, silk, denim, ribbon, and so on.

Really special; don't miss it.

Note: There's a separate trade resource; call ✆ **020/7622-5735** for details.

BARGAINS ON BASICS

Aside from sales seasons and the big outlet malls, there are a few outlets that specialize in discounted home furnishings and design items. Most of the china companies have outlet stores in **The Potteries,** a district of seven villages located around Stoke-on-Trent (1 hr. south of Manchester and 3 hr. from London by train), although a few factories have packed up.

There's a chain of DIY (do-it-yourself) stores around the United Kingdom called **Home Base** (there's one in London in W. Kensington), but I don't find them as much fun as Home Depot in the United States.

For those with a car or a way to get around, there's **Discount Decorating,** a 279-sq.-m (3,000-sq.-ft.) warehouse on the edge of London. It's about an hour's drive from Mayfair. It discounts all major U.K. brands in wallpapers and so on and has a selection of discontinued styles and paints. Call for more details before you trek over (© **020/7732-3986**).

Chapter Nine

....

ANTIQUES, USED BOOKS & COLLECTIBLES

LONDON, QUEEN OF IT ALL

It isn't possible to write a chapter that completely covers the antiques-and-collectibles scene in London. There's just too much of it: the specialty dealers, the collectibles, the books and musical recordings—not to mention the fun you can have every minute of every day, even Sunday, shopping these sources!

This directory, though not complete, should provide enough to satisfy the novice shopper and to give the accomplished shopper (or dealer) a more than adequate overview.

The best thing for an American to remember about shopping for used items in London is that all prices are possible. Although a lot of people pooh-pooh Portobello Road and say the bargains are gone, I disagree strongly. In fact, I have two things to say about Portobello:

- It ain't 1969 anymore.
- There's still plenty to buy.

As for me, I adore Saturdays at Portobello Road. I do not own museum-quality items, nor am I particularly interested in what the trade calls "important" pieces. I just buy fun stuff that I can afford.

When you shop London, try to get a mix of everything—
and remember: You cannot get a good price until you know
what the going price is; you cannot get a "bargain" until you
know exactly what you are buying. Only by studying the
finest examples can you decide whether an item is a fake, a
copy, a handsome repro, or a deal.

Spend time seeing and learning. Ask a lot of questions.

ANTIQUES

Booking Antiques

The London and Provincial Antique Dealers Association
(LAPADA) publishes a paperback book called *Buying Antiques
in Britain,* which is filled with advice, tips, resources, and
advertising. Most of the ads have pictures. This is an invalu-
able little guide for those just getting started. You can buy it
at antiques markets or through the association at 535 King's
Rd., London SW10.

There are also several collectors' magazines sold on newsstands; they have information on fairs and auctions, and edi-
torials about collecting. They usually cost about £2 to £3
($3.30–$4.95) an issue, but you'll enjoy them heartily. Try the
Antique Dealer and Collector's Guide (U.S. subscriptions cost
$50 a year); *London & Southern Antiques Diary; Antique and
Collectors' Fayre,* a more low-end collectors' magazine; and
Antique Collector, published by the National Magazine Company and our favorite of the bunch (U.S. subscriptions cost $30).
The Collector is a small-size freebie published by Barrington
Publications and is often given away in shops; it includes maps
of London's antiques areas, as well as the usual advertising and
lists. A consumer magazine called *Miller's Magazine,* for £2
($3.30) and published by the famous antiques experts, is
on newsstands; the BBC also has its own antiques magazine,
price guide, and editorial, based on its *Antiques Roadshow*
experiences.

Defining Antiques

The U.S. government defines an antique as any object that is 100 years old or older. There is some discussion that this rule will be changed to use the beginning of the 20th century as the new cutoff point. If you are sweating it, ask before you leave home.

If your purchase does not meet this definition, it is merely "used," and you must pay duty on it at the regular rate.

Most important to the trade is a tabloid newspaper called *Antiques Trade Gazette,* published each Wednesday by Metropress Ltd., 17 Whitcomb St., London WC2. You can buy a single copy at some West End news agents or kiosks, or apply for an American subscription through Joyce Golden & Associates, 551 Fifth Ave., New York, NY 10176.

On the Web, visit the Antiques World site at **www.antiques world.co.uk/antiquesdiary/index.html** for a complete directory of local antiques events.

Antiques Fairs

One of the best ways of learning something about the London antiques market is to attend a few antiques fairs. Antiques fairs come in several categories; most of the London ones are *vetted* (a committee certifies that all goods are genuine) and cost several pounds for admission. They may be associated with a charity or fancy-dress ball on opening night. Some fairs are vetted but less formal, and others are just plain old country fairs where anyone can show. By and large, the antiques-fair scene in London is serious, and normally the country shows are held in the country. In the city, it's strictly the big time.

Although goods are sold at these fairs, I certainly don't buy them. In fact, I use these big-name fairs merely as an educational device to learn about quality; I cannot begin to afford to buy at these fairs. To be quite honest about it all, I some-times find the price of admission to such an event more than I can bear—the thought of actually buying an item is almost obscene. On the other hand, CNN reported that a Georgian table that sold in London for £30,000 ($50,000) some 15 years ago is today worth £90,000 ($150,000). Go figure.

Some fairs are fancy-shmancy (June is chockablock with these events, which are almost part of The Season), while some are ragtag affairs. Anything at **Alexandra Palace** (locals call it "Ally Pally") is my kind of fair; it has the largest fairs in London (www.allypally-uk.com). Anything at the **Grosvenor House** is not my kind of fair (although I do appreciate that Grosvenor House is about the social season first, and antiques are just a means to an end).

Only you know what's inside your wallet and your living room.

ANTIQUARIAN BOOK FAIR
Park Lane, Piccadilly, W1 (Tube: Green Park or Hyde Park).

This fair does not have much to do with furnishings; however, no good library would be complete without a rare book or two in its collection. Collectors and dealers swap stories and collection items, including book illustrations and prints.

THE BRITISH ANTIQUE DEALERS' ASSOCIATION FAIR
The Duke of York's Headquarters, SW3 (Tube: Sloane Sq.).

Another Chelsea fair, it's held in early May and usually kicks off with a big charity gala.

CHELSEA ANTIQUES FAIR
Chelsea Old Town Hall, King's Rd., SW3 (Tube: Sloane Sq.).

This vetted fair is held twice yearly, in March and September. Our favorite time to go is September because the weather usually is wonderful and most of the tourists have left town. However, the March fair is not as crowded, and better deals might be made then. This fair has been going on for more than 60 years and will probably continue for another 260. Note that this venue is near several King's Road antiques galleries.

GROSVENOR HOUSE ANTIQUES FAIR
Grosvenor House Hotel, Park Lane, W1 (Tube: Hyde Park Corner).

One of the best antiques fairs held in London, it's timed each year to run after the Derby (say *Darby*, darling) and before Ascot and Wimbledon. This is "The Season," my dears. The top antiques dealers from all over Britain are invited to exhibit their best pieces, and everything except paintings has to be more than 100 years old. A committee reviews all items for authenticity. This is also one of the top social events of The Season, and watching the crowds is as much fun as examining the antiquities—some are the same vintage. There is a preview night before opening; it's a formal gala at £500 ($825) a pop.

INTERNATIONAL CERAMICS FAIR
Held at the Dorchester hotel, Park Lane, W1 (Tube: Marble Arch or Hyde Park).

This has become an annual event with a substantial following. The fair usually coincides with the **Grosvenor House Antiques Fair** (see above) because they complement each other. Some of the antique glass pieces on exhibit here are so delicate that the technique of getting them from the fair to your home would pose an interesting problem. All forms of ceramics are on exhibit, including some from other countries.

THE LITTLE CHELSEA ANTIQUES FAIR
Chelsea Old Town Hall, King's Rd., SW3 (Tube: Sloane Sq.).

This vetted fair is held twice a year with less than 100 participating dealers, and should not be confused with the Chelsea Antiques Fair (see above), a bigger and fancier show.

OLYMPIA DECORATIVE ARTS AND ANTIQUES FAIR
Earls Court Exhibition Centre, SW5 (Tube: Kensington Olympia).

This is an international fair; several hundred dealers participate. Stands are most often arranged as room sets. The date of the event is often piggybacked with another big fair so that people can plan to attend both. Olympia is usually considered a less expensive fair than some of the other high-end ones, but it is not a jumble sale. It is a vetted event. Call © 020/8385-1200 for more information, or contact Philbeach Events Ltd., Earls Court Exhibition Centre, London SW5.

WEST LONDON ANTIQUES FAIR
Kensington Town Hall, off Kensington High St., W8 (Tube: High St. Kensington).

One of two fairs run by the Penman Antiques Fairs Company, which also runs the Chelsea Antiques Fair (see above). This fair, like the Chelsea, is held twice yearly (Aug is the second time) and attracts good-quality dealers.

Street Markets

In London, many market areas are so famous that they have no specific street address. Although it's usually enough to name the market to a cabbie, ask your concierge whether you need more in the way of directions. Buses usually service market areas, as may the Tube. There are markets that have everything from clothing to jewelry to books and art. Some specialize in antiques; see more on antiques beginning on p. 253.

APPLE MARKET
Covent Garden, WC2 (Tube: Covent Garden or Charing Cross).

The Apple Market is the official name of the marketplace held under the rooftops of Covent Garden in the courtyard space between the brick lanes of stores. This is a rotating affair that usually houses craftspeople, so this is the part where you get out the highlighter: Antiques are sold on Monday only in order to coordinate with the antiques goings-on across the way at the **Jubilee Market.**

Note that, with the reconstruction of the ballet/opera house, one of the markets in the Covent Garden area has closed up shop, so now there are just two. It's easiest to understand what the Apple Market is in contrast to the Jubilee Market. Jubilee is often junky; Apple is always classy, and it offers some of the best prices on British crafts.

The courtyard space is filled with vendors who set up little stalls and pin their wares to backdrops; sometimes boxes of loot are under the tables. The market is vetted, so the participants must apply for permission to sell and be granted an official space and day. If they show up on other days—which many do—they set up in stalls other than their regular ones.

Many vendors take plastic; some will bargain if you buy a lot. They don't get set up before 10am, and many are still setting up at 11am. They do stay there until dark, which is, obviously, later in summer than in winter.

BERMONDSEY MARKET
Corner of Long Lane and Bermondsey St. at Bermondsey Sq., SE1 (Tube: Bermondsey).

Also known as the **New Caledonian Market,** Bermondsey is open Friday only, from 5am until 2pm. Go early for the best deals. Take a torch (flashlight) and elbow the dealers who are there to buy it all. Many of the deals are done either out of the trunks of cars or in the indoor cafe across the street.

The dealers who are buying arrive as early as 5am and leave early, too. The official market opens at 7am, but by this time, the good pieces will have left, only to appear the next day on **Portobello Road** or in **Camden Passage.** It's pretty hard to convince anyone that you are a dealer after 7am, when prices go up noticeably. This is very much an insider's scene; if you aren't a regular, you will just have to do the time until you get the respect, and the price breaks, you desire.

There is a covered market building across the street called the **Bermondsey Antiques Market and Warehouse,** which is run by the London Borough of Southwark (say *Suttock*) as a commercial retail operation. There are around 100 stalls. In this building, you will find a *bureau de change* and a cafe (entrance from the outside of the building).

I usually go to this market around 9 or 10am; I am too old to be there before dawn, although I have indeed done it. The market can be cold and nasty in winter, but it's still fun. Dress for the weather, though. I buy oleographs here—they are slightly less expensive than in the Portobello Road market. Should you get there anytime after noon, do send us a postcard and let us know your opinion.

CAMDEN LOCK
Camden High St., NW1 (Tube: Camden Town).

This is definitely the lower end, located in the Regents Canal section of Camden, where canals once provided a practical means to transport goods from the docks in the east to the main canal that carried on to Birmingham. However, the area around the Camden Lock has become the home of black-leather fashions and cheap, old clothes. This is really a teenage-vintage-clothing neighborhood more than anything else—a scene that may not be your cup of tea if you are over 40 and wash your hands regularly. Open Saturday and Sunday from 10am to 5:30pm.

CAMDEN PASSAGE
Upper St., Islington, N1 (Tube: Angel).

There are more than 200 antiques stores open every day in Camden Passage, and on Wednesday and Saturday the area becomes crowded, with hundreds of stalls and stands selling just about everything imaginable. The more permanent shops have a good collection of fine-quality antiques; there are also several vintage-clothing shops. Open Monday, Tuesday, Thursday, and Friday from 10am to 5pm; Wednesday and Saturday from 8am to 4pm.

JUBILEE MARKET
Covent Garden, WC2 (Tube: Covent Garden or Charing Cross).

It's not fair to compare the Jubilee Market to Bermondsey or even to Greenwich (see below), because it's a small-time affair. It's not even fair to compare the Jubilee Market to the Apple Market, a few hundred yards away. Jubilee Market is basically a very touristy, teen-oriented, crass marketplace at the back of Covent Garden. On Monday, however, all the dealers (about 25 of 'em) are antiques dealers, and the market is much more fun. It never turns high-end, but it is affordable and is very much worth a look. Please note this is a dregs-of-the-dealers market, and there's no telling what can be said to you. I had some anti-Semitic comments shouted at me by a very frightening dealer on one of my last visits.

PORTOBELLO ROAD
Portobello Rd., W11 (Tube: Notting Hill Gate or Ladbroke Grove).

Saturday in London means Portobello Road to me. I often choose a hotel—or stay with a friend—to be within walking distance. Yes, it's one more reason to stay at the **Royal Garden Hotel.**

I buy something at Portobello every time I'm in town. Not only antiques, but new items such as hand-knit sweaters and cashmeres, dishes, reproductions of expensive botanicals that look great when framed, old linens, buttons, and more, more, more. As my money has become more scarce, I enjoy the "cheap" end of the market more and more, finding the regular end a tad touristy. I also like the upper reaches of Portobello on a weekday, when you can really get into the funky shops.

Here's the skinny: The people with the stands and tables and stalls are just there on Saturday. The shops behind them are also open on Saturday but do not sell the stuff you see in the streets, so don't get your vendors mixed up. If you are a more serious antiques shopper, come back during the week and explore the three or four dozen serious shops (see reviews beginning on p. 253). Note that Fridays are growing in popularity with serious shoppers and dealers; I checked out the Sunday action to find a mere three tables.

Don't forget to explore the shops on Pembridge Road and Westbourne Grove after you've shopped the full range of Portobello Road, and be sure to read chapter 5, "Shopping Neighborhoods," because there's some very exciting retail going on to either side of Portobello Market—in Holland Park (p. 107) or in Notting Hill, which I call Ledbury Grove (p. 99)—which can lead you right over to Bayswater Road. There's also Golborne Road (p. 107).

Now then, because I no longer consider myself a tourist, I have a new routine for going to this market. Instead of following the herd at Notting Hill Gate, I arrive via Ladbroke Grove, right under the railroad trestle. I go to the market via what I call Young Stuff Alley (you can't miss it) and then turn left on Portobello Road, heading what I call "uptown." This is the funky part of the market where real junk is sold. Then I segue onto Golborne Road, go back to Portobello Road, and work my way against the throng as I head "downtown" toward Notting Hill Gate.

GREENWICH MARKETS

I used to think there was nothing better than a Sunday in Greenwich spent at the flea markets. Although I still do it every now and then, on my last trip I found myself a bit bored and worn out—you can find just about all of this stuff elsewhere. But then, there's a lot of fleas here and you may be tempted.

If you are staying in Canary Wharf, want a day out with a boat ride, or are doing the historical sites, there are plenty of markets to enjoy, both Saturday and Sunday. I have been on a Saturday and find that I slightly prefer the vendors on Sunday (they are elsewhere on Sat).

There are several markets in Greenwich, so the idea is to spend the day going from one to the next. The fact that Greenwich houses museums, ships, and sights of historical interest means little to me, even if there's no time like mean time. If you want to combine culture and shopping, arrange your schedule accordingly.

Crafts Market

The Crafts Market in Greenwich is held under a covered roof in the center of "downtown" and consists of rows of stalls selling merchandise much like that at Covent Garden. The prices are slightly less than in London.

Bosun's Yard

Around the corner from the Crafts Market, right at the waterfront, Bosun's Yard holds the overflow from the Crafts Market. It's a little too much for me: These are the dealers who just came back from Tibet and think they have something to sell, but it's a cute place, and you can get an ice-cream cone here.

Canopy Antiques Market

You will not like this market if you don't like junk. This is of less standard quality than your average flea market or jumble sale. But I love it. The market sprawls for quite some bit; I enter at the far end—not where the truck says BEIGELS *[sic]* SOLD HERE.

The reason I enter from the far end is that this is where the jumble is; if you enter the first gateway, you have regular market stalls with new goods. I don't like these as much. The dealers in the back specialize in vintage clothing (there's an entire shed of it), home decor from the 1950s, costume jewelry, and junk.

Greenwich Antiques Market

This market is not huge, but it's packed with fun. The dealers farthest from the street specialize in vintage clothing. The quality of the merchandise here cannot be classified as junk; there may even be a few true antiques.

To get there: Take BritRail from Charing Cross Station, take the boat from Westminster Pier, or take the Jubilee Line to Canary Wharf and transfer to Docklands Railway. *Note:* Do not take the Jubilee Line to North Greenwich, as you will be in the wrong place. Your stop in Greenwich is Gipsy Moth.

MONSTER MARKETS
....

Just about every major British city has markets and fairs. Many are easily reached on BritRail and aren't that far away— Brighton and Bath are two cities (different directions) that make good day trips for flea-market lovers.

There are also some enormous fairs—held mostly for dealers—that are the kind of things legends are made of. There are over 1,000 dealers at these events, so I call them the Monster Markets. The two biggies are Newark and Ardingly. Here are the facts:

- Newark has some 4,000 stands and is the largest market in Europe. Ardingly is a baby with about half that. However, Ardingly is closer to London.
- These markets are actually for professionals, although anyone can go. There is an entrance charge—you can buy a multiday pass, usually for about £20 ($33).
- The first day of the market usually begins at dawn, or earlier. Bring a torch (flashlight).

- Both fairs are organized by DMG Antiques Fairs (© **1636/ 702-326;** www.dmgantiquefairs.com).
- Markets are held several times a year but are never in conflict with each other.

ANTIQUES & COLLECTIBLE SUPERMARKETS

Antiques supermarkets have been created to give the smaller but established dealers a permanent place to set up and display their wares. They are covered shopping centers for antiques, collectibles, and junk. The fun is figuring out which is which. Very often, the dealer stalls change, especially in these hard times; therefore, I'm not really pointing out faves. Because the buildings are not going anywhere fast, I suggest that you plow through. Don't forget that if you catch a rainy day in London town, an antiques gallery or supermarket can keep you busy for hours. The other advantage to shopping at a covered market is that very often other services are offered: There are repair shops at **Grays**, *bureaux de change* at **Antiquarius** and **Grays**, and places to eat at all of them.

ALFIE'S ANTIQUES MARKET
13–25 Church St., NW8 (Tube: Edgware Rd. or Marylebone).

Alfie's is under the same ownership as Grays and houses 150 stalls. It's a series of blue town houses now joined together higgledy-piggledy, so you weave around a bit when you shop. This is well worth the trip; prices are moderate and dealers will deal. Because the location is a tad offbeat, the dealers tend to be a little funkier, so you get high quality and some value. This is perhaps one of the best supermarkets for seeing a lot and feeling that you're getting good value. Not far from The Landmark Hotel. Closed Sunday and Monday. Open Tuesday through Saturday from 10am to 5:30pm.

Antiquarius
135–141 King's Rd., SW3 (Tube: Sloane Sq.).

Located right on King's Road in Chelsea in the thick of several antiques venues, Antiquarius could be mistaken for a theater from the outside. In actuality, it was constructed in an old snooker-hall building dating to way back when. With more than 200 stalls, Antiquarius has gained a reputation for being the place to go for Art Nouveau and Art Deco pieces of every variety, from jewelry to furniture. There's also a very famous dealer (Sue Norman) for blue-and-white porcelain. Now then, I have it from an inside London source that if you are into celebrity spotting, all the big-time stars shop at this market (this is their idea of slumming it), but they never come on weekends. Open Monday through Saturday from 10am to 6pm.

Bond Street Antiques Centre
124 New Bond St., W1 (Tube: Bond St.).

Like Grays (see below), the Bond Street Antiques Centre is located amid the finest in fashion and specializes in the finest of miniatures, porcelain, jewelry, silver, and paintings. This one is a tad fancy for my taste. Open Monday through Friday from 10am to 5:30pm.

Chenil Galleries
181–183 King's Rd., SW3 (Tube: Sloane Sq.).

Chenil Galleries is more of a shopping arcade with a long, thin thrust to the floor pattern and a swell chance to browse in good merchandise; it's not intimidating at all. They have an art gallery and are known for being a good place for antique medical instruments, as well as 17th- and 18th-century paintings and smaller items. There's a sensational dealer for costume jewelry. Another one of the Chelsea galleries, this one should be combined with your visit to **Antiquarius.** Another celebrity shopping venue. Open Monday through Saturday from 10am to 6pm.

GRAYS

1–7 Davies Mews, 58 Davies St., W1 (Tube: Bond St.).

These two buildings, located on the opposite ends of the same block, house more than 300 antiques stalls containing every variety of item, large and small. Davies Street conveniently intersects South Molton Street at one end and Brook Street at the other, placing it directly in the heart of the big-name-designer section of London.

When you need a break from fashion, it is easy to breeze over to Grays and rest your eyes on some breathtaking antique jewelry, bound to coordinate with any purchase you have made on Bond Street. Don't miss the river tributary that runs decoratively through the basement of the Davies Mews building. The shops are open Monday through Friday from 10am to 6pm only. They are not open Saturday or Sunday.

You can grab a bite in the cute cafe on the lowest floor.

ANTIQUES NEIGHBORHOODS

The best thing about antiques neighborhoods is that the good shops stay for a long while, and they attract other shops. High rents plague London, like any big city, but these neighborhoods are nuggets where you can just wander and gawk.

Church Street/Marylebone (NW8)

This antiques area, on the way to Alfie's Antiques Market (see earlier in this chapter), is fun and pretty much affordable. It's open Tuesday through Saturday from 10am to 6pm. Aside from Alfie's, there's the **Gallery Of Antique Costume & Textiles** (2 Church St.), as well as **Simon Tracy** (no. 18), **Beverley** (no. 32), **Bizarre** (no. 24), **Risky Business** (two shops at nos. 34 and 46), and **Pillows** (no. 48). This is kind of a funky neighborhood where you can wear casual clothes and not have to worry about the posh, but be sure to also wander over to Marylebone High Street, the latest new Yuppie area for chic (Tube: Edgware or Marylebone).

Covent Garden (WC2)

The neighborhoods surrounding Covent Garden, from Charing Cross to The Strand and over to Leicester Square, are known as important haunts for those interested in antique books, used books, stamps, records, and ephemera. There are some famous antiques stores sprinkled in here, and many vintage-clothing shops, but it's mostly a paper-goods neighborhood.

But wait: On Mondays, there are two markets at Covent Garden—**Apple Market** and **Jubilee Market** (which is about 90m/100 yards away from Apple Market). The stalls at Apple Market, which are normally devoted to craftspeople, are taken over by rather high-end antiques dealers. Jubilee Market is more open—many price ranges are available, and there's more room for bargaining and fun. You may also find local publications about other markets and fairs at some of the dealers at Jubilee. I'm not talking hoity-toity antiques here, but you can have fun anyway (Tube: Covent Garden).

Fulham Road

This is another way to get to the upper King's Road area, then the Fulham Road area, and then over toward Brompton Cross, depending on which way you want to walk. Look at a map!

There's a lot of stuff in the Fulham area between the Gloucester Road Tube stop and Brompton Cross, but within a special block or two of Fulham Road you'll find either an antiques shop or a decorator showroom behind every door. Look in at **Peter Lipiteh** (no. 120), **Today's Interiors** (no. 122), **Michael Foster** (no. 118), **Christophe Gollut** (no. 116), **Colefax & Fowler** (no. 110), **John Stefanidis** (no. 253), and **Clifford Wright** (nos. 104–106). If you keep walking you'll hit **Michelin House,** which is where **The Conran Shop** has made history (no. 81; Tube: Fulham Broadway or S. Kensington).

Kensington Church Street (W8)

Shoppers, please note that few of these stores are open all day—if at all—on Saturday, so despite the fact that you're a stone's throw from Portobello Road, Saturday is not really the day to combine these neighborhoods.

Of course, a lot of serious Portobello Road dealers are open during the week (without the stalls and stands of Sat), and you can combine the two neighborhoods that way. The best way to do so is to exit the Tube at Kensington High Street, cross the street at the light, and head slightly to your right before you zig up Kensington Church Street.

A small gallery and a zillion shops line Kensington Church Street. Many of the stores are the small, fancy kind that make you nervous to even press your nose to the glass. The closer you get to Notting Hill Gate (at the top of the hill you are climbing), the funkier the stores get.

The month of June can be tricky for shopping this area, as most of the good stores exhibit at the important shows and close up shop.

Oliver Sutton (34 Kensington Church St.) sells only Staffordshire figurines; pressing your nose to the glass may suffice, as you can see quite a selection from the street. At no. 58 is a small gallery with very serious dealers in their tiny glass cubbyholes. **Jonathan Horne** (no. 66) is another famous dealer for pottery, tiles, and ceramics—also very serious. **Simon Spero** (no. 109) has more pottery. For a slight change of pottery pace, pop in at **New Century,** a gallery that sells new art pottery that is hoped will become collectible (no. 69).

Don't miss three little dealers in a row along Peel Street, who have Kensington Church Street addresses (it's a corner junction)—among them **Hope & Glory** (no. 131A), which specializes in royal porcelain memorabilia (Tube: Kensington High St. or Notting Hill Gate).

Portobello Road (W11)

I just love this Saturday market event (p. 249). But don't think that this is just a flea-market scene or that Saturday is the only day. Saturday is the main event, but during the week, especially on Friday, the regular shops are open without the Saturday circus atmosphere. And yep, there is a ton to see, even on a weekday.

Warning: A few arcade galleries open Friday from noon to 4pm as well as Saturday, but are not otherwise open; there's some vintage-clothing action on Sunday.

There are many enclosed antiques markets here, with many stalls and dealers, as well as some free-standing shops on Portobello Road and on Westbourne Grove. Get there via Pembridge Road to check out a few more shops (especially strong for vintage clothing) or by walking up the hill via Kensington Church Street, where there are a few more dealers (see above). Note a change in postal codes; this is nothing to be alarmed about (Tube: Notting Hill Gate or Kensington High St.).

Without the Saturday circus, the main action on Portobello Road is the number of galleries packed with dealers. These galleries are often called arcades. Check out **Alice's** (no. 77), **Chelsea Galleries** (no. 67), **Geoffrey Van** (no. 105), **Portobello Antique Arcade** (no. 139), and **Lipka Arcade** (284 Westbourne Grove).

King's Road (SW3)

For upscale shoppers, the better part of King's Road is the middle 200 to 300 range. There are several antiques malls here and lots of showrooms. In terms of visual stimulation and the possibility of affording something nice, this neighborhood may offer the best combination of the right things. Other neighborhoods are cheaper, but this one has a trendiness that can't be ignored, even in antiques.

Whatever you do, check out **Steinberg & Tolkien** (193 King's Rd.), extraordinary dealers in vintage clothing, costume jewelry, and the like, with two floors of space and drool-over pieces, including old Chanel and tons o' Pucci. The owner is American (Tube: Fulham Broadway or Sloane Sq.).

Lower Sloane (SW3)

I call the area including Pimlico Road, Ebury Road, and Lower Sloane Street simply Lower Sloane. It is an extension of Sloane Street, after you pass Sloane Square. Most of the dealers here are fancy, as is the clientele, but everyone is a tad more approachable than the high-end, don't-touch crowd. There are a lot of showrooms here, as well as antiques shops. If you're on Sloane Street, instead of turning to the right to get to King's Road, walk straight and follow Lower Sloane Street to Pimlico Road. Convenient for cutting back to King's Road and Chelsea antiques shops (Tube: Sloane Sq.).

Mayfair & Mount Streets (W1)

This is the most expensive part of London; the prices in the antiques shops reflect the rents and the unwritten law that objects displayed in windows must be dripping with ormolu. New Bond Street is the main source, but don't forget side streets such as Conduit Street, Old Bond Street, Vigo Street, and Jermyn Street. Mayfair is also headquarters for several auction houses, decorating firms, and big-time dealers. If you're just looking, make sure you're dressed to kill. If you're serious, you should probably have an appointment or a letter of introduction or both (Tube: Bond St. or Green Park).

If you like a fancy but good market, don't miss Grays, the market (p. 255). If you like hoity with your toity, don't miss **Mallett & Son** (141 New Bond St.), **S. J. Phillips Ltd.** (139 New Bond St.), or **Wartski** (14 Grafton St.).

Mount Street begins, appropriately enough, with an **American Express** office (no. 89), where you will undoubtedly have to go for more cash. As a shopping destination, Mount Street is easy to miss because it's set back a little bit. It's sort of a 2-block job, stretching from behind The Dorchester to Berkeley Square, a sneeze from Bond Street.

Here you can find a group of excellent antiques shops; my favorite on this street is **Stair & Co.** (no. 14). Then you pass The Connaught to connect to more of Mount Street and **Blairman and Sons** (no. 119) and **John Sparks Limited** (no. 128).

ANTIQUARIAN BOOKS, MAPS & AUTOGRAPHS
....

If you collect first editions or antiquarian books, or even if you're just seeking a title that's currently out of print, flip this way.

In addition to perusing these listings, collectors of antiquarian books should also consult two new magazines devoted to the topic—*Driff's* and *Slightly Soiled*—which are available at **Sotheran's of Sackville Street** and the Cecil Court stores. Both carry news of auctions, sales, and book fairs, not to mention gossip about booksellers.

The West End

BERNARD QUARITCH LTD.
5–8 Lower John St., Golden Sq., W1 (Tube: Piccadilly Circus).

In October 1847, Bernard Quaritch came to London, determined to become a bookseller. He succeeded, attracting along the way clients such as prime ministers William Gladstone and Benjamin Disraeli, publishing Edward FitzGerald's *The Rubáiyát of Omar Khayyám,* and being eulogized by the *Times* as "the greatest bookseller who ever lived."

Quaritch Ltd. has attained an international reputation. Boasting perhaps the largest stock of antiquarian books in London and 32 experts in fields as diverse as Arabic, bibliography, and psychiatry, Quaritch maintains an atmosphere that is quiet but not formal. The firm attends auctions on the Continent (sometimes bidding for the British Museum) and assembles collections that can run the gamut from Tibet and Henry James to rigging and shipbuilding.

Because of its size, Quaritch is able to airfreight its own crate of books to New York once a week; the contents are then sent separately to clients via UPS, bypassing the post office and possibly careless (and financially damaging) handling.

G. HEYWOOD HILL LTD.
10 Curzon St., W1 (Tube: Green Park).

If Maggs (see below) is a showplace for books and autographs of the illustrious, nearby G. Heywood Hill on Curzon Street represents the cramped, Dickensian bookshop most visitors associate with literary London. For 50 years, Heywood has been a beacon to authors, librarians, and collectors around the world.

Although space is limited, the shop is packed to the rafters with books that meet the standards of its knowledgeable staff. Although antiquarian books pay the light bills, Heywood stocks contemporary books on a variety of subjects merely to satisfy its clients' needs. (It is also probably the only bookseller that will refuse to sell books that don't meet its Olympian standards.)

The shop specializes in books on design, architecture, gardening, and the allied decorative arts. There's also an extensive collection of biographies and a subspecialty in literary criticism. Heywood's bookishness has attracted many writers as steady customers, including Evelyn Waugh, Anthony Powell, Nancy Mitford (who worked there during World War II), and other Waughs, Mitfords, and Sitwells for several generations.

The shop's family feeling, as well as its terrifically high standards, often ensure it first crack at extensive private libraries when they become available. The location is right around the corner from the Hilton Park Lane and The Connaught, off Berkeley Square.

Jonathan Potter
125 New Bond St., W1. (Tube: Bond St.).

I got a letter from William Latey asking that Jonathan Potter, a gallery specializing in antique maps, be included in these pages. This firm is 20 years old, as opposed to 120 as some of the other sources are, but exhibits regularly in the United States. They also stock atlases, antique globes, and books on cartography. Member, BADA (that's British Association of Dealers of Antiques).

Maggs Brothers Ltd.
50 Berkeley Sq., W1 (Tube: Green Park).

Although it had been rumored for years that the Maggs mansion, built in 1740, was haunted, no ghosts were spotted during World War II, when fire-watch rules required at least one Maggs employee to sleep on the premises each night. Of course, the house next door was completely destroyed, and the one across Berkeley Square suffered heavy damage—but there are no ghosts.

Such eccentricities are allowed any bookseller with an enormous collection of travel books, militaria, maps, illuminated manuscripts, autographs, and Orientalia. Maggs's travel section alone would fill the average bookstore with first-edition, on-the-spot reminiscences by the likes of Stanley, Livingstone, Robert Falcon Scott, and Admiral Byrd. Ten specialists attend auctions around the world on a regular basis.

Maggs also boasts of a sizable autograph collection.

Sotheran's of Sackville Street
2–5 Sackville St., Piccadilly, W1 (Tube: Piccadilly Circus).

Sotheran's has been selling books since 1761 in York and has been established in London since 1815. Charles Dickens was a regular customer, and when he died, Sotheran's sold his library. The firm also purchased a number of volumes from

Winston Churchill's library and was the agent for the sale of Sir Isaac Newton's library to Cambridge. The firm specializes in ornithology and natural science.

The atmosphere is neat, formal, and as silent as a library. A lower floor is given over exclusively to antiquarian prints and maps, drawings by book illustrators such as Kate Greenaway and Arthur Rackham, sporting prints, and military and naval subjects.

Sotheran's offers search service; hand-binds serial publications, such as the Bills and Acts of Parliament; restores books; and also maintains subscriptions to overseas periodicals for its customers.

Charing Cross Road

Visitors searching for 84 Charing Cross Rd. will be disappointed to find a record store, not the bookshop that inspired Helene Hanff's bestseller; nevertheless, the long street is filled with other equally engaging book emporiums, all of which are open Monday through Saturday from 9am to 6pm.

Cecil Court, a block-long street between Charing Cross Road and St. Martin's Lane, has some charming secondhand bookshops. Most are open Monday through Saturday from 9:30am to 6pm. Start with **Tindley & Chapman** (4 Cecil Court, WC2; Tube: Leicester Sq.).

Long Acre, the "Main Street" of Covent Garden, is also lined with bookstores on both sides of the road; it is a block from Cecil Court.

EDWARD STANFORD
12–14 Long Acre, WC2 (Tube: Covent Garden).

Stanford is a mecca for maps, charts, atlases, and travel books. A particular specialty is guides for mountain climbers, skiers, and other outdoor types. Open Monday through Friday from 9am to 5:30pm, Saturday from 10am to 4pm.

Foyle
119 Charing Cross Rd., WC2 (Tube: Leicester Sq.).

There's a small antiquarian library here in London's largest bookstore. See chapter 6, "London Resources A to Z," for more details.

Francis Edwards
48A Charing Cross Rd., WC2 (Tube: Leicester Sq.).

Francis Edwards is the leading antiquarian bookseller on the street and carries natural history and militaria. Open Monday through Friday from 9am to 5pm.

COLLECTIBLES

Shopping for the real thing in London is a tricky business. Remember:

- England is indeed a nation of shopkeepers.
- Many of the shops they keep are crammed with collectibles.
- Some of these collectibles are as real as St. George's dragon or that grand old American collectible, the Brooklyn Bridge.

Coins & Medals

Collectors' note: In addition to the Spink and Seaby publications, there's also a periodical called *Coin Monthly*.

The Arches
Villiers St., WC2 (Tube: Charing Cross).

Soaring rents have forced small-time dealers out of Cutler Street, long a Sunday-morning fixture at the Petticoat Lane market; however, inexpensive coins still are available by the bagful at The Arches on Villiers Street, beneath the Charing Cross Road Tube stop. This is where we got 20 coins from around the world for about 90p ($1.50). This is decidedly low end, and major collectors will not be interested; however, the place is a lot of fun. In addition to coins, there are comic books, cigarette cards, military insignia, and used romance novels in this covey of little dealers nestled beneath and beside the Tube station. Most proprietors are open Monday through Saturday from 9am to 6pm.

ARMADA ANTIQUES
Grays Antiques Market, Stand 122, 58 Davies St., W1 (Tube: Bond St.).

One of two important stalls in **Grays Antiques Market,** Armada Antiques is crammed with militaria of all kinds. Armada Antiques (Stand 122) carries mostly edged weapons, such as stilettos and sabers, but also has some medals. For the total effect, shop also at **Seidler** (Stand 120)—together, these two fabulous dealers give you a nice overview.

B. A. SEABY LTD.
7 Davies St., W1 (Tube: Bond St.).

Early coins bearing the likenesses of royalty from Corinth, Phoenicia, and Rome rub shoulders with tradesmen's tokens issued by coopers in Dover and fishmongers in Margate; each is presented with care, panache, and the necessary historical background.

The firm is deep in antiquarian coins, and that interest has led to sidelines such as collections of jewelry and copperplate from ancient Greece, Rome, and Jerusalem. Seaby publishes a magazine, the bimonthly *Coin & Medal Bulletin,* which is likely to contain scholarly pieces related to archaeological finds, as well as price lists of coins. Open Monday through Friday from 9:30am to 5pm.

FORMAN PICCADILLY LTD.
99 Mount St., W1 (Tube: Bond St.).

Forman specializes in medals but also sells carved ivories (made by soldiers and sailors) and other specialized antiquities. But it's the gorgeous colored ribbons and enamel medals that drew us into the shop, to peer hungrily into the large wooden case. If you brush up on your Russian, you can read the inscriptions on medals awarded by the czars. We're fond of Napoleonic medals, complete with ribbons or sashes.

SPINK & SON LTD.
5–7 King St., St. James's, SW1 (Tube: Piccadilly Circus or Green Park).

If you've yearned for those glitzy costume-jewelry medals, you'll all-out faint and go stark raving mad with delight when you see the original medals that the current fad was based on. Why was a man always so dashing in his uniform? Because of his medals, of course. And chances are, they came from Spink. Spink has tremendous stock in Orientalia, paperweights, and Greek and Roman coins, as well as an ample supply of early English hammered coins in gold and silver and milled pieces dating back to the late 1600s; however, as Hamley's is to toys, so Spink is to medals. Along with sheer size, Spink offers an expertise born of creating decorations for Great Britain and 65 other countries.

The company also issues the monthly *Spink Numismatic Circular,* which includes large sections on medals, orders, and decorations. Open Monday through Friday from 9:30am to 5:30pm.

Scientific Instruments

Collectors' note: Collectors of scientific instruments should be aware of two specialty publications: *Rittenhouse Journal of the American Scientific Instrument Enterprise,* published by David and Yola Coffeen and Raymond V. Giordano, and *Bulletin of the Scientific Instrument Society,* published by the Scientific Instrument Society.

ARTHUR MIDDLETON
12 New Row, WC2 (Tube: Leicester Sq.).

Located between Leicester Square and Covent Garden, this shop is chockablock with antique clocks, telescopes, surgical instruments, and early dental equipment, all in splendid condition. Even if you're not a collector, you'll enjoy the spit and polish of these fascinating pieces. Open Monday through Friday from 10am to 6pm, Saturday from 11am to 5:30pm.

STEPHEN O'DONNELL
Grays Antiques Market, Stand 156, 58 Davies St., W1 (Tube: Bond St.).

An interest in navigation led O'Donnell to begin collecting and restoring sextants, spyglasses, and telescopes. By this time, his collection is extensive, as is a fairly new sideline in antique postage scales. The scales run from £90 to £600 ($150–$1,000), while telescopes start at £150 ($250), and sextants run anywhere from £425 to £1,800 ($700–$3,000). Open Monday through Friday from 10am to 6pm.

TREVOR PHILIPS & SONS LTD.
75A Jermyn St., SW1 (Tube: Piccadilly Circus).

A smaller version of Arthur Middleton (see above), Philips carries gyroscopes, English drafting instruments, sundials, stethoscopes, and a selection of books about scientific instruments. The shop also carries miniature instruments, such as pocket botanical microscopes, pocket globes, and exquisite orreries—small clockwork representations of the solar system. Open Monday through Friday from 10am to 6pm.

Stamps

The Strand (and offshoots such as King St. and Cecil Court) is a magnet for philatelists in London. All the shops are in the Strand area, although we label some as in Charing Cross Road/Covent Garden—this is the same neighborhood and is an easy walk (Tube: Charing Cross).

Collectors' and shoppers' note: All these shops are open Monday through Friday from 10am to 5pm (Gibbons opens at 9am) and the same hours Saturday, except for Strand and Gibbons, which close at 1pm. David Brandon is closed all day Saturday.

There are several periodicals for stamp collectors, including *Stamp News*. Collectors also should keep in mind the large auction houses: Phillips has a postage-stamp auction nearly every Thursday, and Christie's recently offered a collection that included proofs and essays from Bradbury, Wilkinson & Co., which has printed British stamps and bank notes for nearly 150 years.

DAVID BRANDON
77 The Strand, WC2 (Tube: Charing Cross).

The second in a row of three shops across from Gibbons, Brandon has a large stock of classic material and is particularly up on postal-history items of Great Britain and the Continent.

STANLEY GIBBONS LTD.
399 The Strand, WC2 (Tube: Charing Cross).

The shop has the largest collection of British Empire stamp material in the world, as well as the most complete selection of stamp accessories—albums, tweezers, and perforation gauges—and its own well-researched catalogs.

Gibbons also sells extraordinary philatelic material. We were once shown an issued but unused full block of 12 of the Twopenny Blue with the original gum. Brilliantly colored and lettered "SG-TL" in the lower left- and right-hand corners (to prevent counterfeiting), this museum-quality piece was offered at a mere £12,000 ($20,000).

Such lofty material is viewed in private, secure surroundings on the second floor. On a more mundane level—the ground floor—Gibbons stocks a few topics such as birds and the royal family, and has specialists in first-day covers, plate blocks, precancels, overprints, color variations, and so on.

The firm gave up the coin and medal business several years ago but now carries a full selection of postcards and pertinent literature.

Gibbons is impossibly famous and therefore impossibly crowded—you may get less service, and they may not have what you are looking for. Don't be afraid to wander around the neighborhood and try the competition. Smaller and less-known dealers may be more fun.

STRAND STAMPS
79 The Strand, WC2 (Tube: Charing Cross).

Three dealers operate as Strand and deal in Commonwealth material. Even though Gibbons has a larger stock in this area, the Strand dealers often come up with particular items from India or Australia that the big kid on the block doesn't stock. Moreover, Strand isn't pricey and is particularly patient with younger collectors. If you've gone to the trouble to seek the neighborhood, don't blow it now—you must stop in here.

Also try:

CHRISTIE'S
8 King St., St. James's, SW1 (Tube: Piccadilly Circus).

HARMER'S
91 New Bond St., W1 (Tube: Bond St.).

SOTHEBY'S
34–35 New Bond St., W1 (Tube: Bond St.).

SPINK & SON LTD.
5-7 King St., St. James's, SW1 (Tube: Piccadilly Circus or Green Park).

Dolls & Toys

Parents and grandparents, please note: This section, in keeping with this chapter's theme, covers only collectible dolls and toys. *Collectors' note: Doll & Toy World* covers these collectibles on a monthly basis, as does *Antique Toy World*.

LONDON TOY AND MODEL MUSEUM
23 Craven Hill Rd., W2 (Tube: Paddington).

In a case devoted to dolls based on the royal family, a German-made Princess Elizabeth doll from 1932 sits next to a Princess Anne doll made in 1953.

This royal rite of passage from child to queen is nearly over-shadowed by other dolls at the museum—poured-wax dolls; bisque (china) dolls; a wax-headed Quaker lady in her original costume from 1840; and a Topsy Turvy doll, which can be either white or black, depending on the owner's fancy. In addition to dolls, the museum has 25,000 Matchbox and Corgi miniature cars, several working rocking horses, a collection of Paddington bears, an entire room of toy trains, and a display of toy soldiers from Pierce Carlson (see below).

The latest addition is the Baywest exhibit, a computer-controlled model of 1,000 houses, 50,000 lights, a railway system, and a helicopter that requires a separate admission charge. There also are two smaller, coin-operated versions by the same designer—a snow scene and a small town at twilight. Open Tuesday through Saturday from 10am to 5:30pm, Sunday from 11am to 5pm. Admission: £4.95 ($8.15) adults, £2.95 ($4.85) children.

PIERCE CARLSON
Portobello Rd. Market, Stall 27, NW11 (Tube: Notting Hill Gate).

There's a windowful of Britain soldiers at the **London Toy and Model Museum** on loan from Pierce Carlson. He runs a retail shop near the British Model Soldier Society and also maintains a stall on Portobello Road.

POLLOCK'S TOY MUSEUM
1 Scala St., W1 (Tube: Goodge St.).

POLLOCK'S TOY THEATRES
44 The Market, Covent Garden, WC2 (Tube: Covent Garden).

Nearly 100 years ago, Robert Louis Stevenson wrote, "If you love art, folly, or the bright eyes of children, speed to Pollock's." Thousands still do and find a treasure island of toys housed in two adjoining buildings overflowing with dolls, teddy bears, tin toys, puppets, and folk toys from Europe, India, Africa, China, and Japan.

Exhibits of mechanical toys and construction sets fill the lower floor of Pollock's Toy Museum, and the second story has exhibits of the paper "toy theaters" and cutout actors and actresses that have fired the imaginations of British children for generations.

In addition to the museum, there's a second Pollock's, a toyshop that was set up in Covent Garden after the original was destroyed in the Blitz. The shop sells the theaters, popguns, and dolls, and there's no admission charge. The shop is open Monday through Saturday from 10am to 8pm.

The museum is at the corner of Scala and Whitfield streets and is open Monday through Saturday from 10am to 5pm. Admission: 50p (85¢) adults, 20p (35¢) children and students. The museum also holds parties for up to 30 children.

Toy Soldiers

UNDER TWO FLAGS
4 St. Christopher's Place, W1 (Tube: Bond St.).

By the time toy soldiers became popular in America (during World War II), English children were celebrating the 50th anniversary of William Britain & Co. Britain went into the toy-soldier business in 1893, creating a set of the Life Guards to honor Queen Victoria's forthcoming Diamond Jubilee in 1897.

Many Britain sets (including the first) are available at Under Two Flags on colorful St. Christopher's Place between Wigmore and Regent streets, just a stone's throw from Oxford Street and Selfridges.

The store also offers inexpensive lead soldiers for do-it-your-self painters; a selection of military books; magazines and prints; bronzes; porcelains; and curios, such as a chess set made of toy soldiers.

Open Monday through Saturday from 10am to 6pm.

Comic Books

Twenty years ago, there were small comic-book departments in some of the better bookstores. Now, according to the comic cognoscenti, there are more than 40 comic-book specialty stores in Great Britain and a baker's dozen in London, each with a slightly different appeal.

FORBIDDEN PLANET
71 New Oxford St., WC1 (Tube: Tottenham Court Rd.).

You are about to enter three strange worlds, one inhabited by aliens, a second in which fantasy princes and monsters reign supreme, and yet a third where comic-book characters rule, but that's not all. At Forbidden Planet you'll also find video-tapes of all 20 James Bond movies, trading cards from the original *Batman* movie, and the complete works of Al Capp *(Li'l Abner)*. It's a comic-aholic's dream. Where else would you find the unauthorized biography of *Superman* baddie Lex Luthor? The stock is vast, with some 10,000 different titles available. (Parents dragging kids should be aware that some items are decidedly not for family consumption, such as *The Adventures of Johnny Condom*.)

Although the emphasis is on new comic heroes, Dick Tracy, Superman, and Little Lulu are represented, as is, believe it or not, cowboy hero Tom Mix, who died 40 years before current comic collectors were born. The shop also has a limited stock of back issues and offers fantasy masks, an incredibly complete assortment of science-fiction books and videos, and toys, such as miniature versions of the original starship *Enterprise*.

GOSH!
39 Great Russell St., WC1 (Tube: Holborn).

Across from the British Museum on Great Russell Street is
Gosh!, which dispensed with signs during the *Batman* craze
and just hung an image of the Caped Crusader to attract
passersby. Gosh! has a serene atmosphere very much in tune
with museum-goers. An employee confided, "We're depend-
ent on the museum trade." As a result, you'll find, along with
comics, complete histories of faded favorites, such as *Captain
Easy* and *Wash Tubbs* in eight volumes, and scholarly histories about cartoon strips and comic books. Gosh! is open
Monday through Saturday from 10am to 6pm, Sunday 1 to
6pm.

Cigarette Cards

Just as baseball cards became wildly popular in the United States
beginning in 1981, so cigarette cards have become highly
collectible in England. Sets that used to sell for £3 or £4.25
($5–$7) in 1986 are now fetching £6 or £7.25 ($10–$12).

You might expect that cigarette-card dealers would be pro-
liferating; just the reverse is true. With more cards being held
by collectors (and investors), the number of sets that used to
turn over at flea markets and in antiques stores specializing in
ephemera has decreased. One of the best shops specializing in
cards is:

MURRAY & CO.
*20 Cecil Court, WC2 (Tube: Leicester Sq.); 51 Watford
Way, Hendon Central, NW4 (Tube: Hendon Central).*

Murray & Co. has become the mecca for cigarette-card collectors around the world. Since 1967, the company has published the only annual price catalog in the field. Murray has
also been active reprinting valuable old sets (clearly marked
reprint) and publishing its own checklists and books; a recent
one, *Half Time,* covers English football (soccer) cards.

Murray has two shops in London, one on Cecil Court just
off Charing Cross Road, the other in Hendon, served by the
Hendon Central stop on the Northern Line. The Hendon shop

has far greater stock in all respects, while the Cecil Court shop is more convenient to central London (less than 90m/100 yd. from Trafalgar Sq.) and offers a brief overview of what's available. If you've got any idea at all of becoming serious about cigarette cards, however, the trip to Hendon is an absolute must. To save time for all concerned, come equipped with a list of the sets you want and their manufacturers' names.

CDs & Records for Collectors

If the impersonality and sheer size of **HMV, Tower,** and **Virgin** have got you down, consider the following specialty sources for new and used CDs, LPs, and rare 78s. Otherwise, turn to chapter 6, "London Resources A to Z," for the address of the megastore near you.

JAZZ & CLASSICAL SPECIALTY SHOPS

RAY'S JAZZ SHOP
180 Shaftesbury Ave., WC2 (Tube: Tottenham Court Rd.).

Wallow here in all things jazz: new and used LPs and CDs, jazz books, magazines, and rare 78s. Some of the records are so rare that Ray's regularly auctions them off. Every month, new records come up for auction, and bidders submit offers in person. The staff is more knowledgeable than employees in the jazz departments at the megastores and very helpful. When a tourist asked to hear a used Billie Holiday CD, the manager sampled every cut on the compact disc to make sure it was all playable. Open Monday through Saturday from 10am to 6:30pm.

TEMPLAR RECORDS
9 Irving St., WC2 (Tube: Leicester Sq.).

Although rock, pop, and jazz fans have been unabashedly pro-compact disc, classical-music lovers have often been astonished at CD prices.

Jean-Louis Ginibre's List of Jazzy Dealers

Jean-Louis Ginibre, the editorial director of Hachette-Filipacchi Magazines in New York, has passed on to me his favorite sources for secondhand LPs and current CDs. What friends will do! They all deal exclusively in jazz, except for Honest Jon, who also sells rock and reggae. Direct from Jean-Louis:

JAMES ASMAN'S RECORD CENTRE
23A New Row, St. Martin's Lane, WC2 (Tube: Leicester Sq. or Covent Garden).

HONEST JON RECORDS
278 Portobello Rd., WC2 (Tube: Ladbroke Grove).

MOLE JAZZ
311 Grays Inn Rd., WC1 (Tube: King's Cross).

RAY'S JAZZ SHOP
180 Shaftesbury Ave., W2 (Tube: Tottenham Court Rd.). See listing in this chapter.

There are, however, classical-CD bargains out there. Templar Records, an unprepossessing classical-CD specialist, features the work of name artists for as low as £5 ($8), while double-disc operas run upwards of £18 ($30). Open Monday through Saturday from 10am to 6pm.

SECONDHAND RECORDS

If the record you're looking for can't be found by browsing the specialty stores, there are always secondhand shops; however, such stores are almost as used as the merchandise they sell. They're generally dirty, dusty, and jumbled up. (We like that in bookstores but hate it in record stores.)

Gramophone Exchange may have that record of "My Tears Have Washed 'I Love You' from the Blackboard of My Heart" you've been looking for all these years.

58 DEAN STREET RECORDS
58 Dean St., W1 (Tube: Green Park).

When was the last time you saw a store display devoted to Doris Day's records? If you answered, "1958," you're halfway there. At 58 Dean St., near Piccadilly Circus, you can check out Doris's greatest—"Que Sera Sera," and "A Guy Is a Guy"— recorded before she was a virgin.

GRAMOPHONE EXCHANGE
3 Betterton St., WC2 (Tube: Covent Garden).

If you don't mind shopping for secondhand records in a place that's also devoted to Albanian trinkets, hit the Gramophone Exchange. It's covered with authentic dust and crammed full of records, and one of the house specialties is wind-up gramophones.

VINYL EXPERIENCE
18 Hanway St., W1 (Tube: Tottenham Court Rd.).

Maybe this is simply the vinyl word: The shop offers Beatles memorabilia and hard-to-find oldies. The records are downstairs, the ephemera on street level.

Chapter Ten

· · · · · · · · · · · · · · · ·

LONDON SHOPPING TOURS

LET'S TOUR THE TOWN

If your idea of a landmark is **Liberty of London,** Carnaby Street, or even **Harrods,** well, who am I to differ with you? Pick a store and start marching. Or charging, perhaps.

Should your time be limited, you will have to pick and choose. Some of the suggestions in chapter 1 should help you with this—or you may want to try these tours. They are devised to get you to a lot of places in a hurry. So grab your brolly, and maybe a tote bag for carrying your packages, and let's go shopping.

Do "look right"—no, I'm not referring to the dress code in Britain, I'm talking about the instructions printed on the curb. It's no fair if you get run over by a taxi just because you don't know how to cross the streets in Britain.

Public Transportation   In more complicated tours, you will want to jump between different neighborhoods by either taxi or public transportation. Before you begin your day, you may want to check routing for the number of times you will be on and off the Tube (or bus) to see if an all-day **Travelcard** is a worthwhile investment. You need to use it at least three times for the pass to pay for itself. See chapter 2 for more on Travelcards.

Also note, these days you may be happier on a bus than in the Tube—plot your day and ask your hotel concierge for the right bus stops. One of the reasons we now use the Royal Garden as our main squeeze is that they have direct buses in front of the hotel to almost every listing in this book.

TOUR ONE: MAYFAIR MAYHEM DAY TOUR

This is a complete tour of Mayfair, with plenty of stops for real-people shopping, so don't be frightened away. Sure, lots of the stores on Bond Street and even Regent Street are out-of-bounds from a budget point of view, but I'm going to give you a little of everything, so hang on tight. A lot of the fun of being in London is window-shopping, so don't fret. Have I got windows for you.

Feel free to pop into stores that interest you, as this tour will take you right by just about every store in London.

1. Begin at Marks & Spencer on Oxford Street (no. 458) near Marble Arch. The British fondly refer to this store as "Marks & Sparks" or even "M&S." Don't miss the basement, where you will want to buy ready-cooked foods in order to save money for clothes. I suggest the chicken tikka or the tandoori chicken followed by a tin of "Curiously Strong Mints." You may want to buy it now and keep it in your tote bag for a picnic lunch later. I do that all the time—honest.

    While at M & S, you may want to look at the men's department, where you can get an awfully nice silk tie for £12 ($20). The women's underwear, the St. Michael's brand, is a legend in our own time. I also like the housewares department. The designer clothes and Autograph Line are on the ground floor. Autograph is the unbranded M&S designer label, mind you.

2. Next, cross Orchard Street and explore **Selfridges** (400 Oxford St.), a great British example of one-stop shopping. Selfridges has totally redone itself and is probably now the best department store in London.

Tour One: Mayfair Mayhem Day Tour

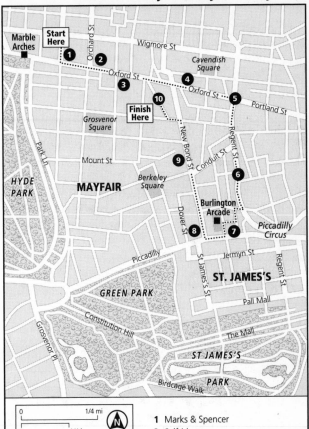

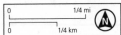

1 Marks & Spencer
2 Selfridges
3 Tesco Metro
4 Body Shop
5 H&M, TopShop, and SuperDrug
6 Regent Street Shops:
   Hamley's, Zara, and Mango
7 Waterstone's, Hatchards,
   and Fortnum & Mason
8 Old Bond Street shops
9 New Bond Street shops
10 Browns

Don't miss **Miss Selfridge,** young and kicky—perfect for the teen-and-'tweens set. It's on the ground floor. I buy stuff for myself here all the time. I'm a teenager at heart. So far, prices have been moderate. I also buy a lot of magazines at the kiosk, where there's an enormous international selection.

3. Leaving Selfridges, go back onto Oxford Street. Proceed away from Marble Arch (turn left) on Oxford Street, and cross to the other side. Be sure you look the right way. This street is crammed with buses, and I don't want you crushed beneath a double-decker. Look right!

   See that grocery store now? **Tesco Metro?** That's your next destination. You can take a miss on the street level if you aren't inclined to love grocery stores (I love them as long as they aren't in my hometown), proceed downstairs, and right into the health and beauty aids and the house-brand makeup products. I buy Indian spices for cooking and Virgin Cola and all sorts of other yummies for me to eat and take home as gifts.

4. Finished at Tesco, walk back across the street (look right) and right into **The Body Shop.** It's always worth a quick browse.

5. Follow Oxford Street, shopping as you go, to Regent Street. On the corner is **H&M,** a must-do if you are a teen or teen at heart. When you finish shopping here, cross Regent Street but stay on Oxford Street and visit **TopShop** for more teeny-bopper cheap clothing. (Go downstairs.) When you're done here, go across the street to **SuperDrug,** my favorite drugstore, where I load up on Original Source, about £2.30 ($3.80) per bottle.

6. Shop your way along Regent Street. For young women, I suggest you ignore the American brands and save yourself for **Zara,** the Spanish retailer that makes great but well-priced clothes with a fashion bite (but not too outré) and also **Mango,**

another Spanish brand, where the clothes are indeed flashy, but fun and inexpensive.

7. When you get to Piccadilly, pop into the flagship of the bookstore **Waterstone's** (where Simpson's used to be) or follow Piccadilly until you get to **Hatchards,** an old-fashioned bookstore with new titles. After Hatchards, stop at **Fortnum & Mason,** perhaps the world's fanciest grocery store.

   From Hatchards, push onward and enter the **Burlington Arcade** and shop your heart out. Don't miss **Pickett's** here, as well as **Georgina von Etzdorf.** Come out the back end of the Burlington Arcade, make a quick left for a few feet, and you are on Bond Street.

8. Follow Old Bond Street toward Oxford Street, shopping as you go. It will become New Bond Street right around **Tiffany & Co.** and a little pedestrian square and flower stall. You will be passing some of the world's fanciest antiques stores, all the major international brand names, and every now and then, a few affordable stores.

9. Continue moving along New Bond Street until you get to Brook Street; here, you'll turn left and then make a quick right onto South Molton Street. While on Brook, you can check out the new **Sonia Rykiel,** the **LK Bennett,** and the tiny but handy **Jo Malone** shop. Then you zig onto South Molton.

10. South Molton is no longer a wonderful shopping street, but there are some branches of multiples and some antiques galleries here. Most important is **Browns,** the leading designer store in London.

    If you get the feeling that I've sent you in a circle, I have. The last part of the route has been a bit of a loop-the-loop. You aren't dizzy, are you? If you're feeling faint, grab a taxi and head for **Claridge's,** 1 block away, where tea will be a memorable experience.

TOUR TWO: KNIGHTSBRIDGE & CHELSEA

1. Begin at **Harrods** (Knightsbridge). Your visit here is optional—
   it's not un-American to bypass Harrods. If you've never seen
   it, tour the food halls; if you're looking for china or souvenirs, or a wheel of Stilton, get them now.

   If you've done it, and the store unnerves you, don't feel
   obligated to try again. Frankly, this place is a zoo.

   Leave Harrods via the front door—or begin the tour without having gone into Harrods—and cross the street (look
   right!). Walk to the corner, which is Montpelier Street, cross
   this street, then turn right on Montpelier.

2. Go for a short block and turn left onto a tiny street called Cheval
   Place. I call it "Pandora's Alley." Shop this entire block for gen-
   tly worn designer bargains—a bargain being a Chanel sweater
   for under £300 ($495). Every store has a selection; the most
   famous address is **Pandora,** no. 16.

3. Return to Harrods, but pass it as if headed to Mayfair along
   Brompton Road. Walk to **Harvey Nichols,** a smaller and
   more fashionable department store (corner of Knightsbridge
   and Sloane sts.), known for its great selection of designer
   fashions.

   If you are hungry, stop at the coffee shop or sushi bar
   on the fifth floor; you can browse the food halls after you've
   been fortified. Harvey Nichols is a lot easier to handle than
   Harrods; they have a nice home-furnishings floor.

4. Now you are ready to take the Sloane Street exit and walk
   toward Sloane Square. Sloane Street is a long, straight shopping avenue filled with fun, chic boutiques and all of Europe's
   big names from **Chanel** (do stare at the new flagship store)
   to **Prada** to **Valentino.**

Tour Two: Knightsbridge & Chelsea

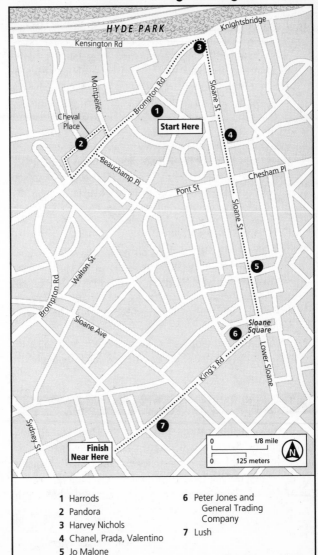

HYDE PARK

Knightsbridge

Kensington Rd

Montpelier

Brompton Rd

3

Sloane St

Cheval Place

1

Start Here

2

4

Beauchamp Pl

Chesham Pl

Pont St

Sloane St

Walton St

5

Brompton Rd

Sloane Ave

Sloane Square

6

Lower Sloane

King's Rd

7

Sydney St

Finish Near Here

| 0 | 1/8 mile |
| 0 | 125 meters |

1 Harrods
2 Pandora
3 Harvey Nichols
4 Chanel, Prada, Valentino
5 Jo Malone
6 Peter Jones and General Trading Company
7 Lush

5. Continue on Sloane Street, past the stores; past **Jo Malone,** the famed bath and fragrance resource; and, at Sloane Square itself, look for the department store **Peter Jones.** Use the department store so that you can find the new building where **General Trading Company** has set up housekeeping; have a look inside General Trading Company. Then you are ready to tour Peter Jones, which is best for home style.

6. When finished there, you're surely in the mood for King's Road, on the other side of **Peter Jones.** Turn right on King's Road, where you can walk for a mile or two and see everything trendy in fashion and furnishings. I walk King's Road up into the 500 block; most people will quit way before then. Hail a taxi to your next stop, as there is no nearby Tube stop.

7. Your next stop will undoubtedly be your hotel and a hot bath or a stiff drink (consider both) because you have just had one helluva day. But wait: Whatever you do, don't bail out or quit King's Road before you've gotten to no. 123, **Lush,** my favorite deli-cum-aromatherapy bath-and-beauty-goop shop. Huh? Trust me and do it!

   Once you've shopped at Lush you can indeed collapse, hopefully to test one of the bath bombs you just bought.

TOUR THREE: THE HOME-STYLE DAY TOUR

Put on those walking shoes. I'm going to march you around town like the Black Watch Guards. Leave your bagpipes at home, but take along any swatches you might have brought with you, or a notepad to write down things of interest as you pass by. If you have business cards or credentials that admit you to the trade, bring 'em along.

1. Take the Tube to Knightsbridge; enter **Harvey Nichols,** the department store; and take the escalator right upstairs to the home-furnishings floor. Tour it slowly, taking mental notes. Then walk out of Harvey Nichols and onto Sloane Street. Ignore the fashion boutiques; this is a home-furnishings tour.

Tour Three: The Home-Style Day Tour

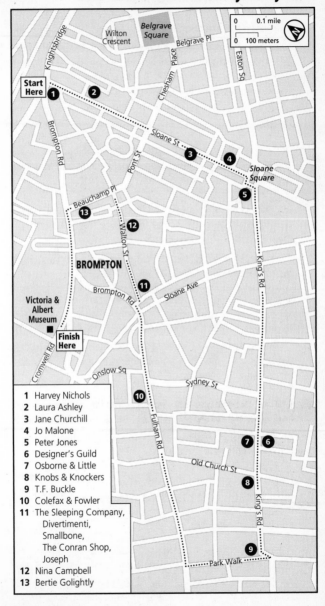

0   0.1 mile
0   100 meters

Wilton Crescent
Belgrave Square
Belgrave Pl
Knightsbridge
Chesham Place
Eaton Sq

Start Here 1
2
Brompton Rd
Sloane St
3
4
Sloane Square
5
Pont St
Beauchamp Pl
13
12
Walton St
King's Rd
BROMPTON
11
Brompton Rd
Sloane Ave
Victoria & Albert Museum
Finish Here
Cromwell Rd
Onslow Sq
Sydney St
10
Fulham Rd
7   6
Old Church St
8
9
Park Walk

1 Harvey Nichols
2 Laura Ashley
3 Jane Churchill
4 Jo Malone
5 Peter Jones
6 Designer's Guild
7 Osborne & Little
8 Knobs & Knockers
9 T.F. Buckle
10 Colefax & Fowler
11 The Sleeping Company,
   Divertimenti,
   Smallbone,
   The Conran Shop,
   Joseph
12 Nina Campbell
13 Bertie Golightly

2. Turn left on Harriet Street, right off Sloane Street, and walk right into the **Laura Ashley** shop. This is a giant home-furnishings store (it does not sell fashion) and will give you many ideas. Be sure to check the bins for sale items. As you leave the store, walk along Sloane Street toward Sloane Square (and away from Knightsbridge).

3–4. Things will be dull for a few seconds but will warm up quickly when you get to **Jane Churchill** at no. 135. And across the street but farther along Sloane Street is **Jo Malone,** before you reach Sloane Square.

5. Dive into **Peter Jones,** the department store, to check out sheets, duvet covers, bed linens, and trimmings; then come out of the store on the King's Road side and head to the right. King's Road is very long, and the design sources are far-flung (the reason I told you to wear sensible shoes).

6. You'll pass several good antiques galleries on King's Road and should be quite warmed up for the chase by the time you hit **Designer's Guild,** one of the two Tricia Guild shops. You'll be panting when you leave (it's so exciting), but don't miss the second shop a few doors farther down, where the fabrics are (no. 271 and no. 277).

7. **Osborne & Little** has a showroom across the street (no. 304), and there are many antiques shops here that you'll want to browse. Keep on moving, even if things get a little boring as the really chic stuff thins out.

8–9. **Knobs & Knockers** is a shop (no. 385) for brass fixtures; **T. F. Buckle** (no. 427) has the reproduction fireplaces that are all the rage. Of course, you'll dive into the antiques galleries as you walk past them.

10. Cut over to Fulham Road, which parallels King's Road, and find yourself more or less in the mid-200 block. **Colefax & Fowler,** an interior-design store, has a branch at no. 110.

11. Continue toward Knightsbridge now, on Fulham Road, taking in **The Sleeping Company, Divertimenti,** and maybe even **Smallbone,** where you'll see kitchens that will make you want to remodel right away. Finish up with a strong espresso at **Michelin House,** now known for **The Conran Shop.** You are now at the famed Brompton Cross. Restored from your coffee, go out the side door of The Conran Shop; visit **Joseph** right there across the street.

12. At the point of Brompton Cross, head for Walton Street. You'll find more decorative shops (remember your trip to Harvey Nichols? All the **Nina Campbell** you didn't buy is still available at her shop at 9 Walton St.) and several jewelry shops and just plain old neat places to look at.

13. You might want to consult our little map here, as there are some choices—you can connect from Walton Street onto Beauchamp and even pop into **Bertie Golightly,** a snazzy resale shop, and then do more of Brompton Cross (new Chanel shop, anyone?). Or you can simply wander directly into the **Victoria & Albert Museum,** where you'll find decorative arts that will inspire you in your design decisions. Learn to copy the best and you'll never go wrong.

TOUR FOUR: OUTLETS 'R' US

I feel very mixed about sending you to a factory-outlet village when you have only a few days in London, so I'll just give you some information and let you decide. For me, I find few outings are more fun, partly because I am a sucker for a price break and a name brand. Ruth and I frequently go out to Bicester Village (say *Bista*), which is in Oxfordshire and slightly more than an hour's drive from London. They do have a bus (see below). Eat lunch at any of the quick lunch stops; the branch of **Carducci's** is new.

Bistro

Earl Jeans

BICESTER VILLAGE
Bicester, Oxfordshire.

This center is co-owned by an American firm and looks like other American outlet villages . . . although, frankly, I think they should change the name to Bicester Town. The place is now huge. The parking lot is usually full, to give some indication of how hot this place is. For me, part of the thrill is the giant supermarket next door. I am quite content with this type of shopping—the best of Britain in flavors and prices, with a little Ferragamo thrown in.

There are now some 90 tenants, so it's impossible to list them. The concept is that there are global names, British names (**Ted Baker, Earl Jeans, Kenneth Turner**), and a few international brands that you may not have heard of, such as the Danish brand **Sand.** The selection is not terribly strong on housewares, but there are a handful of sources (don't miss **The White Company,** which is kind of hidden), so don't fret. Do remember that bed sizes in the U.K. and U.S. are not the same. The selection for teens and 'tweens is excellent; the selection for designer-brand have-to-haves is mind boggling.

There is free parking; shuttle bus from London or train.

Take the train from Marylebone Station to Bicester North Station. There are taxis available as well as a free station bus that runs Thursday through Sunday. Train fare, round trip, is about £13 ($22). Trains have been privatized in the U.K., so you want Chiltern Railways.

The Bicester Coach runs every Wednesday and Saturday morning from the Golden Tours Terminal at Victoria Coach Station and/or the Cumberland Hotel at Marble Arch. The phone for Golden Tours is **020/7233-7030.** The cost of the bus trip is about £15 ($25) per adult.

Open daily from 10am to 6pm, Thursday until 8pm.

TOUR FIVE: PARIS IN A DAY

I think Paris deserves more than a day, but lots of people like to take the Chunnel train—zip into Paris for lunch, spend a few hours shopping, and return to London. Note that the best prices on train tickets, especially when there is no Saturday-night stay, are on tickets bought in the U.S. through Rail-Europe before departure, unless you qualify for a senior or student fare or luck into promotional deals on Eurostar, especially on day-return fares or weekend deals.

Note that as we go to press, the Eurostar has cut a half hour off the travel time, so London and Paris are now only 2 hours and 35 minutes apart. There is a 1-hour time change.

Although there are two classes of service, I see no reason to spring for the first-class seat. And don't forget your passport; there are formalities, even for E.U. residents.

Size Conversion Chart

Women's Clothing

American	8	10	12	14	16	18
Continental	38	40	42	44	46	48
British	10	12	14	16	18	20

Women's Shoes

American	5	6	7	8	9	10
Continental	36	37	38	39	40	41
British	4	5	6	7	8	9

Children's Clothing

American	3	4	5	6	6X
Continental	98	104	110	116	122
British	18	20	22	24	26

Children's Shoes

American	8	9	10	11	12	13	1	2	3
Continental	24	25	27	28	29	30	32	33	34
British	7	8	9	10	11	12	13	1	2

Men's Suits

American	34	36	38	40	42	44	46	48
Continental	44	46	48	50	52	54	56	58
British	34	36	38	40	42	44	46	48

Men's Shirts

American	$14\frac{1}{2}$	15	$15\frac{1}{2}$	16	$16\frac{1}{2}$	17	$17\frac{1}{2}$	18
Continental	37	38	39	41	42	43	44	45
British	$14\frac{1}{2}$	15	$15\frac{1}{2}$	16	$16\frac{1}{2}$	17	$17\frac{1}{2}$	18

Men's Shoes

American	7	8	9	10	11	12	13
Continental	$39\frac{1}{2}$	41	42	43	$44\frac{1}{2}$	46	47
British	6	7	8	9	10	11	12

INDEX

A

Accessories, 119–120
Accessorize, 109, 119
Accommodations. *See* Hotels
Adolfo Dominguez, 131
Afternoon tea (tea rooms), 10, 13, 76–79
Agent Provocateur, 181
Agnes B., 131
Airfares, 17
Air France, 24
Airfreight, 224–225
Airlines
  from continental Europe, 24
  from the United States, 20–22
Airport hotels, 70–71
Airports
  alternative, 25
  duty-free shopping, 40–41
Alberta Ferretti, 131
Alexander McQueen, 121–122
Alfie's Antiques Market, 253
Amanda Wakely, 122
Amazing Nails, 206
American Airlines, 21
American brand names, 47
American Express, currency exchange, 44, 45
Angela Flanders, 189
Anna French, 233

Ann Harvey, 162
Annie's, 182
Antiquarian Book Fair, 244
Antiquarius, 254
Antiques, 241–260
  books, maps, and autographs, 260–264
  books and magazines on, 242
  duty-free, 54
  Greenwich markets, 250–252
  "Monster Markets," 252–253
  neighborhoods for, 255–260
  street markets, 246–251
  supermarkets, 253–255
Antiques fairs, 243–246
The Apartment Company, 70
Apple Market, 246–247, 256
Aquascutum, 122
The Arches, 264–265
Ardingly antiques market, 252–253
Armada Antiques, 265
Aroma Cushion, 10
Aromatherapy, 9, 191–194
Arsenal team luggage, 115
Arthur Middleton, 266–267
Arts and crafts, 142–143
Asprey, 122
ATMs (automated-teller machines), 43, 46
Auctions, 219–223